BODY'S A BAD
MONSTER

Andrews McMeel Publishing
a division of Andrews McMeel Universal
1130 Walnut Street, Kansas City, Missouri 64106

www.andrewsmcmeel.com

24 25 26 27 28 TEN 10 9 8 7 6 5 4 3 2 1

ISBN: 978-1-5248-9225-8

Library of Congress Control Number: 2024931574

Editor: Danys Mares
Art Director: Tiffany Meairs
Production Editor: Elizabeth A. Garcia
Production Manager: Shona Burns

BODY'S A BAD MONSTER

Rowan Perez

Andrews McMeel
PUBLISHING®

BEFORE I BEGIN.

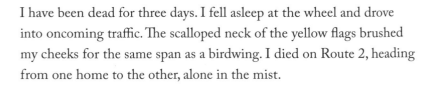

I have been dead for three days. I fell asleep at the wheel and drove into oncoming traffic. The scalloped neck of the yellow flags brushed my cheeks for the same span as a birdwing. I died on Route 2, heading from one home to the other, alone in the mist.

i began to seriously collect monstrosities three years ago. it was, of course, a sunday.

it's important to collect things wisely. my therapist has said something beautiful about a gratitude inventory, but my ocd acts as a rabbit and kicks any tenderness out of her warren. i cannot remember important dates or names, but i do store rocks in a rusted red pail. my memories collide and panic, bleed together in the shower. their colors mute the water into fawn skin.

my childhood is a statue of the virgin mary. she stood in our back garden, round ceramic sparrows broken at her feet. underneath their overturned pottery wings, all the worms went to church. she was ensconced in poison ivy.

there are three similar stones on the beach. i have to take *only one* of the rocks, and i *must* take one. but what if there's no one to comfort their grieving rock family. what if i make the other rocks jealous. what if i take the wrong rock and now the universe will have to end.

i cry about the oracle of delphi, and how she was alone over an open grate, breathing in poison. i cry about cassandra, and how she was telling the truth. i cry about the skeleton rinds of sand dollars, and how they become buried under the stars, in the foreignness of open air. i cry about how we, with our flesh bodies, will be buried under stone instead, with our faces unable to see the horizon.

my friend has to carry me home. pallbearer, she tucks my hair behind my ear while shushing my personal funeral. when i remember this, sometimes i remember her dying here because i killed her because i took the wrong rock.

my sister says the holes in the tops of seashells are due to the tongues of other mollusks —something else had drilled through to suck out the organs.

this is worship.

there is a mythology: *que sera, sera.* god tips his hand, and the plan rolls out along the tongue of our spine, unfolding.

FAREWELL,

Before the road comes down your throat and you snap your own spine and die there; what you had meant to do was to protect the body you had taken residence in. You had often heard *our bodies are our temples.* Echoing, empty spaces, full of prayer and pretension. The good among us kept our bodies like lockets, perfect and somewhat sanctimonious. We were to exude grace, and glide from encounter to encounter on our modesty and virtue. To cast our eyes away from sin.

But whatever shout lived in you was not one of fervor. You are still trying to figure out the exact name of that sound. You only know it is tremendous and horrible.

Something too ugly even for a howl.

ocd comes with built-in sainthood. martyr child, i cannot help but pray about things, an endless stereotypical loop. condensed panic, real/unreal, felt/unfelt. i can no longer remember what i actually experienced and what i feared i would experience. when they crack open the geode of my skull, they will not be able to pick out the raw fruit of *trauma* from the rotten gore of *imagined truth*. if i never move and am very lucky, no one will know what was memory and what was invention. if i never look directly, the viscera cannot take a name— only lie there, ambivalent and twitching.

greek mythology divides the soul into disparate halves. a soulmate is "the soul's recognition of its counterpoint," at least according to my bible school.

we are sent to the earth horrifically decentered. we arrive only half-there, and we must seek that which completes us. in many ways, this is framed as a bittersweet arrangement. it is lonely, after all, to have not-met the *one* spirit.

but i like it. it implies our first and most basic purpose is to seek love. no matter how full we are, love always fits.

we might spend months or years collecting seashells, just for the hope we will one day find *the one* beautiful and perfect enough to string along on a necklace. in the meantime, we have still collected something. and it's lovely, the act of collecting.

the formula of living is just what we do with each selected piece.

◇

my childhood cat is currently flat against a table, dying alone. this will be important later.

  for now, let's leave him alive. let's leave him at home.

◇

i love that we say a light touch is *ghosting your hands over.* i love that the living assume that death presses her gray hands only softly, so that the whisper of her fingers is only ever a veil. a silken comfort.

  there are many mythologies about what happens after.

  in this life, in my life: the next step is clear.

  always a road, the way home covered in mist.

◆

PART ONE:

I DON'T KILL MYSELF YET.

RESIDENTIAL LEASE AGREEMENT

I. THE PARTIES This Residential Lease Agreement ("Agreement") made this November 21 between:

Landlord: ▮▮▮▮▮ with a mailing address of ▮▮▮▮▮ ("Landlord"), AND

Tenant(s): Mouse ("Tenant").

Landlord and Tenant are each referred to herein as a "Party" and, collectively, as the "Parties."

NOW, THEREFORE, FOR AND IN CONSIDERATION of the mutual promises and agreements contained herein, the Tenant agrees to lease the Premises from the Landlord under the following terms and conditions:

II. LEASE TYPE. This Agreement shall be considered a: (check one)

☐ - Fixed Lease. The Tenant shall be allowed to occupy the Premises starting on [LEASE START DATE] and end on [LEASE END DATE] ("Lease Term"). At the end of the Lease Term and no renewal is made, the Tenant: (check one)
☐ - May continue to lease the Premises under the same terms of this Agreement under a month-to-month arrangement.
☐ - Must vacate the Premises.

☑ - Month-to-Month Lease. The Tenant shall be allowed to occupy the Premises on a month-to-month arrangement starting on December 1 and ending upon notice of 30 days from either Party to the other Party ("Lease Term").

III. OCCUPANT(S). The Premises is to be occupied strictly as a residential dwelling with the following individual(s) in addition to the Tenant: (check one)

☐ - [OCCUPANT(S) NAME(S)] ("Occupant(s)")

☑ - There are no Occupant(s).

IV. THE PROPERTY. The Landlord agrees to lease the described property below to the Tenant: (enter the property information)

a.) Mailing Address: Holy rotten. Cannot continue.
b.) Residence Type: ☐ Apartment ☐ House ☐ Condo ☑ Other: Single Hispanic female, Earth Years 19. Average height and stocky build. Unremarkable for her

species, requires low maintenance but some tolerance towards proper communication.
c.) Bedroom(s): 1
d.) Bathroom(s): 1

The aforementioned property shall be leased wholly by the Tenant ("Premises").

V. PURPOSE. The Tenant and Occupant(s) may only use the Premises as: (check one)

☐ - A residential dwelling only.

☑ - A residential dwelling and: bag, sack, holder. Lease will not be broken under circumstances such as sex, pain, or self-harm.

VI. FURNISHINGS. The Premises is: (check one)

☑ - To be furnished with the following items: Severe OCD, Depression, and other misalignments. Plants, artwork, and other "unnecessary" survival items will be present; the Tenant might experience hardship (to one's own) as a result. The Landlord will not be at fault for pre-existing conditions (inability to reproduce, etc). All other damages, responsibilities, and requirements Tenant seeks to undertake will not be at the fault of the Tenant.

☐ - Not furnished.

VII. APPLIANCES. The Landlord shall: (check one)

Provide the following appliances: Human Body, slight scarring on thighs and

◇

i was required to memorize the apostles' creed. to be fair, it wouldn't have been proper for me to obtain first communion without it. i didn't study hard enough; i cried between each stanza, sliced open on words that held too much weight and slipped their fish bellies between my fingers. what does a seven-year-old know about *pontius pilate.*

i knew i couldn't do it; howled my sorrow while my father turned the tv up. i sat in the reek of every horrid stanza until the consonants could slurry over my tongue.

i did not just *go to church.* church came home with us. church hovered inside of me, bloating the space.

i had been *in a church* my whole life; assigned *of* the church, almost like a species.

my family was so catholic that we were *that* catholic. a painting of angels hung in our entry hall; paired finely by jesus and crosses and mary and crosses and the saints and crosses and doves and crosses on every available wall—*that* catholic. we were ask-saint-anthony-if-it's-lost—*that* catholic. at-least-one-seventh-of-my-life-in-a-pew—*that* catholic. i-can't-stay-over-we-have-church—*that* catholic.

with authority, then, i can confirm: one can craft a church. they can be pocket-size. some churches are robust, come with a personal stamp that *this* church will be *your* church forever—the church of the wild, the church of coffee, the church of hating traffic. some churches wilt; are sustained only by the playacting of the universe and the unreal sweat of the participants.

my research has concluded that a church may only really require a few simple traits:

- it must be insular.
- it must have an element of theater.
- it must be incalculable.
- it must contain answers that only *it* provides; it must require the routine of sacrifice, praise, and devotion in order to *give* these answers.
- it must have rules, and it must motivate the audience to *follow* these rules, lest punishment occur—shame, horror, guilt.
- and, of course, above all: it must be beautiful.

i chose girls.

girls as an attic; secret and sublime. girls with magic wands. girls who chewed their hair and girls who kept their spat gum in their back pocket and girls that wore exclusive shades of pink. girls who hid during recess and girls who ate their scabs off and girls who were bad at math.

girls who forced the heads off of their barbies with a butter knife and threw the plastic viscera against the ceiling fan to see what would happen. girls who established long bloody backstories for their beanie babies. girls who gave mud magic potion powers and served it out of pink teacups and who wrote in floaty-hearted letters and who fried the face off their brand-partnered happy meal magenta troll dolls in their easy-bake ovens.

we curled our bodies into corners and organized the laws of magic, holding meetings with serious tones as we drafted theatrical debuts featuring our untold power. we made codes and banished curses, knowing *someone* was watching, although we shouldn't and couldn't speak the name of that *someone*. we finished our science homework after burning our hair over candles we stole from our mothers.

this is where the memory of me will begin, then. in the palm of her hand.

FROM THE DESK OF MOUSE
MEMO RE: *WHILE YOU WERE OUT*

The wind comes in through the pine trees and the sun gets tangled in the doors. The next gallery's glass turbine entryway is titled *Come Back Soon*.

She ties her shoes.

You guys accidentally match again. Typical. She always looks better than you, but that's probably her confidence. You have the same type of black, chunky, high-heeled boot. New England almost feminine.

One long semester of college left, and then you will both graduate. And after that—well, *who knows.*

You have made your entire family promise not to give you *Oh, the Places You'll Go!* You barely want to be *here.*

"Fucking Professor Shaw," she says again. "How many do we have left?" She cracks her back when she stands up.

You check the sheet. "Fourteen. And the three essays."

"I'm going to take a shit on his desk." She shuffles through her tiny backpack, sniffing.

"I'm not gonna do the essays." You are absolutely going to do the essays.

Marlowe's recently refreshed her undercut and the purple of her hair catches the edge of the dark brown underneath. You can't stop reaching out to shush your hand over the caterpillar back of her head. She purrs whenever you do, joking. Sometimes not joking. "His pants were too tight on Thursday. Did you see that?"

A yellow scowl in his crotch. Not that you were looking. You hack a laugh. "The next gallery is supposed to have, like, six of them."

"I'm hungry."

So are you. "Hmm. I had too much coffee."

"I drank like twelve cups this morning and now my skeleton is tapdancing." Marlowe finds the assignment you are both doing wadded at the bottom of her bag. She sighs at it, her lip curling into a tiny sneer.

You have both spent what feels like an eternity hunting for specific art pieces in a specific museum that your professor *specifically* has had a job at. Your mouth is dry but at least your headache is abating.

You met her at a mixer for other incoming freshmen. You liked her hair; she liked your jacket. After that it was just survival—she was your *person,* and you were, usually, hers.

She smooths the paper against her thin thigh. "I have literally been here for like, six hours. It's a fucking Friday."

It's only been three hours, and neither of you have class on Friday. It's also only a quarter past noon.

But the assignment is getting old for you too. She has a point. You look behind you as if a map will appear. "I think there's like a cafeteria somewhere in the B Wing."

She stamps her tiny foot. You do not smirk at it. She rubs her eyes, smudging her makeup. "I'm so fucking hungover."

"It's the mixed drinks." And drinking on a Thursday. It had been your mother's specific request that you *just let loose* for once. Marlowe had been happy to oblige, delighted by what she called *any opportunity to distract a good student.*

"How are you *standing* right now?" She squints at you. "Full and entire offense, but you look almost fucking *chipper.*"

You laugh. "Okay, but . . . okay, so. Don't freak out when I tell you this. But—" You hold the door to the gallery open, and she dip-dives gracefully under your arm, scooting her free hand over the small of your back while she passes you. You rub your nose. "I'm tellin' ya. It's the ultimate hangover cure."

Her eyes twinkle. It's darker in this gallery. It smells like shoe polish and wet paint. "Wait, is it now? Are you going to tell me this evil little secret *now?* Wait. Wait. I don't know if I'm ready."

The paintings are full of frowning people in thick black clothes. They swim out of focus around her, chameleoned against her glow.

"Progresso chicken noodle soup."

Her brow furrows. "Okay, that doesn't sound so ba—"

"Straight out of the can. Unheated."

Marlowe cackles. "Stop. Do not tell me right now you—"

"I grip it and rip it. Just yank the pull tab and drain it."

She retches and grabs your hand. "No, you do *not.*"

"It's legitimately pretty dangerous because the can is sharp?

So I've cut myself on it, like, a bunch of times—just, like, trying to suck down one of these bad boys."

"I'm literally so disgusted with you right now." The radio beam of her smile plunges into your heart and eats out all the cartilage. She steps closer. She smells like rain and lilacs. "Okay, but it works? Like, it *works?*"

"I think it's the salt level."

"Hang on, hang on. This is one of them, right?" Marlowe puts herself under the frame of a Renaissance mastery. You check your copy of the list, carefully folded and continuously updated. You triple-check the artist and the painting name, and then give her a nod of *good job* while also checking a fourth time, just in case.

You both follow Professor Shaw's instructions and snap a picture of yourself in front of it. She throws up peace signs, you look uncomfortable and unsure.

You check off the respective box on one piece of paper and also cross it off on a second list you'd handwritten. Marlowe doesn't bother making a note. She hums to herself while you pull out your spiral-bound and jot down something passingly intelligent-sounding about the work—*dark, dangerous, yet full of careful brushstrokes. Pushes the boundaries of the form while encouraging the audience to participate in the challenge.*

Even though the assignment is just to take a picture of yourself with the painting, you also snap one of the whole piece, the information next to it, and the area in general—just in case. A few more pictures just feature Marlowe, head tilted back to look at the work, the soft light on her small nose—for Instagram purposes only.

She looks back at you and reaches out her hand, giving you a gesture you taught her because your mom taught you. You take her fingers in yours and come stand next to her.

"Art is good," she sighs.

"Art is good." You aren't looking at it. You're thinking about the term *chiaroscuro*. The play of shadows and light. You are never really sure how to pronounce it.

She blinks up at the wall. "It's kind of crazy to think about, like, how these people were alive so long ago and they were all real and had real people problems and real people lives—and, like, somebody sat with them for hours and hours."

You turn to actually study the work. "Yeah." You are never going to be able to understand art like a good artist should. Pieces like this are uninteresting to you and always will be—huge swatches of white faces and deep, light-eating color. You had no one like this back on the home world, so you cannot recognize yourself in their fleshy pink cheeks.

Her fingers tighten around yours. "I just spend so much time wondering who they were and what they wanted and who they were going out with and who their parents were and if they ever, like, did drag or anything."

"It kinda seems like the dude over there is wearing a dress, to be honest. And he *does* rock that wig. And the *smolder* on him?"

"It's like, this whole room is *people*, and the paint is just *chemicals* and, like, not to sound like a Hot Topic T-shirt but, like, love is chemicals too."

"Paintings are love," you answer, trying out her equation, not seeing the solution, knowing it is likely due to a failure of your mathematics. You point to a portrait. "This baby is, like, super beefy."

She laughs. "He could arm wrestle me, yeah."

"He's got his *oats* in him."

You look over for a response, but Marlowe is on her phone, texting someone. To you, she says, "We have thirteen left?"

"I think I saw one on the other wall. So, like, twelve."

She groans, follows while you lead her over to the other painting, not looking up from the iPhone. "Okay, by the way, we're invited to Henry's tonight. And also I guess next weekend, which is a bit presumptuous."

She means *she* was invited, but this is not a new thing. In the last four years, it has become unspoken, easy, rote: if one of you shows up, so does the other one. You are a package deal often enough that your shared friends have pointed it out. You can't tell if they think it's charming or genuinely kind of annoying.

Your heart is tight about the idea of a party. You shouldn't be drinking so much. You should be studying for your test on Wednesday. "I could do, like, an hour of partying next week. Like, particularly if we go out this weekend. My body is just like . . . it's not as young as it used to be."

She angles you both into the next obligatory picture (you do a peace sign this time, but she doesn't, so you look immature and weird) and then goes back to typing. She frowns at the phone. "And like, just to be honest? Henry is literally the worst. While you were in the bathroom last night, Kaisa said he suplexed a dude, like, through a table last weekend."

Kaisa is your roommate and is also, unlike you, actually a reliable narrator. You picture what suplexing someone through a table even looks like. "What the fuck?"

"Yeah, dude. He almost got arrested."

"Is everyone okay?"

"Can I be honest? It kind of bothers me that he keeps bringing up how gay we are." She cuts her eyes up to you. "Like, he's so *weird* about me kissing you."

You wrinkle your nose. "Wait, what? Like in a—*sex* way 'weird about it' or like in a *homophobia* way?" You don't actually know which option would be worse. Being perceived at all makes your skin crawl.

Marlowe mirrors your look of disgust. "That's what I *mean*, I legit don't *know*. I'll be walking to class and Henry will be like, *Marlowe are you gonna kiss your friend tonight?* And I'm like, can straight men leave me the fuck alone for like *two minutes.*"

Marlowe didn't teach you to friend-kiss, that was someone many years ago. She had actually already believed in friend-kissing when you met her, which was perfect. It required no explanation.

A friend-kiss doesn't count; is almost plastic and *straight* by how sexless it is. A friend-kiss is because all guys are kind of gross and you just want to make out with *someone*, without the risk of being kidnapped. And girls are soft! Girls are fun to play with! A friend-kiss is so bereft of romantic intention that sometimes a *hug* means more.

You kiss a lot of other people at any opportunity, but okay, objectively speaking, you and Marlowe friend-kiss a *lot* at *every* party. It is maybe codependent. You should google if you are codependent; you might secretly be manipulating her. Why else do you feel violated by this man? It's because you're probably possessive of her, you creep.

"What in the ever-fuck." Your mouth turns into a snarl. You are eleven years old and pretending to be a wolf. You can't stop it, because you react strongly any time something happens to her, because maybe you *are* codependent.

"And I'm like, it's none of your business." She points to a different painting, but you shake your head—it's the wrong year. "And I like *yelled* at him about it, actually."

"Fuck, I'm sorry. You shouldn't have had to—"

"I'm like. Bro, it's the year of Our Lord ▮, are we still *doing* this? Are we still fucking making girls kissing their friends *weird?* Is this the first time you have even seen two women in the wild, literally at all?"

"Patron Mother Lady Gaga did not create *Born This Way* for him to be like this."

She whirls on you, her anger so obvious it actually makes you take a step back. "I'm so fucking *done* with men. I am like, I'm sorry I drunk-kiss my friends. It's fucking *platonic*, it doesn't fucking *mean* anything, and the *reason* that I kiss my *friends* and not *people like him* is because he's like *this*."

Your brows furrow. "Yeah." You search for the right thing to say, floundering, alarmed by her sudden flash-fire temper. You don't know how, but *you're* responsible for this. You did this to her. "We can stop kissing, if, like—?"

She throws her hands up and paces an angry circle around herself. "I'm like, it shouldn't fucking *belong* to him! *I* should get to *kiss you* without *worrying* about it. Like, why is he so fucking okay with just *bothering* me about it."

You start nodding, unsure what to say. You should calm her down. This is *your fault*; you should have figured out how to avoid this. *You* kissed her; therefore, *you* put her in this situation. Make her feel better, you owe her that. "No, you definitely—"

"I, like, *just* figured out I'm into women—and, like, anyone—and not just men. And now I wish I wasn't into *any* man. Because they do shit like *this*. Like, you know he wouldn't say *shit* if it was me just kissing my guy friends."

"Right, and—"

"And you know I can't *even* kiss my guy friends, because they're fucking *weird* about it, and it always has to *mean* something. And I don't fucking want to be in a relationship. I've said this *so* many times. I just want to have fun."

"Which, like—"

"Which I've told him," she says, and then blows out a sigh. She gives herself a little shake, and that shake travels down her whole body, out through her left leg. She flutters her hands. "Wow, okay, sorry. He just pisses me off. Like, I'm not trying to fucking date you. Can he stop making everything fucking *sexual*."

You hold your hands up. "No, dude, I get it."

She doesn't answer. Her hair falls in front of her face. She has a habit of chewing her lips while she focuses. She sighs while she texts.

You try to navigate the shift in tone, but your heart is racing. You long-stare at the wall, not seeing. Wait, do you kiss her too much? Are you being a predator? Are you pushing her to kiss you? Is Henry actually trying to *warn* her? You've been out of the closet longer than she's been; he knows you're bisexual. What if he's worried you *forced* her into coming out too?

Maybe you *did,* is the problem. Maybe she was just influenced by you, pressuring her to kiss you. Yes, she usually makes the first move. But you're uptight and Catholic. *You're* the problem here, probably.

"Lacey's coming tonight, right?" Marlowe doesn't look up from her phone.

"She won't be in until, like, *late* tonight, though." Long after dinner. "She has to work. She said start without her."

"I love her." Marlowe has never met her. "I'm telling Henry she's coming and he should kiss her."

"Babe," you say.

"We hate her boyfriend," she says, which is a good point, and also extremely charming that she remembered. But also, you would prefer Lacey kiss *literally* anyone else.

You find another assignment painting and drag her over to it. Snap a picture in which you look ugly. Whatever. It's for a class project, you shouldn't care this much. Your skin is bad under your makeup, patchy and raw from the sugar in the alcohol. You'll have to reapply your foundation before tonight. An expensive hobby.

"Oh, hey, I forgot to ask," you rest your palm on her bicep. She's boney. You drop your hand immediately. "Did you ever hear back about that French internship?"

"Yeah, I think I'm gonna skip it." She doesn't look up. "Can I ask you a personal question?"

Yes, you still shoplift. No, the sleeping hasn't gotten any better. Yes, you know that you're annoying and kind of terrible to be around because you're the worst; anxious, pretentious, uptight, possessive, overbearing. "Ominous."

"When did you come out?"

Your reorientation occurs in a single surprised blink. "Like. Gay?"

"Like gay."

"Uh." You fool with the edge of your primary checklist. "It was awkward. I was 18—maybe 19?" Throw her a grin. Her eyes catch yours and then you pretend to be looking at anything else instead.

The wall is a deep forest green. Does that affect how dark the paintings look? "It was by accident," you admit. "In Boston's most popular gay club: a Wendy's."

She doesn't laugh, but you said it like that to make her laugh. You try to read one of the white placards, but take in none of the information.

She considers you for a second and then nods once. "Were they okay with it?"

"My parents?" The placard's first four words are the furthest you seem to be able to get. *Beginning in the early.* Maybe you have never been able to read and have just been faking it this whole time.

You dart your eyes to Marlowe. Her screen is reflecting against her cheekbones. She is strangely still, just watching you. Waiting.

The letters of *beginning in the early* can be rearranged into *ringing in an eel, thy be.* You love the word *eel.* "Uh . . . they were, like, talking about how stupid the Gay-Straight Alliance was at my high school, I don't know."

Eel is almost direct from the Germanic. You like the idea of a German person just, like, finding an eel in the wild and saying—*this glistening tube fish will be called . . .* and then naming it so perfectly. The moniker is almost an onomatopoeia for the sound many people make when seeing their first: *eehck.*

Marlowe doesn't say anything. Just keeps watching.

You swallow loudly. Play with your hair. "So, like, I hadn't been home in a while, right? But I'm, like, super out at college—obviously—and this is in . . . I think spring break of freshman year? And, like, you remember—like, I was had-a-butch-girlfriend *out*. And while I'm home and we're talking in this Wendy's—I just, like . . . forgot they didn't know? For a second? Like, everyone *here* knows. I forgot that my parents *didn't*, that I'd never officially said anything." You hold up a finger. "Although to be fair? I never really came out in college either, I was just never *in the closet*."

"I get that." Her voice is soft. She scoops one hand around your arm and rests her cheek against your shoulder. ". . . So they were talking about the Gay-Straight Alliance . . . ?"

Certain eel species can live up to eighty years. That has to be impossible—they're just snakes that are doing a bad job of being a snake.

You blow out a breath at her prompt. "Yeah, so like, my dad is talking about—oh, you know, the GSA is pointless, that we're kids in high school and shouldn't be thinking about that stuff, that it's not regulated, blah, blah, blah. I'm deep in my chicken sandwich and just like—I'm thinking we're having a normal conversation. So I say, like, *oh it's not that bad, I think it's, like, meant to help people. Like, they weren't that helpful with me but at least they were trying.* Literally just outed myself completely by accident." You wiggle your foot for no reason, just to have something to do, or maybe to test if you can become an eel with the right movements. You send Marlowe a look. "I mean, like, again, to be fair—I was like super bullied by some of those kids, but it's fine. Like, the GSA as a program is fine, I mean."

"Do you still talk to any of them?"

"The kids?" You snort. "No. *Super* bullied."

She doesn't say anything. You realize with a vague sense of almost-dread that she is the first person you've ever told this story to.

You pick an invisible thread off your shirt. You should stop talking now. "But yeah, like, I was like—*oh, it's not so bad.* And my parents were like, *why not?* And I was like, *well it was fine when I dropped in.* And they were like, *wait why were you there,* and I just, kind of, blurted—*well, because I'm bisexual*—and then realized, like—oops! Fuck! There was, like, this long awkward pause where all of us kind of just, like—froze. Like—*oh shit, did she just admit to it?*"

"Does Lacey know?"

"Yeah." Lacey lied for you a lot, when the two of you were growing up together. A *lot.* "She's cool with it."

"Yeah, she's, like. Your best friend, right?"

You pause before just nodding. There's something in Marlowe's tone that seems dangerous, but you can't place it.

"Hang on, I think this one is on the list." She gestures to a painting in a corner, and takes you over to it gently, her thumb rubbing the back of your hand. "So, like, were your *parents* okay with it?"

"Mostly they just, like . . . ignore it? A lot."

In the parking lot afterward, cheeks burning, you had asked them—*do you still love me?* like some kind of dumb lamb, bleating out a horrible possibility that shook in the air. Your mother had said *of course we do, honey.* Your father had notably (and for once) said nothing.

You chew the cuticle on your left thumb. "They, like, don't want to, like, deal with it, basically. Like, I still like guys—so it's like, *straight until proven guilty.*"

"My dad told me it was a phase." She wraps her arm around your shoulder again and gives you a kiss on the cheek during the picture she snaps. "I'm sorry they're not being cool about it."

Her sincerity sends some kind of a rot through your organs. "It's okay." Actually, things are kind of fine at home. Since your parents are ignoring it, you just don't bring it up. You have learned the ability to sidestep anything uncomfortable in the house simply by not looking directly at it. It solves a lot of problems. "Sorry, uh . . ." How do you even say this. ". . . Like, your dad sucks."

"Honestly, it was just, like . . . par for the course. I was kind of angry about it just for, like, how stereotypical it was. Like, at least be homophobic in a less cliché way. Make something up. Call me a slur."

She pulls you into a hug and sighs into your shoulder. You wrap yourself around her, feeling the shift of her back muscles against your arms as she leans deep into you. "I don't want to do this fucking homework." Her words are muffled.

"You like art, though. Love is painted chemicals, or whatever."

She doesn't remove her face from you. "I don't want to fucking do this homework. I want to hold your hand and walk around the museum and just look at stuff and not write a stupid fucking essay and not be here for-fucking-*ever*."

You stroke the back of her head, walking your fingers over the line between her undercut and her long hair. She groans. You shush her gently. "We can go get, like, a sandwich or something after this gallery, maybe that will help."

She groans again, nuzzling deeper into the hug.

You pick a piece of lint out of her hair, flicking it to the ground. "Did you ever read that book about the kids that sleep over in the museum and, like, get coins out of the fountain to survive?"

"I saw *Night at the Museum.*" She groans a third time and then fake-bites your collarbone before pulling back to make eye contact. "I'm gonna eat, like, four sandwiches."

She is very close to you, but you are used to how close she gets. The two of you are just touchy people. You would swear this with your hand on a Bible: *it's just that we're close friends.* Not *all* queer girls have to date.

You duck your nose down to her ear and grin, whispering low in your throat: "They sell wine here, we could pregame."

She gags and shoves you away. "Don't even—"

You adopt a witch persona. "Don't be a coward, child! Drink the wretched poison! Embrace death! Allow it to rise within you!"

Marlowe laughs and adopts the same hunched stance and gnarled voice. "I shall never succumb to your evil ways, oh foul one. You must best me upon the spell field."

You wiggle your hands, declaring, "I shall turn thee into a—" when the door opens, and more people come in. Both you and Marlowe stand up straight and then throw each other a look and immediately hush the fit of giggles.

"Okay. I hate this, but least you're fun," she whispers. "Thank you for taking me." She grabs your hand, and, for the rest of the gallery, refuses to drop it.

You text Lacey—*Let me know when you're on your way. We cannot wait to see you, bb!*

i tell people—haha! *despite all appearances, i went to bible school.*

i was sixteen when i was forced back into it. the curriculum was for second graders. my siblings and i were carted in, coaxed by the notion of *attending a real summer camp.* i sat in the back of classrooms, already confirmed, sweating and bored. the lord was a stained-glass coloring page. everyone wore sandals in the line art. i wrote bad poems as marginalia.

at the end of six weeks of summer sainthood, i came home early and found my father on the floor of my bedroom. he was sorting through my personal notebooks, their crinkled spiral-bound spines pulled from my bookshelf and piled on the floor around his body. his hands on my crude anime-style eye drawings and hundreds of pages of scratchy, violent stories.

he didn't like what i had been making, because it was *troubling*. i didn't like that it had been mine, and was now instead *his*, in a way. he didn't like that i kept nasty little secrets. i didn't like that he didn't *let* me keep secrets. he didn't like that i had spent time in vacation bible school *mouthing off* and disrespecting my teachers and, worse, disrespecting *god* by writing all these gruesome, meaningless stories instead of *learning*.

my punishment is to memorize mark and john from *king james*. i am still not sure if this is because i hadn't been listening in class or if he was just disappointed in my extremely bad margin doodles.

the eye twitch that followed this argument lasted for six months. at one point i asked the school nurse if i should be worried—she said, *do you have a real problem, or can i go on break?* i kept making people put their fingers on my cheek so they could feel the muscle spasming.

i don't know when the ocd really *started*. i was always an anxious kid. the belief that *clean* and *ocd* are synonyms is not relatable to my lived experience. it was simply a taskforce of intricate scaffolding—a harness. any compulsion i developed usually began as a form of protection charm. *tender* to me.

turn, for example, to the *magical thinking* that sprouted whole-hand from this single teenage interaction; my father on the floor, my writing at his feet.

convinced *anyone could be looking*, i now feared the single-minded peace that had previously come from writing. i no longer believed that writing was safe—there was simply no guarantee of privacy in *anything*.

and, at the same time: i couldn't *stop* writing, it was too precious to me.

i developed three sets of handwriting. one for notes: pristine and linear, in formidable capital letters. one for rushing: a more scrawled, a jaunty still-legible, half-cursive, half-ugly. and, holy, the third: the ghost. entirely illegible. safely messy. jagged scribbles that overlap in a code only i recognize.

i cannot write any harsh truth legibly, all of my skin starts frying. there are counter spells for it, but the easiest is to just cross it out and pretend it never happened.

at home, i was handed worksheets on *lord jesus*. when i crossed my eyes, i could make the lines flip over each other into the same static i taste at the back of my throat. dutiful, chided, obedient to a fault: i wrote in capital letters and filled in the blanks.

my father had signed us up for bible school exactly two weeks after i had asked: *what would you do if i was gay?*

◇

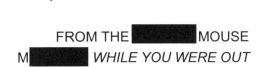

"Wet is worse than creepy. I'm literally positive." Marlowe is navigating a nail clipper around her toes, artfully catching slivers in the scoop of one hand. Her music plays off the scrangly speakers of her old phone.

You sit at her college-provided desk, turned halfway on the college-provided chair so you can see her. You are managing the absolutely herculean task of navigating sticky plastic ovals, slowly applying fake nails, a nice white-blue you picked up at CVS while getting mixer for tonight. You like it when one color is actually two colors at once.

This whole thing is very practiced and familiar. While Kaisa is very cool and you're *so* fucking lucky that you got a roommate like *her*, Marlowe has a single dorm. You tend to disappear to Marlowe's for hours on end. Kaisa, meanwhile, gets party ready with her real friends. Plus, you're having Lacey over later—you want Kaisa to have the room to herself for as long as possible as penance.

Your beautification process is not going well. You have shaky hands—and you buy the good brand, the one that comes with a sassy pink superglue that likes to cke out in unmanageable blobs. "Wet things can be good things, though," you argue. "Creepy is worse, I'm telling you."

"Okay, just, like, imagine the pussy joke I'm not gonna lower myself to." Marlowe's music is muffled by her salmon-colored IKEA bedspread. The first time you'd seen her room, you waited for the punch line—it was the same bedding you had in your childhood home. You'd said *my mom picked it out*, and she laughed—*my dad did*.

"Shrimps can be wet." The dry stickiness of the glue smears over your fingertip. Ugh. "Otters. Fish. Whales. Birds can be wet, sometimes."

The clipper in her hands makes a sharp sound as she works it. "Birds aren't, like, known for their wetness."

"But a thing can be wet without being creepy, is what I'm saying."

"But a *wet* creepy thing is way worse than a creepy thing. *Wet* is worse." Marlowe sits back for a second. "A creepy thing is just, like, a spooky mall. A scarecrow. Like, you can walk *around* a creepy thing and, like, keep going with your day. But a creepy *and* wet thing is, like: you lay eyes on that thing, and you're absolutely *fucked*."

"But, like, a thing that is creepy isn't *itself* anymore, you know what I mean? It's, like, the *creepy* thing instead. A wet thing is the *same* thing, but wet. A wet dog is just a dog that is wet. A *creepy* dog is like—the haunted version."

"Creepy Dogs Two: there's ghosts this time." Her hands fan at the fake movie title and then she brushes the toenails off her palm into the bin by the side of her bed.

"Like, a creepy shrimp is like—a completely different genre and species. It's not, like, *shrimp* anymore. It's *creepy shrimp.*" You tilt your head. "Does that make sense?"

"Right. Like, a creepy shrimp is 7-Eleven shrimp."

"Shrimp but it's *homophobic* shrimp."

She shoots you a look. "No shrimp can be homophobic, they're pink."

"I think they're, like, not pink until cooked." At the look on her face, you add, "Yeah. Sorry. But also, like, to be fair: I haven't met every shrimp. So maybe, like, some shrimp *are* pink shrimp."

You have only completed three nails and you're already bored of the application process, even if it is fun to click your new claws onto things.

You tap the desk. "But, like, yeah, I'm saying—creepy shrimp aren't *shrimp*. They're reclassified. They've branched off into like, alien territory. Like, we can discuss Marxism and alienation of the body if you want, but he could have just said—*capitalism makes your body creepy to itself.*"

"Okay, first of all, my body is far too spicy to ever be creepy, which he should have anticipated." She shakes a red polish in the air and then against her palm. "But like . . . this is what I'm saying. A wet, creepy Marx is *so* much creepier than just a creepy Marx. Like picture a room with a creepy Marx—now make him sopping wet. Wet is more powerful, like, it can, like . . . change a creepy thing."

"Oh, like—wet can modify creepy, but creepy can't modify wet?"

"Like, creepy socks. *Wet,* creepy socks." She puts the bottle back down. Maybe not a red night. "Creepy, wet socks?"

You retch. She shudders. You both laugh, and then laugh again only because you laughed at the same time. You test the seashell scoop of fake-nail size against your own, trying to consider if it's better to go bigger or go smaller. "Okay but creepy is, like, a sense. Wet is, like, a scenario. A creepy thing will *be creepy* until it, like, decides not to be, or whatever. It hangs around. Like, okay, maybe a haunted creepy church gets an exorcism. It starts eating right and making good choices. But it'll always be, like—oh that's the church that used to be creepy. But a wet thing just needs, like, a towel. Nobody's like *that church used to be wet.*"

"Okay, to your point—you can't sponge creepy," she agrees. "So, like. Hang on. Hold up." She laughs. "Maybe creepy *can* change wet. Like, a creepy-wet sponge is *way* creepier than a *wet*-wet sponge."

"Right. Like, if creepy spilled everywhere, it would be like—oh fuck, here's all the creepy. What do I do with this?"

"Right. And then that's just a frat party."

You laugh and fuck up the middle-finger installation attempt. You have to bring your hands closer to your face to try to fix it, trying to force your tremor to chill out. You're never going to be a surgeon, not when you can't even angle a fake nail correctly.

Marlowe jumps off the bed, pulling herself into a goblin crouch, miming skimming her hands through thick jungle. "Here we are," her faux English accent is both horrible and absolutely perfect, "Navigating the stank wasteland of the frat house—where someone has spilled the creepy all over the floor. Ah! Behold! The frat boys have smelled it and are running toward it, sensing their calling. This is their natural secretion."

You laugh, which gets glue everywhere. Your yank to remove the off-center nail somehow manages to straight-up flick it *directly* into your eye, and then you are both laughing too hard to talk. She kneels next to you, grabs your hand, tries to ask if you're alright, which you are, and then she gives you a single star kiss, right next to your affected eye—perfectly soothing the area, as if you had pointed it out with a target.

"Useless gay activity," she says through her laughing. Her hand comes up and she rubs at your cheek. "Want me to put those on?"

"Oh my God. Yes please." You scoot the chair so you are fully facing her, offering her your mottled blue-cold hands. "I have some kind of witch curse. I cannot get them straight the first time." At her look, you add, "No pun intended."

"I literally always need someone to do them for me." She pearls the glue into the back of the selected plastic, blowing on it to set it. She sits down in front of you, but then it's weird to be sitting up on a chair with her kneeling at your feet, so you get down too, awkwardly navigating the unpackaged nails in their little tray down along with you.

She puts on the next two acrylics, her dark brows wrinkled in concentration. You are both so focused on the task that no time is passing. She got her blue area carpet from a dumpster and washed it three times in the dorm laundry. It smells like the soap she borrowed from you.

You hear your phone buzz on the desk, and you kind of crane to glance at it, even though you absolutely cannot see it from here. "Lacey should be here by, like, seven, by the way."

"Dude, I'm kind of, like," Marlowe clears her throat. "I'm kind of nervous to meet your friends." She laughs in a high and tight way. "I don't, like, even know what to say."

But Marlowe always seems to understand something *other* about being in a room: she fills it up effortlessly. She always knows someone, somewhere, and those people always seem to love her. She is always laughing. Always dancing. Marlowe is infectious. Marlowe doesn't get nervous, Marlowe just *is*. It's part of what has made your college experience so charming—you just follow along, and Marlowe does all the talking.

You're baffled by her nervousness. "Like, Lacey?" Lacey, who is extremely funny and was your friend without question even when you were weird and bullied. "She's, like, she's okay? She's nice. She's fun. You'll—like, you'll get along."

"She's your childhood best friend." Something in her tone sounds heavy, dark.

It is a tone you haven't heard before, and you don't know how to walk with it. "Uh. Are you . . . like, okay?"

Marlowe shrugs and gives you a half smile. "I didn't, like, have one." She motions for you to tilt your hand so she can apply the thumbnail. Her hands are cold too, but she's not clammy like you.

"Like, a best friend?"

"Yeah, I like—I didn't . . . like, have that."

"I mean, like, Lacey and I were, like—not best friends at first, but like," you hold up the left hand for her to start, "I don't know, I didn't really, like—I got bullied a lot, so." You don't know what you're trying to communicate, but it's absolutely not helpful.

"Yeah, I mean, I didn't have, like, *any friends.*" She says it almost cheerfully.

You have no idea how to help. "Oh, honey, no. High schoolers are . . . like they fucking suck, dude."

"I mean they, like, absolutely do." She puts on your pinky finger. "I think it was me, though."

You don't know what to say to this. Marlowe stares at her task. Doesn't look at you. "I mean, I sucked a lot in high school. Like. Pretty much until I was twenty-two."

"You *are* twenty-two."

"It's, like, a process." She gives you a half smile, but you sense you fumbled something.

You try again. "Fuck those guys."

"I mean, yeah." She finished your right hand and takes your left again, working the clippers over the extended claws without you asking, filing them down to a manageable level.

The music changes songs. You are suddenly very aware of how small the room is. "I'm . . . really sorry, Mars. That shouldn't have happened."

"I mean, like. Like, I had some friends, but they were, like, not my *friends*. Like, I was in a circle of people, and those people all super loved each other, and I was just—there. Like, I was *there*. And nobody, like—" she takes a deep breath.

You're an idiot. She looks like she's about to cry, and you're just sitting there letting her do your nails.

"Like, nobody was *mine*," she blurts it like a bell. Like, spilling over.

You grab her hand. Hold it hard. Wait until her eyes meet yours. She offers you a weak, fake smile, wobbling over her lips.

"Hey." You find yourself whispering. "*I'm* yours."

She clutches your hand hard, squeezing her eyes shut. "You, like—" she half laughs, "You like me?" You can tell she meant it in a funny voice, but the honesty of it makes her pitch wobble.

"I super like you." You were expecting to exaggerate, but it comes out all soft, all accurate. Your vulnerability surprises even you. "Like, *super*. Like, *so much*, dude."

She doesn't open her eyes, but her vice grip relaxes a little. "Good, because, like, you're, like. Probably my best friend."

You make a noise from an unplanned place and then forget about the nails, awkwardly tackling her to the ground in a hug, wrapping her tiny body in your arms. She shrieks and splays out her limbs, trying to navigate the clippers away from your face.

"You're *my* best friend," you say into her shoulder.

"It's fine. I know there's, like, Lacey."

"Like, she's fine. But, like—" you don't know how to say it. "It's different with you."

The words are loud, even though she said them softly. They hang in the air like snow.

Neither of you move for a moment, and then Marlowe puts down the clippers and wraps her arms around you. After a moment, her hands start working idly through your hair.

She's warm, and softer than you expected. You can feel her hip bone through her jeans, but the angle you're at is pretty comfortable, actually. She sighs loudly. "Sor-*ry*." She sighs again. "Like, I didn't mean to get, all, like, weird and weepy."

"It's okay." You wrap her tighter for a moment, but you can tell she wants this to be over.

You sit back up and she swipes at her eyes, groaning. "This is, like, so ugly, sorry."

"I cry literally at anything and it looks *so* much worse."

She rolls her eyes. "I've, like, never even seen you cry, ever."

"I cried at that dog video, like, three days ago."

Marlowe rolls her eyes. "You only, like, teared up." She waves at you to give back over your hands, and you gladly do. You like feeling her fingers around you. She returns to shaping the nails. "It was, like, sociopathic, actually." She wrinkles her nose. "Wait. Do we still say sociopathic?"

"It's because I hate crying." You want to make her happy again. You scramble. "I just, like, pour out of my whole face in an ooze. *Blargh*," you say, rolling your body in an example undulating *blargh*.

"You do *not*, shut up."

"I gush, dude. Water everywhere. They have to call the DPW." You can't mime a phone with your hands in hers, so you just trust her to know what gag you're doing. You choose a bad approximation of a New York accent. "Hello, is this Tony? Yeah, she's at it again. Lady's gotten the whole district shut down—yeah, Tony, she's a real piece of work, huh? Send in all the clowns ya got."

She laughs, and you see her shoulders relax. She runs a file over the edges of her work for a second before sniffing quietly and looking up to you. "Hang on—did you call me *Mars* earlier?"

You wrinkle your nose. "Uh, yeah. Sorry."

She laughs. "Is it weird I kind of like it? Usually people shorten it to Lo or something."

"I could go with, like, Mar-Mar."

"I'll actually kill you. Like, I will sneak into your room at night and *kill you.*"

"If we take the 's' from Mars and put it on the last syllable instead, you'd be Lowe's," you offer.

"Oh my God, how am I just noticing this now?" She smiles with that particular glint in her eye, and then she catches *your* expression. Her mouth drops open like she is reading your mind. "Don't you dare. You fucking English major, don't—don't look at me like that— no! Don't you *dare.* I will reciprocate and only introduce you as Home Depot."

"That's my family name. You can just call me Depot, miss."

"I hate you," she says.

And then she leans in, and her hands wrap around the back of your head. For a second, you flinch, and then she is kissing you fully on the lips, deep and passionate.

Your heart leaps into your throat. She rushes over you in an anchor. You put your fingers into her hair. She gasps and pulls at the front of your shirt, dragging you closer. You snake your arms around her small body. She crushes against you, organza petals as she sighs into your mouth, skating her nails up your back.

She groans and pulls back, pushing the heel of her palm against her eyes. Sighs. "God. Sorry. Sorry. I wasn't supposed to do that."

"No," you say, hearing your stutter barely cap over the roar in your ears, "Like, please do that any time, for any reason. Like, any time. Literally."

She laughs. Leaves a peck on your cheek. "Okay, for real, we need to start, like, getting ready. I want it to be, like, go time for Lacey."

"Okay," you say. "Yes." You say. "Okay." You say. "Yes. Getting . . . ready."
Marlowe gets up and gives you a hand to help you to your feet.
"Any time?" she asks with a wink. She seems to be handling this so
casually.

"Uh, yeah. Yes. Absolutely." You feel yourself blushing, and she
laughs when she sees, patting your cheeks.

"I didn't think you blushed!"

"I don't, usually." It makes you blush harder, which makes her
laugh harder.

"You're *so* gay."

"Uh, yeah. Yes. Despite my best intentions. Some would say
unfortunately."

Marlowe laughs again. "Sorry. I'm just like—I like kissing you,
okay? I don't get why we only do it when we're drunk. Like. I like
kissing you too much to ever, like, actually stop."

"Yes," you squeak. "Uh."

"It's very French of us," she begins to collect things around her
room, grinning. "This is my best friend, whom I kiss a lot. Get used to
it. Like, it's strictly platonic."

"Yeah," you say. "Strictly. Uh. Platonic."

i can talk for hours about the sexism of lycanthropy, but the
calculation has such clear variables—any woman can tell you about
being a werewolf. ask her about having fur. ask her about having too
much howl. ask her about the fountain of her mooning, miserable
loneliness. ask her what it is like to want something so loudly that
she turns feral for it. ask her what it is like when she loses control.
ask her about how they look at her, when she finally turns on them
and snaps *not like this, no you don't.* ask her about being polite. ask

her what it feels like when she comes home and finally takes her smile off. ask her about her childhood. ask her how many rotisserie chickens she has torn apart with nothing but her fingernails. ask her about the last time she felt something build inside of her, vicious, angry, lonely.

ask her how she hid what was overwhelming, painful, bloody.

◇

FROM ▮▮ ▮▮▮▮▮ MOUSE
ME▮▮▮▮▮: *WHILE YOU*▮▮▮▮▮

You are all stomping in the kind-of-a-fun way from one party to the next, chilly in your bodycon dresses and boot heels and no tights, New England winter whistling around your pinking ears. *Hoes don't get cold.* You have all thickly applied *the liquor coat.*

Lacey is humming, dancing as she walks, talking about the school she goes to. Kaisa walks next to her, and the two of them occasionally walk close enough that they hip check. You keep grinning about it. Two years ago, Lacey admitted *your roommate is like, so pretty.* You have been trying to set them up ever since.

"But yeah," Lacey is saying, "It's technically only houses run by team sports, not frat houses, but honestly? There's no appreciable difference." Lacey is drunk too, she's just smart as a whip, and can use words like *appreciable* while absolutely twisted.

Kaisa is nodding and smiling in that small, beautiful way she has, like she's holding in a laugh or about to tell a secret. Meanwhile, around the three of you, Greek row is disgusting as usual, packed with people and litter and graying snow. Kaisa promised she'd check in on a friend, and then the plan is that you'll all pack into an Uber to go to Henry's place.

If you were seventeen again, you'd be baffled by your own behavior. You actually in the real life go to *actual* frat house parties. This is functionally at odds for *literally everything* that is true about you. Worse: you even *legitimately* have some friends at these houses; people you take classes with and have hung out to do homework with. So much for pretending to be a feminist: if a man is ever nice to you, you immediately believe the best in him.

Kaisa gently leads Lacey around a puddle, and leans in to whisper something into her ear. Lacey lets out a sparkle of surprised laughter.

You grin like an idiot, weirdly proud that your friends are all getting along. Look! You are pretty and popular and you have *three* friends who all like each other!

Marlowe grabs your hand and pulls your ear down too. "Sorry, can I just . . ." She giggles. "Can we just address—like, I can't believe I kissed you earlier," she whispers.

A chill goes through you, her breath on your neck. You slide your eyes to her, maybe too-drunk to be clever with an answer. "I liked it," you manage.

She wrinkles her nose up at you, but not in a "gross" way, in the way that is *her* language specifically—she means *you're being cute.* "I liked it."

You kick a rock by accident, stumble. She catches you.

"We should have rules," she says.

"Rules," you repeat. "For—oh, for the kissing?"

"Like," she laughs once, like a bark, "I'm *gonna* do it again. I just want to be, like, honest about it."

Your eyebrows skyrocket, can't stop the look of utter joy that spreads across your face. "You have my . . . full attention."

The four of you have to pause to let a group of girls pass in the other direction. They compliment Marlowe's hair, she does a little shimmy for them, everyone starts laughing.

She tugs your hand again while you all start walking. "I just, like. Not to be like a stickler or something. I just. Don't want it to be a weird thing."

"It's not a weird thing."

"I don't want it to *become*, like. A weird thing."

You are too drunk for this. "Yes."

She holds up her hand, thumb extended, like she's about to start counting. "Okay, so."

"So, okay." You steady yourself as you all file into a line waiting at the front of the frat house. Kaisa and Lacey peel off into the lawn, talking closely. You navigate one eye carefully at Marlowe, trying to force yourself into appearing sober.

She pauses to send a text message and then hums thoughtfully. "Okay. I'm gonna shoot off at the hip here, so don't freak out."

A prickle of fear collapses an ice shelf down your thigh bone. "I'm not freaked out."

"*Promise* you won't freak out, though." She points at you. "Like, I'm just saying what's right for *me* and for what *I* want."

You hold up your hands like you're at gunpoint. "Yeah, dude."

She stares at you for a moment, and then nods. "Okay. Rule one—I don't think we should ever have sex. I'm just gonna say that right now, off the bat. I love kissing you, but I want it on record we are *not* gonna do that."

You're staring at her hand.

Once when you were twelve, you held a pair of scissors tilted at a particular angle. The whole world got really quiet.

This isn't happening right now. You are actually back in the same blue plastic chair you once began ███ing in.

How come you started that shit so *young?* At a distance, it looks fake. Kids don't *do* that, right? You're probably misremembering. You had a really beautiful childhood, and you're not being fair to your parents, who are good people, and who did their best by you, despite your fucking horrific personality.

Marlowe peers up at you, her brow knitting. How long have you been silent for. She narrows her eyes. "Is that, like? Okay? I just, like, I don't want to be stupid about this."

You remember to be on the planet. "I think our first rule should be that if you make a *Fight Club* reference, you need to, like, be ready to . . . like," you search around your slippery brain, "write an essay about how it's been misunderstood. Or something." You know the joke you're trying to make, but you're fucking up the timing.

She points to you. "No talking about *Fight Club*, then."

You mock-flinch, groaning. "Fuck. *I* did it."

"But, so. Rule one." She makes her hand bounce, as if recounting *one* on her fingers. "No sex," she repeats. "It literally always ruins things. And, like, you mean too much to me. We are *not* going to be those gay people who, like, fuck their friends and can never speak to them again. I am not gonna be that stereotype."

You look at your shoes and then at your hands and then at Lacey and then at the clouded sky and then at the wet and littered grass underfoot. "It's, I mean. It's just kissing, right? Do we need to . . . like, take it this seriously?"

She points at you. "Rule two. It's just kissing. We do not take it seriously."

"I think I take kissing . . . as more like . . . a sacred duty?"

Marlowe doesn't answer you, she's on her phone, texting. She puts the phone back into her dress, in the place she calls her *bra pocket*. You keep your stuff in the same place on *your* body, because honestly, it's a really good place for it. "Okay. So, no sex, and don't take it seriously. Does that feel good?"

For some reason, the problem is actually that there's only two rules. You don't like this number, but your OCD hasn't been diagnosed yet, so instead ants gutter their way over your skin, their little talons clicking. Even through the softening of the alcohol, that horrible knowledge that two isn't *right*.

There's a tradition: *bad things come in threes.* "Rule three," you say, slowly, trying to figure it out while you speak, "We should have something about . . . how frisky."

Marlowe snorts. "You still say *frisky?*"

"Like the . . . cat food."

"Over the shirt? Nothing under the belt, right. I don't know, I'm like—I just want this to be fun for both of us, and, like. I don't know, I want to be serious about boundaries."

You peer down at her, closing one eye. You're swishy. "Okay border control. We get it. No funny business."

"No, actually. It *has* to be funny, is the thing." She tilts her head. "Actually, I said that as a joke, but I think I actually mean it? Does that make sense? Like rule three would be—this is only for the laugh of it?"

You should take a moment and make a note on your phone about the feeling you're having right now, because in the morning, you will have forgotten it. You should let your future self know exactly what she's dealing with.

"I think I was scared of the Teletubbies as a kid," you admit. "Do you think they put their televisions *in* their stomach, or do you think they grow *around* the television?" You like the idea of a perfectly sized hole to fit a moving image. You pantomime the square around your stomach, but then realize you've brought attention to your considerable midsection, so you wiggle your hands up your body in a sparkly jazz motion to distract from it.

She grabs your floating hands, leans in, kisses you, smooth and deep and painless, like the whole compass forgot north. She wraps her fingers into your hair, traces your cheekbones, guides you against her. Kisses you like you're not in public, like nobody is around to see, like nobody exists except you two and the way she leans into you.

Then she steps back, grinning. "God, I fucking love having you as a girlfriend. I fucking love this."

"I think they might grow *around* the television," you say. "I'm worried that would make them, like, a topiary? But they've got to be mammalian, right? Or are they egg-laying?"

She squeezes your hands, lowers her voice, brings herself up onto her toes, nuzzles into your neck. "Seriously, thank you for talking with me about this. I was, like, freaked out. Like genuinely convinced I ruined it."

Did you really start at *twelve?* That has *got* to be the wrong number. Isn't that, like, seventh grade? What could you *possibly* have been going through? Okay, yes, you were bullied, but, like—wasn't it mostly just normal shit, like how you never seemed to know which clothes to wear or how to fit in? Like, you had a pretty easy life, all things considered. Always had a roof over your head and you had your photography and your writing. And now you're about to graduate *college.* Like, you're fucking *lucky.* People *wish* they had your life. You have no excuse. In some ways, you're kind of co-opting the language of suffering. Like, you never *actually* had anything bad happen to you.

(God, wouldn't that have been nice, though? If you'd had a fucking *excuse?*)

Marlowe wrinkles her nose. "Isn't a platypus still a mammal even though it lays eggs? Maybe they're like that."

The platypus is the last living member of the genus Ornithorhynchus. Maybe the Teletubbies are dinosaurs, then, and you grew up watching a fossil record of old giants. Maybe that whole show is just a dream by something that is already extinct.

"I'm going to go check on Lacey," you say, because the inhuman parts of yourself are pushing up against your skin, and if you stay still any longer, something might slip.

1 corinthians 7:9 reads: "if they cannot control themselves, they should marry, for it is better to marry than to burn with passion."

only a few paragraphs after this, paul states he has "no word from god" about virgins, which made me laugh out loud the first time i read it. i pictured a weary monk, bent over his table, getting to the part where he's asked about god's views on sex—and that paul ends up just kind of shrugging about it.

i like the causality—*if* they cannot control themselves, *then* they should marry. the implication that it is far less sinful to act on your desires than it is to tremble in anticipation of sin. even the bible has to admit—humans cannot be stopped from loving each other so tangibly that it *burns* through us; alters our hardwiring.

in marriage, we codify love as a perpetual condition. we agree: every morning, every evening, through happiness and anger. we tie ourselves together, knowing the way might be difficult. the alternative is hell on earth: wanting and not having.

the first time you hang out one-on-one, you are nervous about sitting near her. she is delicate, and you're big in comparison. you'd been close for a while, but not *too* close. she offers to start watching a show with you and another girl; the other girl ends up canceling.

playacting your casual self, you sit on her dorm bed and loosely let your legs touch hers. in other (straight) friendships, this is nothing. later in your life, someone will call this *breaking the touch barrier.* the moment you test her: a distinct moment of decision.

you both pretend. it is different when you are both queer. the silence from your body is an astounding, precarious illness. this moment is incredibly tenuous—who pulls away, who allows it to continue, who snuggles closer.

neither body moves, which is, of course, a move you're both making.

◇

You're the wrong kind of drunk: bored and angry. Two hours ago, you guys got sidetracked, and now you're somewhere new, in somebody's basement with a bad DJ. Lots of weird esoteric European ska—and not the fun kind. You want to take the aux cord just to play literally anything else.

Not that you're looking for her, but Marlowe's across the floor from you, separated by an undulating crowd, doing the same thing she's always done at parties: making friends, making advances. You've seen this a million times and never had a problem with it. You'll just meet back up with her at the end of the night like usual. The two of you almost never stay together once you're inside. This is a normal day.

You're lucky, actually. She could have left you. Things could have changed. You know how she is; she could have just ditched you without incident, and then you'd have lost a best friend. She even *admitted* it—that it could be ruined by something like this. You're lucky she even speaks to you, much less wants to kiss you.

You go find Lacey where she is nodding politely to someone in another corner of the party, tilting her head to hear him over the pounding music. She doesn't resist when you make some purposefully quiet excuse to him, knowing he can't hear over the weird drum solo currently blasting.

You interlace your fingers with hers and she lets you drag her over to the room next door where random people are just standing around and chatting over Pabst beers. There's a singular laundry machine and rust on the floor and a silver exhaust pipe overhead. You make a note to breathe less, suspecting mildew among all of it.

Lacey has a hickey blooming on the side of her neck. She bends to look behind her at the dancing. "I love Marlowe, can I say that?"

"Are you having fun?" You need to remember to start applying for jobs soon, before the semester is done. *And* you need to figure out where to live. Shit.

She grins at you. "You've asked me that, like, seven times."

"But *are* you?"

Lacey always makes this strange space around her, like you've been holding your breath for a really long time, and she's got the last supply of oxygen left. She's seen you as a weird teen and she's seen you get bangs and she's seen you try out nicknames and she's seen you in a panic attack and she's seen you throwing up. You picked each other, is the thing. The two of you just instantly understood you were both operating on the same level, some kind of plane where you were both the same kind of *something*.

Also, she's extraordinarily pretty. So being seen with her is a good thing. You get to point to her and say *that's my best friend* and feel exceptionally cool about it.

She elbows you gently. "I'm having fun."

"*Please* tell me you weren't making out with Kaisa in a closet again." You meant it to sound playful, but it comes off sort of aggressive. The liquor gives your words a metallic, sullen edge. You try: "You absolute whore," as a joke to soften it, but it actually makes the comment somehow *worse*. "I love it."

She gives you a giggly shrug, making a kind of noncommittal *ehh* sound. "Would you be mad if I said yes but not in a *closet?*"

"You're such a whore," you repeat, managing to soothe the venom out of it so it comes out the way you'd originally intended—affectionate, loving.

Lacey looks more triumphant than sheepish, gives another shrug, this one to cover her blushing. "*What!* They're a good kisser! And they're *so* pretty. Holy shit. Did you see they got a new tattoo?"

Kaisa *is* so pretty. You'd both been randomly matched up for the room assignment during freshman year, but had actually liked each other's living styles enough to keep up the arrangement. You aren't exactly *friends*, but you've also never gotten into an actual argument. In part this is probably because you are both middle children, and therefore would rather die than make unnecessary conflict.

Kaisa is fun, and out of the closet, and openly identifies with she/they pronouns, and is unflappable, and likes coconut candy. She always offers you one out of her jar when she's eating, even though you've never actually accepted. She dyes her hair fun colors and has an assortment of incredible tattoos and plays softball and does cool indie stuff and everyone loves her. Kaisa doesn't shave her legs, but she is the kind of person who can pull it off—you're too noticeable for that. It would seem like you're just messy.

"I mean," you have to pause to consider. "Like, I *guess* she's cute, but I don't think, she's, like, *for* me." You don't know how to language it

When you look up, you have the misfortune of glancing around the corner to where Marlowe is now grinding on a guy's leg and making out with tongue visible from across the floor. Oh, come *on*.

You drag Lacey back to the music and do your stupid purposefully bad-dad-at-a-party dance moves and shake your hair and laugh and sway your hips and pretend *this is it!* so loudly that you eventually convince the liquor too.

Kaisa ends up going home and people trickle out of the room and then it is basically just you and Lacey and three of the guys from the house. Suddenly the basement is very big and it's stupid to be here. They're just too polite to officially kick you out. One of the guys tries to impress Lacey by doing a handstand against the wall and managing to flip a cup off his ass cheek, and you have to admit—actually that was pretty fucking cool, if extremely weird of him.

You're starting to shiver as you sober up. They didn't heat the basement. Someone has taken the aux cord and is now exclusively playing "Build Me Up Buttercup" on repeat.

Marlowe usually goes home with you, is the thing. You keep checking your phone, waiting to hear from her. You don't want to call her: that would be desperate, attention-seeking.

The flipcup guy advises you not to, but you go upstairs, hunting for her. Sure enough, they're further into the event than you'd expected, splayed out on the couch. You blink stupidly at them for a second, and then whip back around the corner.

"Uh," you call out. "We're about to head out."

You hear silence and then quick shuffling, and the guy says, "█████████!" and Marlowe shushes him, giggling.

Your whole face is hot, horrible. You are so *fucking* embarrassing. Why can't you just figure out how to be a *normal person?*

Marlowe leans around the doorjamb. Her lipstick is smeared, and she's only in her bra. "Hi, hi. Sorry." She winks at you. "I'm staying."

Your heart is racing. "Are you sure? I feel bad about leaving."

She rolls her eyes.

You gesture vaguely. "Are you, like, actually okay to stay? I mean, like . . . ?" Like, you've both been drinking pretty heavily. Like, you're worried about her. Like, she's in danger.

She snorts. "I'm a grown-up, babe. I can make smart choices."

Your brow furrows. "Are you sure? I just—"

She must misunderstand where your hesitation is coming from, because now she looks angry. "Dude. Seriously, get the fuck out of here. I'm in the middle of something. I don't need you hanging around. You're here with Lacey and Kaisa, they'll get you home safe."

You stare at her, feeling your mouth hang open. You can't even think to stutter a response. A thin silver blade stabs into your gut.

"I . . ."

You should explain where you're coming from. Talk fast. You're a bad friend. Instead of comforting her, you're just focused on the act of swallowing instead of throwing up.

Maybe she thought you were judging her? Maybe it seemed like you were calling her a slut. God, nobody actually likes you, you know that, right? Everyone is just *pretending* to be your friend. You're actually super unlovable and awkward and a huge burden. And now you're making it *worse*. You did the wrong thing.

You want to fix this, right now, immediately, but you can't get the correct command prompt running and she just looks so fucking *angry*, and you ruined *everything*.

"██████████!" The guy calls.

Marlowe, laughing, throws him the middle finger.

She turns back to you, and maybe it all shows on the body before you can stop it, because she finally softens. "Go," she whispers, "I'll be okay, I promise. Love you." She darts out, kisses you quickly, and then jumps back into the living room. You hear her cackle and shriek. The couch squeaks and the dude grunts with surprise—it sounds like she threw herself into his lap again.

You are standing in a hallway, and your best friend since high school is in the basement under you, and you've accidentally abandoned her. Go get her, you're horrible. Stop looking at the floor with its yellowed tile. Stop staring at the cracked plastic molding.

There's a single nail that's been pounded in wrong but never fixed. Its thin and rusted body is bent at an angle.

In the morning, you text her first. Something vague about getting breakfast.

Marlowe shows up with her guy, and you show up with Lacey and Kaisa. Marlowe holds his hand and laughs loudly at all of his jokes, her laughter big and bold and brassy. You are hangover-hungry but you can't eat.

The entire meal, Marlowe keeps making comments like—"But what do I know, I'm just a little gay person," and then cracking up.

You bend your fork out of shape, which feels dramatic and violent.

You're an adult now, Mouse. Start acting like one.

i had *a lot* of collections, actually. i collected art supplies which i did not use. i collected the phrases from fortune cookies. i collected cutout pictures from magazines.

my current collection is a messy horde in a pantry. items that are too hot for me to touch, loaded with emotional damage. one of them is a letter from a friend. i couldn't get past the part that says *i'm worried about you. i heard what happened.* i lied and told them i didn't get the message.

my ocd got very bad at nineteen. i started having to hiss or bite my tongue any time someone promised something they couldn't necessarily see through—*it'll be okay* or *of course she'll forgive you.* my skin peeled off whenever someone used an absolute—*you'll be fine* as a platitude made me actively retch. i'd make my ears ring trying to find the thought and trap it before it could get inside of me. i'd spend hours pulling out the hair on my legs, hazy with some kind of bloodlust. greed. a need to devour something.

i knew i was weird, so i took allergy pills to be normal. when you live in extremes, dullness is an exactitude of self-possession. allergy pills had a consistent, timed effect. i would take them and drift into a noiseless, perfect calm of too-drowsy-for-much. there isn't room for anxiety in the weariness—everything was flat, manageable, perfect.

the broken hand of my life was a tipping scale of indulgence and restriction, an endless aura of desperation versus gluttony without any singular and clear sustained *want*.

a habit of fostered trauma: if you do not want things, they cannot be denied to you.

i did want a connection with others, sure, on some level—but rather than cultivate rejection via honesty, i would absolve myself preternaturally by the body of a claritin. *they don't know me; they only know the drugged version of me.* therefore, i am not truly there, nor do i truly exist. if they realize i am weird, and shy, and awkward—well, i wasn't really *there*. i wasn't really *trying*. it wasn't really *me*, was it?

the sacrament was dry. i would, many times, forget i'd taken it. i'd sip hard liquor and stupor myself in seconds, miracle water sloshing through my gut. in alcohol i accidentally discover the perfect antianxiety drug: one that makes you *fun!*

from the mouth of others i loved: *i have no idea who you are.* is that a compliment?

i'd see myself in the mirror and catastrophize about her. *that is a ghost. that is not myself. that is the uncomfortable, unknown, unfamiliar.*

un; meaning "anti." the whitened, christened specter of my own mind.

◇

You realize about thirty minutes into the conversation that he might actually believe the thing he's saying about the Pope. You missed the first part, but you're pretty sure it's all uncited.

So the last two months, it's been . . . fine! It's even been *good*. She just kisses you whenever she wants, leaning over in the middle of the day. In the middle of homework. In the middle of texting.

Spookily, she'll be turning twenty-three almost *exactly* six months after you—she's younger by six months and six days. She's a Sagittarius, which is your rising sign. November feels a shocking amount of distance away now, even despite the snow in spring.

You are so fucking lucky she hasn't gotten bored of you. This is probably because you two are definitely *not* dating. You both laugh about it whenever you are asked. You have even developed a cyst of a boyfriend. He thinks Marlowe is hot and that you kissing Marlowe is hotter. He used to be nice, to be fair. Now he's just nicely long distance.

Sure, okay, you're the only girl she kisses—and lately, she's the only *person* you kiss. You both tag each other on Insta #mygirlfriend. You both hold hands in public. You spend weekends on dates and get drunk and have sleepovers but the whole time—you follow the three rules. Neither of you touch each other like you *actually* want anything from it. All flirty comments are ironic or overtly lusty and aren't meant to *mean* anything.

The rules are almost seductive.

To push the boundaries on this thing would be to make it come into focus. To define it would be to give it shape. On the good days, you actually kind of like the sketchiness of it, how the outline undulates and flexes. You tell Lacey *we're both just enjoying whatever it is.*

On the bad days: the loneliness gets so loud, and you kind of want to vomit.

And there are these *moments*. Little flashes. How she texts you first. How she sends you pictures of herself in nothing but a bra, asking you if it looks good. How she calls you whenever she's driving. She wants you to meet her family. She wants to hear your secrets. She asks you to teach her how to write poetry.

In these moments, you're horribly aware: *you* can't ask, but God, wouldn't it be so good and easy if it was actually *real?*

But she doesn't ask, so you don't say anything. You write angsty, longing poetry that all has the same mantra: *she needs to come of her own accord.*

Sometimes it's even *you* who puts a stop to it. Sitting up, scrubbing your hair back from your face. You'd kind of groan about it, growling low in your chest. She'd float a hand up to you and bring you back down for more kisses. In the morning you always have to figure out what exactly had made you pause *this* time—but you never want to look too closely at it.

So you're *hers,* but she isn't *your* girlfriend.

The party is so loud, and you don't like the song that keeps coming back on. Marlowe spits the last half of her green apple into your hand. It is covered in drool. Someone shouts in another room. "It's supposed to cure nausea," she's saying, "but it's mealy."

Your phone rings. Marlowe pulls a disappearing act between you swiping to answer and you looking up.

You plug one ear and shush the guy. Hunt half-heartedly for a trash can to organize the apple better. You two are at Henry's place a *lot* these days, just because it's further off campus and has more friends from Marlowe's major.

"Hi? Hang on, Mom."

"Is that a party? Are you at a party?"

The guy follows you into the kitchen. It's quieter in here, and the lights are brighter. Flipcup is in the corner, but it's a chill version;

most of the people in here are mellowed into their drinks. You try
to turn so you can block the guy from talking to you, but he backs
you against the fridge, so you give up. You hand him the apple half,
which he stares at. You wipe your hands on your stupid little black
dress. You've been getting kind of chubby lately—you should keep
an eye on that.

To your mom, you say: "I saw your text. So, hang on, *what* did
Grandma do with your knives?"

"I'm not kidding. Just the way I said it. She used the Ginsu I gave
her—*to borrow*—to lift her flooring."

"She's eighty-eight years old. How is she even—"

A snort. "It's been exactly seven hours since she started a project
and the floor was dirty and it was bothering her. You know."

"Okay. Go back and explain what you meant about *lifting* the
flooring." You check your reflection in a spoon from the sink.

The guy shifts to lean against the counter, casually putting the
apple down among the other dishes. His rant, as far as you can tell, is
a conspiracy about popes and their many fingers in different parts of
the world. Something about mind control. Something about hats.

Your mother sighs. "She didn't need a spatula or a real tool to lift
it because she had a knife." The line fills with rustling. "When I hang
up, I'll send you pictures. And yes—it comes with pictures."

"Hang on. Are you saying she actually—like, she peeled the floors
like they're—"

"And you know your grandmother—"

"Like a *grape?* Like a, like—some kind of motherfucking *fruit?*"

"She did all of this without calling me or your father or your
brother first. So I find out about it because I call her to ask if she
got snowed in because she lives, you know, in the middle of godless
country, USA, where it snows in fucking *April.* Forty minutes into the
conversation—I mean, it's a conversation about *birds*—I find out she's

filming *Extreme Home Makeover: Senior Edition*. With! Mind you. The ninety-dollar Ginsu I lent her. I *lent* her."

You tap the spoon tunelessly against the counter. "Weren't her floors wood? How does she get even get under—like, is she a *spider?*"

"This was her kitchen; it's—it *was*—tile. Linoleum."

"The kitchen would be where one would find a Ginsu knife, I guess. Easy access."

"I'm going to kill her."

"With the Ginsu?"

A girl comes to fill her Sprite bottle with water. Pope guy restarts the whole conspiracy theory from the top, and you nod to him so she can escape toward the side. Martyr complex.

"Are we going to visit her?" You draw a tiny heart in the water on the crusty yellow peel-and-stick counter tiles. The cold New England spring wind blows in from the front porch. All the cool kids are smoking out there and talking about the not-cool kids who can't smoke because they have asthma and a victim complex. Someone shouts and slams the glass door shut.

You should probably go look for Marlowe.

You roll up your sleeves and start washing a mason jar. Flipcup suddenly erupts into cheers behind you.

"Honey, if you're at a party, I want you to go have fun."

"I can be home next weekend."

"You should go and make friends. You don't have a lot of time left in the semester. This is your *senior year*, sweetheart."

You begin to wiggle apart the artfully stacked plastic *Frozen* cups you recognize from the dollar store down the street—pink and blue with ice princesses. They make octopus sounds when separated.

"Maybe we could go get lunch with her?"

"The last time we went out she only ordered a coffee. Black. Said she's on a liquid diet these days. I said—oh, honey, hang on."

You hang on, shake the finished cups dry, place them in delicate wet rings in an uneven ant line of Olaf and Elsa and . . . what's the reindeer's name?

A hand scoops up your back. Your shoulders crackle up around your ears, but when you cut your eyes to Pope guy, you find you've been unfair—it was Marlowe, not him. She tucks herself against you, nibbling the side of your neck.

"I'm sorry, I'm so drunk."

"It's okay." You don't want to touch her with wet hands. You twist, gently tap her with the toe of your wedge-heeled boots. "It's cute, babe."

"I am like, the fucking *worst*." She rubs her cheek. Wraps her arms around your throat and wiggles her tiny nose against your ear. "You're my *best friend* and I *love* you and I'm *so* drunk right now."

"Want to talk to my mom?"

"Oh my God, no." Marlowe pulls back and shakes her head about three times more than necessary. "You already probably, like, hate me for being, like. *Such* a shitty friend. Like, I promised I'd take care of you today so you could have *fun* and I'm just like, I'm *so* sorry."

"I don't hate you."

"I think I'm gonna, like, dye my hair the same color as you. We could match. We could have, like, such cute pictures together. For graduation."

She would look better with the red than you do—she's got fair skin, and you have a weird almost olive undertone that never seems to settle in any particular classification. She pats around her tiny dress—one she borrowed from you two years ago and looked too good in, which meant you could never ask her to return it. "Oh shit . . . have you seen my keys?"

"I have them." You've had them every time she's asked for the past three hours.

"I love you *so* much." She puts her palms on the side of your face and makes concentrated eye contact. "You are *amazing.*" Someone she knows shows up and her mouth breaks into a toothy grin. "Oh my God. That's fucking Jason. I *told* you he'd be here. I fucking told you. I'm gonna do shots with him really quick, gimme a second."

Marlowe kisses your hand and runs into the hoofbeat section of the house. You've been over there, and a lava lamp is the only lighting. You felt too sober.

Pope guy is affirming that the pope thing goes back to the *sixteenth century.* You actually answer him a few times, even though you know better than to feed these kinds of things. You're just impressed, is all. Usually, people notice if you're ignoring them completely.

You put your hands back into the sink and get back to cleaning. Fourteen plates and another mason jar, all ogre mouth filled with green discharge.

Then another mason jar. Then another mason jar. Then another mason jar, but textured. Mason jar, mason jar, three plastic bottles. Mason jar.

You get one side of the sink empty. Start on the other.

Rustling from the phone. "Sorry to make you wait so long. Your father just got home. Do you want to talk to him?"

"He's home late."

"Are you sure you're not busy? It sounds like you're busy."

"So are we not going to visit her?" You frown at the dishes. Where are they even getting the mason jars. There are just so many. Are the people who live here picklers? Farmers? Fancy jam crafters? Mason himself?

"Well. You know how your grandmother is."

One jar has a crack. You want to keep it, but don't want it to be confused when it wakes up alone. You put it back with the others.

"Right. And what would be the current grandma availability hours?"

"Oh, you know. The normal ones, for normal old people. Two in the morning, she says."

"What could possibly be happening at two in the morning that requires her to be awake for it?"

"She says it's the cat. She needs to get up and feed him."

Pope guy starts drying the cups you put down in front of him. He looks you dead in the eye for the first time and says that the Pope's hat is called a zucchetto.

There are six dishes left, stacked primly between icing layers of brown sludge. "Like that cat needs more food."

"Last time she took him, the vet said, direct quote: *this is an obese monstrosity.*"

"Is her bedtime the crack of dawn?"

"Close. Last time I called she was going down after one thirty in the afternoon. After her soaps."

"Is she a fucking *vampire?*"

There's only one cup left. You won't go look for Marlowe after this. You'll get in the car and you'll go eat cake by yourself on the floor of your bedroom while watching *Criminal Minds.* You kind of like that show, right? It's watchable, at least. You two shouldn't have driven here, you should have just sprung for the Uber.

You tap this glass a few times more than the rest, listening to your mother's breathing on the other end of the phone. "Hey, what's the name of the pope's hat?"

"Uh. I think it's. Hmm." She pauses. "A miter."

You hold the phone to your chest. "My mom says it's a miter and she's like, super Catholic." You put the speaker back up. "Sorry. A kid I'm talking to says it's a zucchetto."

"I don't know! Ask your father. Maybe that's the Italian name for it. Look it up. Who are you talking to?"

Pope guy looks undefeated. You pass him the cup. He goes back to talking. You wipe your wet hands on your bare legs. You shouldn't have worn this short of a dress. "Hey, Mere, how do you spell *miter*?"

"Honey, I have no idea. Are you sure you're not busy?"

"So am I coming home next weekend? This weekend? Right now? Preventatively before Grandma literally tears apart every corner of her house?"

"Let me ask your father if we're busy."

You turn your back to the sink. Fold one arm. Flipcup has evolved into beer pong. Someone chucks it directly in, no rim. Great shot. "Nah, don't. I just, like I'm—I worry Grandmother will, like, weaponize her crochet next. It's like watching a tiger in the wild. I don't trust it. She's going to escape and vampire us all any day now."

"God, I hope not. May the seventh seal remain unbroken."

You can't think of anything else to say. "How's the dog?"

"Oh, you know. Doing doggy things, thinking doggy thoughts. Very busy."

You pull the phone away briefly to check Facebook for a notification that doesn't come.

Your mother gasps. "Now *there's* a photography series for you to make. 'Why does my dog keep taking knives out of the knife block?'"

The phone is wet now and you have to wipe it off. "Oh, I saw your Snap! Was—"

"If he spends any more time with knives and tuna cans, he's going to invent a weapon."

You look at Pope guy. Without dishes to do, he's counting evidence on his fingertips, weighing each down like a springboard. The burden of truth, ever so heavy.

Maybe you should stay here where Marlowe left you. Maybe if you just wait, she'll show up, drag you with her into the violent snow, alight and dancing. Maybe she'll come back and tell you she missed you and say you look cute.

You walk toward the other room, darker and quieter. Beer on the floor. Sticky. You switch the phone to the other ear. "You named the dog Mercutio, I mean. You manifested this. Don't let him near the can opener."

"Like I ever *let* him do anything. You know he has a doggy will of his own."

"Maybe he can be a doggy chef. Maybe you should stop stifling his doggy artistic talents."

"Your father says he's plotting something against us."

You stop at the deck's sliding door. Someone you don't know is laughing and blowing smoke up and out next to your roommate. Kaisa is always like this—cool poet in the middle of an indie film where all of their friends are half wiccans and have hanging gardens with interesting plant names and a very good sense of individual fashion. They all probably have cool and unusual pets and never need to dress up to feel sexy. And they all probably know where to get mason jars.

Pope guy has followed you and is now talking about the fingers of rats. Dexterous. He wiggles at you.

You look at your own hand. Unratlike. Where the hell is Marlowe.

"Mother, in dog years, hear me out—I think Mercutio is kind of, like, *thirty*. Maybe, like, it's just time for him to learn how to hold a knife."

"Oh! The photo series could be named *Knife to Meet You*."

"What does that have to do with dogs?" You open and close your hand. You think: *this is how to hold nothing, and thereby never let go.* That is pretentious. You should write that down, put it in your poetry class's final project. Shit, you need to remember to get that done.

"I don't know!" Your mother sounds a little miffed, "I'm workshopping. It's something, though, right? You said you were stuck;

I'm just trying to give you an idea about stuff. You know, you should really talk to your father about that."

"How about the *Fur-y of the Blade*?"

"I'm serious. He hasn't heard from you in a while. He knows you call me. He's very lonely. Hey, have you applied for the gallery I sent you?"

"I don't really do that kind of photography." Well, you're just not *good* enough for that kind of photography.

As if she read your thoughts, she says, "You shouldn't be nervous about applying. I love your pictures. You gotta try, at least. No harm in trying."

The people on the deck all laugh at once. The cold air explodes in a joyous froth. The floor under you has a thin wooden barrier between threadbare rug and cracked kitchen linoleum. You run your toe along it. "Yeah, maybe."

"Honey, you need to call your father. You know he—I mean, your father gets anxious. Hang on, sweetheart, let me get him."

"No— I. I need to go soon, I think. I'm kind of in the middle of something."

"Are you sure you're not spending too much time studying? It's not healthy. And, oh, hang on, here he is."

You start walking. Your father says,

"   small   mouse   ."

He is on the phone for the duration of your slow walk through the living room, a bedroom where Pope guy grabs a half-empty tequila bottle, bathroom where a line is suffering, up the forbidden stairs. Henry has fallen in unreciprocated love with Marlowe and lets her anywhere in the house—and everyone knows you're her echo.

"Honey?"

"Hey, Mom. Hey, how'd the meeting go?"

"You know the client. Jeff is calling me from *Singapore.* He's chuckling to us about how the company is just *paying for this*—mind you, he moved the call for the *rest* of us to two in the morning. Two."

"Remember last week when HR was like—'oh we *super* respect the time zones of our employees' and you were like *um . . .*" You sigh on behalf of your mother. "They for real need to pay you more."

Pope guy puts himself against the wall while you wrestle the door open to Henry's bedroom. Coats cover every available surface, including the floor.

"They need to do a lot of things," your mother sighs.

"Did he even actually, like, take the contract?"

There's Marlowe. Is she *nesting?* She looks unabashed about it, grins widely at you and pats the coat next to her like you should come join her. Like it's cute to be half passed out in someone's bed, curled under a bunch of stranger's outerwear.

To be fair, it is kind of cute.

Your mom groans. "Two in the morning he is calling us. And, no, he did not."

You suck your teeth. "I'm sorry."

"It is what it is."

You slot next to Marlowe, wiggling so she can be little spoon, flipping your hair over one shoulder and then brushing her hair out of your mouth. She's already talking to the Pope guy, who is perched at the end of the bed, awkward but undaunted.

You have nothing to say again. "You seen *Captain Marvel* yet?"

"Yeah, your father hated it."

You wanted to go as a family to it. "Okay, but was I right about how weird that new *Avengers* trailer is?"

"It looks sad. You know I don't like sad things."

"They're going to make Captain Marvel do exactly nothing that whole movie and then a man is going to win."

"I hope it's Iron Man."

"I think he dies in it."

"They better not kill hi—hang on."

You hang on again, watching people through the half-open door. Pope guy is launching into the description of the conspiracy again. Back to the hats. He says miter this time. You're kind of proud of him.

Marlowe stands up. Takes your hand. "Great news. I am going to puke. Join me for . . . the show." She has the keys to the off-limits bathroom, because of course she does.

The whole tiny bathroom is covered in thin grime. Why is everything slightly broken and slightly orange.

You put the phone on speaker and rest it on the rust-slime sink so you can hold back her hair. "Just letting you know I didn't mute this, so like, don't say swear words, Lowes."

She chuckles and then throws up her spine. You watch the ick travel up and over her skin, and you have to turn away for a second. She spits. Puts one arm around her head. "Fuck. Depot. I'm fucking sorry. I just, like. I *know* I said I would drive and I fucking suck so fucking much. Please don't hate me."

You don't say anything.

"Why did we even fucking—take the minivan? Like, I should have just bought you an Uber. I'm fucking sorry, dude."

"The Uber was fifty-four dollars."

"We could have just walked."

"Okay, one, it's like negative fourteen degrees. Two, this place is literally four miles away, how the fuck would we walk. And three, like—it's fine. I'm okay."

"You have permission to, like, whenever you want—just stab me." And then her back flexes in that cat way again, and you have to flinch and stare at the weird wood paneling covering the bottom half of the wall.

When she's done, you both hunt for toothpaste, and she finds it behind the mirror. She giggles around the finger she sticks in her mouth. Toothpaste bleeds at the corner of her lips.

Her eyeliner is smeared. You fix it for her. She looks up toward the light while you do, still brushing her teeth with her finger, grinning. Says with a sigh she loves you. Says she's sorry about drinking, but her anxiety. Says again she loves you. Finally gets around to asking where you've been all night. Asks if you've met someone. Asks if you like Pope guy because obviously he likes you.

Then she loads her finger with toothpaste again and attacks you, cackling, trying to shove her fingers between your lips. Gets some in despite your protests.

Rustling on the phone. "Hello?"

Marlowe goes *oop!* And freezes.

"Hey, Mom." You spit into the sink. Wet a piece of paper towel to get rid of the mascara marks on your cheeks. Hand it over to Marlowe, who is grinning.

Your mother's end rustles again. "Your father wants to go to bed. I'm gonna have to leave ya."

"Okay."

"Okay, love you."

"Love you too."

She hangs up before you do.

Marlowe lets you wipe off the makeup smeared on her cheeks. "I can't believe Jason actually came. Fuck. Tonight's been so good," she says. She pulls up her phone and angles it at the white-flecked mirror. "Come here, be in this picture with me."

You oblige, you both mostly cover your faces with peace signs. She kicks her leg up to balance her boot on the sink, cackling as you both strike poses. She kisses you on the cheek in one and then turns serious for a moment, despite her slight swaying. The phone even goes down.

She wraps her arms around you and leans in. "Today is your fucking birthday, dude. We graduate in like six weeks."

"It's wild, right?" You steady her subtly, putting your hand to the small of her back. You want to go home suddenly, but you don't know where that would exactly *be*.

"Okay. What do you want for your birthday. Be real. Like, list three things you want in the next year."

"Pussy, weed, money. Sorry I said pussy just then, I didn't like it either."

"Doable, tangible, and goal-oriented. I like it." She leans in close. She smells like tequila and mint toothpaste and a little bit sour. "No, but be real. Be *honest*."

"Um . . ." You look down at her and those stupidly bright eyes. What do normal people usually ask for? "I want to graduate, obviously."

She unwinds and hops up onto the sink, kicking her heels. Your weight would have sent the thin porcelain thing straight to the ground. She ticks off a finger from one hand. "Almost got it. And you're— which one? Magna cum laude?"

"Summa." Not that anyone gives a shit; you're an English major. It's not that hard to spend four years just reading something and then having an opinion about it.

"Perfect." She shakes her head. "Next two, please."

"Um . . . find a job, I guess?" Which reminds you—you're running out of time. You need to keep applying to open positions. *And* you need to figure out a place to live unless you want to be at home with your parents again. Fuck. A weight comes slipping into your chest, pressing downward. *Oh, and remember—*

She reaches out and pulls you closer. You slot between her legs. She grips your dress, and you can tell she's having trouble balancing. "We love a working lady. It's hot. Will you wear like, a sexy office woman outfit?"

You don't feel like responding to this. Flirty banter is fun when you're both on the same level, not while she's stupid drunk. You look up and out the single dingy window. The night is blue-black. Snow is scudding past at high speed. Fuck. Driving in that is going to *suck.*

"I think," Marlowe hiccups and covers her mouth with her hand, which you both pause a second to behold. When it's clear she's not going to throw up again, she continues, "I think your third thing should be to practice relaxing. Like, letting go."

The idea makes you snort. You push her hair back behind her ear. "I'm getting kind of worried about the snow. Do you think we could leave in, like, an hour?"

"Can I bargain for two?"

You roll your eyes and point at her. "Fine. But you're going to read over my Shakespeare essay for me."

She extends her hand solemnly. "I will actively try not to make it worse."

You both shake on it, but she doesn't pull away. Instead, she flips your hand over in hers so that your palm faces the ceiling. She traces her fingernails ever so gently across the geography of your skin lines. Looks carefully, slowly. She runs her thumb over you almost as if she's trying to clear dirt from your hand—but she does it so tenderly, it makes goosebumps break out down your legs.

"I love your hands," she says.

You hate them. "When I was little, I used to think I was a witch because the lines on my left palm make a perfect triangle."

At that, she gestures to you. You give her both hands. She examines them in the yellow light, checking. "Oh. They do." She checks her own palms. "Huh. I don't have that. That's kind of funny." She brings your hands together and folds them over her heart and looks up at you. "Do you know what I just read in your palms?"

You can't really speak. You're very aware of how sober you are. How she is looking up at you, eyes so wide and dark. How her legs wrap so casually around you, warm against your hips. Where your dress has crept up, the press of skin to skin.

You are used to keeping your hands to yourself when it comes to women. And you are particularly used to it when it comes to Marlowe.

She closes her eyes. "I read that . . . you're going to be a magician. You're going to make everyone love you. You're going to . . . build a big ship. And . . . and you'll sail out in it. And everyone will . . . get on the ship. And watch you do beautiful magic tricks. Out on the ocean. Just you and your . . . beautiful words and face and personality." And then she kisses the inside of each of your wrists, one at a time, almost with reverence.

"Oh." You want to say something funny, but the croak in your voice breaks the moment in half as if the moment was less than a figment. "But I—can't swim."

She laughs, and hops off the sink. You take a step back. She fixes her dress, helps you fix yours, fixes her hair in the mirror, uses a little more toothpaste, spits, grins. "Time to go back to it," she announces, picking up her phone again, passing you yours.

You stand there, dumbly sober. Unmoving.

"Oh, hang on," she says, and takes part of your bangs into her fingertips.

She rips out a single strand. It's as white as the moon.

the first time i knew *i liked a girl*, we were coloring in sharpie on our converse. i was drawing music notes. hers were poems. i had said, within the past month, i thought that bisexuals were untrustworthy and needed to just choose something; i was ignoring the mounting evidence that my attentions were similarly split into quadrants of yearning.

in the movie version of this, when she said—*i just like who i like, and that's whatever*—it's how we, the audience, are able to identify how *she* identifies. we know the steps of the dance without ever seeing the ballet. this secret knowledge slinks in from pornography, where the breathy ingenue leans into the camera and says she's *thinking about exploring*. her animal wariness maybe is from literature, where *lesbian* is of course off-limits, but *bisexual* isn't a friendly term either, so the author has to come up with something more cleverly supple.

it isn't permanent like this. it is a question of opportunity, like the lip of a cup. it is a question of harmonics. if put in the right angle of sunlight, any of us might be gay enough; a generally accepted rule of conduct.

any of your straight friends will confirm this, nodding emphatically over liquor so we know they aren't *thinking straight*. they throw a smile. *oh, i mean, if it was a threesome*. it might even be a form of empathy. in extreme conditions, *any* of us would have tumbled unwittingly into gayhood. our straight friends assure us that they have come close: they would have also been gay if it was kristen stewart (post-*twilight*). if it was in the right room and the right drug was involved. if they had just become a falling glass, a single beautiful mistake.

therefore, queerness appears as a *moment,* rather than a constant state of being. it is a diversion from the norm. it is a condition: it could *happen* to you.

i, for my part, did not realize what she was saying with *it's whatever.* i thought she meant: *it's none of your fucking business.*

i respected that attitude.

there are some academic circles that point out the symptoms of lycanthropy might be *too* based in the monthly hormonal cycles of a body to be ignored. a werewolf's aggression, dominance, loss of control—these are all traits each of us should avoid. if monsters exemplify that which we should object to, the myth of the werewolf would be: *come home quietly. leave behind the moon.*

werewolves as i know them from american media are almost entirely depicted as men. in women, the above symptoms (aggression, etc.) are extremely taboo. in *men,* however, they become a clever purr of seduction. it's *hot* when a man loses control, rips off his clothes, takes the girl home. it's *hot* when they give into their most base instincts. after all, we all *know* men aren't *really* above such things— don't we already call men *dogs?* isn't this what they're good for? their *real* soul only full of lust and howling?

a shirtless, dehydrated youth fans his shoulders across *teen vogue.* in my childhood, i stared at the picture and waited for something electric to occur. to pass through the gloss and into my system so i could finally see men differently; turn them sweet, glazed like a donut. most men look like different brands of whiteboard markers to me, even when they are fake growling.

i would turn quickly past the images of girls. i tried to burn *only boys* into myself. in truth, these meditations on various pop singers were just a strange form of studying. i thought i could convince myself out of it. i would close my eyes and flex my hands, murmuring imagined conversations under my breath. if i was ever tested, i'd be able to say *i don't really find women attractive.* the lie would roll right off my tongue while i jumped into a whole separate sentence—*on the other hand, did you see this guy from a boy band?*

werewolves spend the majority of their lives as humans. their entire identity—their label, their species—is based on their behavior of roughly thirteen nights out of the year. if we assume that nighttime lasts an average of twelve hours, werewolves spend roughly 1.6 percent of their year as a beast. most people spend more time stuck in traffic annually.

something about being different marks you, is the thing. once you know you *can* let go, that knowledge never silences. it hunts around in the back of your head. grinning. waiting.

when your nature is one of horror, you often learn to delight in the bloodshed.

◇

It's three days before graduating, and you're half naked on her bed, sprawled lazily over the bedspread so eerily familiar to you. It's May and too hot in her dorm, so you've taken off your shirt— she's already seen you in a bra a million times anyway. You've done this every year you've known her; the two of you sitting around, anticipating the summer, both of you wearing not many clothes by necessity. The dorm building is still blasting heat despite the weather outside—the last time you read the internal temperature, it said *ninety*. You are nostalgic and stressed out and sweaty.

She's on the floor with no pants on, talking about the other senior-year events you will both be drunk at. You're only half listening, scrolling your phone through work application rejections, thinking about memory, thinking about how time is somehow passing both too quickly and too slowly, holding itself up by spider legs.

It takes a second for you to actually hear her. "Hang on," you say. You look up. "Not to be too homosexual about this, but did you just ask me to move in with you?"

Actually, if your auditory recall is correct, what she said was: *and when we move in together, you'd be in charge of that.*

She laughs, clears her throat, says out loud the exact thing you are thinking. "I actually said *when* you do."

You sit all the way up. "Okay. Marlowe, I know you're joking, but I'm not. I would legit love that. It would solve, like, a lot of problems for me." It would actually maybe kill you to move back in with your parents. If you split the rent, you have enough savings to hold you over while you look for a job. Holy shit. It would be *so* much easier.

She looks up at you. Her eyes so clear like that. You are always jealous of her lashes; thick and dark. "I wasn't joking."

You slide off the bed and down onto the floor with her. She drops your gaze suddenly, playing with her fingernails. "I know you're busy and like have a life and a family and, like, probably a hundred other options—"

You kiss her, maybe a little too long and little too serious, over and over and over again, laughing, your hands in her hair. Against her mouth you say, "Fuck yes. Oh my God, *fuck* yes. Thank you."

She laughs too, and your teeth click. She holds you back, her fingers looping into your hands. "I don't know where works for you or if you've been looking or—"

"Shh, shh, shh," you keep kissing her, hard and fast and full of lightning, "We'll resolve it in a second. Less talking, more kissing." You can't stop smiling. "*Fuck*, Marlowe. This makes things *so* much easier for me." You dropped your phone somewhere. You need to tell Lacey. Your hands skim the bedsheets. "Yes, yes, yes, yes." You find the phone and turn back to Marlowe. "Fucking *amazing*."

Her cheeks are pink. She's caught your smile now, too, and her grin is toothy. She tucks her hair behind one ear, and then fixes it back to frame her face. "I'm—I thought you'd—I didn't think you'd be so excited." She laughs softly, blinking.

"It's like, a little last-minute, but you know I love a challenge." You'd already been on about fifteen thousand Facebook pages and Craigslist ads. You had your favorites bookmarked, picked out while wine drunk and stressing. "There's this place in ███████████ and it's *super* cute, it's right down the street from the college. I'll, like—I'll tutor or something, and—ah!" You get too excited, have to dance around, punching the air.

Marlowe laughs. "I don't know how much I can really, like pay for, or anything . . . ?"

You scoop her up into your arms and bury her under kisses. She giggles and reciprocates, and then you spin her around and into a low dip. She shrieks as her hair skims the ground. You drag her back upward, chasing her lips, not letting her catch her breath for an instant. You are glorious, intoxicated. The weight on your chest that has been building for the last semester has just been—erased. And *she* did that. You can't stop kissing her, heart all high and fluttery and free. She holds your biceps and gives you a squeeze.

Her cheeks are a new shade of pink, and her eyelids are fluttery. She looks almost flustered. "It's that easy to make you happy, huh?"

You respond by giving her another peck on the cheek, and then you pick your phone back up, delighted, buzzing. You wrap your free arm around her waist, balancing on your knees. "Okay, fair warning? I'm about to send you about a million listings."

Marlowe puts her hands against your chest and then her eyes drop to your bra, and then she stills for a second.

The air in the room changes.

You drop the phone.

She works her fingers softly over the black velvet that surrounds the powder-blue lace cup. "This is cute," she murmurs, tracing her fingers lightly upward toward the straps. She looks up from under her eyelashes at you, her fingers toying with the band. "Victoria's Secret?"

Your heart is racing in your chest. This is dangerous. "Uh. They. Sale," you half stammer. Fuck. You have done a good job, followed those rules, kept your hands to yourself. This is a test, don't be a creep. She's just being friendly.

Her fingers continue their slow parade across your skin. She murmurs something you don't hear. She traces back down, coming to the curve of your breast. You turn hot and hard and thrumming. You hear yourself gasp as her thumb runs over the part of your bra covering your nipple. She looks up at you again and bites her lower lip, grinning, self-aware.

You reach out, half-blind, needing, desperate—and something in your movement startles her, and she jumps and pulls back, spooking like a rabbit. She gently pushes you away, laughing. Like—maybe this whole thing was a game from the beginning. "I love you, but go put a shirt on, you absolute slut. I can't handle looking at you like that. It makes me insane." She turns her whole body away from you, running her hands through her hair.

Shaking, you pick back up your shirt and put it on. Your knees are weak. Why do you want to cry right now? Fuck, what *was* that? And what if she *was* just playing?

She jumps up on the bed and pats the space next to her like nothing's happening. "Okay. Apartments. Come show me."

You take a few seconds to tuck in your shirt, pausing to go over to the mirror on her closet door, pretending to check your fit even though you don't really need to. For a moment, and only by accident: you catch your own eye contact in the reflection. The dark thing that passes there makes you feel a little sick. You take a deep breath and close all the windows inside of yourself.

You jump up next to her and nudge her over to make room. "Okay," you say, clearing your throat, "So, apartments!"

the first girl to sink her teeth into my neck warned me: *people will think you're gay if you sigh like that.* i think she meant it jokingly. it felt like a benediction instead.

in mythology, biting has a certain power, and it can *pass on* that power. vampires, zombies, rabies. it takes and it gives. historians with a scientific eye might categorize this as early germ folklore—our mouths are dirty places, and bacteria can kill. this is phonetically satisfying; kill/kiss are tender parallels with completely different sonics.

when we lean into our partners and expose our necks, we are saying—*here, here. show me the difference that single sound makes.*

i haven't googled it but in high school someone told me: *if you can bite through a carrot, you can bite through a human finger.* at first this news was sort of delightful, and i chomped carrots with vigor. the potential to do harm is an unreasonable pleasure. it's just the knowledge you *could* if you really *wanted* to, but mostly you won't. but—you *could.*

eating is calculated, kissing is calculated, but *biting* remains personal. i have an affinity for almost-raw meat. i usually blame it on the feminine experience of an iron deficiency.

there are many violences i was not ready for. they did not split apart like a carrot. they folded in my hands, and the marrow was darker than i thought.

◇

You watch her unpack that same salmon pink duvet. You both sleep better when you're next to each other; so you buy the queen mattress to share, stack the "guest" bedroom with her meager twin-XL. You both get cute knickknacks and she helps you hang up your plants and you help her put up her art. The oven timer beeps as your syncopation while she pulls you into dances, you spin her around and make her breakfast. She drags you along to Zumba class and you make her pose for your artsy photography. When you both get a job, the two of you celebrate by getting rip-drunk and then doing bad karaoke. Lacey visits for just you and then both of you and then somehow you're all three best friends, going to carnivals and outdoor markets and big-city adventures. When Lacey comes over, she sleeps in the same bed too, the three of you giggling in a cuddle puddle.

You kiss Marlowe in the rain, on crowded city trains, at a pride parade. She kisses you on her way out the door, while hunting for cookie ingredients, while you both finally finish your *Criminal Minds* binge. She opens the door while you're showering and closes her eyes while she steps in to kiss you and tell you she made you coffee, you both giggle at the absurdity. You write her love poems where the punch line in the volta is *no homo though, I'm joking*. She shyly admits to trying to learn guitar, she plays you a song for your birthday. You learn how to knit just to make her a blanket for the holidays.

Her boyfriend, though, you'd tell anyone—*he's amazing.* You love him! He's *great.*

She threw you a party when you'd finally broken up with that guy. She helps you casually date a rotating list of people of all genders. You keep collapsing on the kitchen floor dramatically, sighing, saying *I think I'm going to die alone,* and, *love isn't real.* She buys you wine and strokes your hair or otherwise puts up with it.

Her boyfriend thinks it's cute that she crawls into bed at night with you. You and Marlowe spoon, lovers without ever stepping over the mark. Platonic, from *Plato.* You feel her breathe against your collarbone at night and try to weave the memory through you like water through a sieve.

On a Tuesday, just before her birthday, the bad thing you've been avoiding happens. The kind of self-realization that should have occurred long before. You are good at not looking directly at the truth.

It's during your normal nightly routine. She's in the other room, brushing her teeth, arguing with you through the door she kept cracked open. "You *can't* be serious." Her words are slushy around her brush. "You believe in metric for *literally* everything else."

"It's a *ratio.*" You have your laptop open in front of you, your legs tucked under you. You're trying to figure out how to French braid your hair, but you simply cannot make your hands figure out the action. You are barely watching a YouTube video about it. "Celsius is not."

You hear her pause to spit into the sink. "*Nobody* uses Fahrenheit, though. Like, you go *anywhere else* in the world, and they have no idea what you're talking about."

"Right, but like. This is the *only* thing Americans are right about. It's not—"

She peeks around the doorframe. "Incorrect. The only other thing is deep-frying food just to see what happens to it."

You blink. For some reason, you didn't expect her to be into fried food.

She shrugs. "I like the spirit of ingenuity." She doesn't pronounce *ingenuity* correctly, but it just makes you smile to yourself.

"Okay but, like, Celsius is for *water*." You have to rewind the video, and then give up and start again from the beginning, your fingers working your hair out of a knot. "Fahrenheit is based on the human body."

"The temperature at which people boil is not a hundred degrees, though, is it."

"No, but like. Eighty degrees Fahrenheit is like. Eighty percent hot. The reason so many people like the 70-degree range is because 70 is only 70 percent hot—not too hot, not too cold. Zero is like *it's not warm anymore.*"

She pads into the room, rubbing lotion onto her hands. "Are you learning to braid your hair again?"

"Also, how do I even dress for like, fourteen degrees Celsius? I can't be like: oh good, it's fourteen degrees outside, that means it's—what, like 50 percent warm? But if it says *fifty* outside, I know to wear pants and a sweater."

She sits beside you and puts her hands into your long hair and starts braiding. "You'd know what to wear because you'd be able to read the fucking thermometer."

"Like you *know* I'm a metric bitch, you know this is true about me."

"It's one of your only redeeming qualities, yes." She takes the offered hair tie out of your hand and gives you a kiss on the cheek, the kind of kiss that means *only kidding.*

"But we cannot use *water* as it relates to our human body because our ambient temperature is like—we are basically one-hundred-degree objects."

"Thirty-seven Celsius, I think, but yeah." She ties your hair up, gives you another kiss, and then stands up, slipping back into the bathroom. "Look, I love you, you're the love of my life and my best friend, but we are *not* gonna agree about this."

"Because you're wrong," you call after her.

"I love you," she repeats, "But *you're* wrong."

You open your mouth to repeat *I love you but you're wrong*, and you find you can't form the words. They are too big in your throat, some strange stopgap that has appeared out of the blue. How many times have you said *I love you* to her?

In relationships, you've frequently had the opposite of this moment—the strange sense that you're about to tell a lie, right before you speak it. How *I love you* in those situations is weird, heavy, better left unsaid.

You can't say it because it's big in the other direction.

Oh no.

Fuck. How long has *that* been a thing?

At night, in phantom script, you spell out the truth in your mind, just to check. Rotating it. Feeling the weight.

Yep, it's accurate.

You fold the truth away, putting it into a pocket for a future self to deal with. You are very, very good at looking away.

sex and death are partners. i could say *lovers* here, right? horror movies love to mix the erotic and the violent—and where else would we find a monster but in a horror movie? an accurate parallel, the unseen and the obscene. love has its own language of violence. we say: *he ripped my heart out.* we say: *she tore me open.*

sex is single-minded passion, the way that fear is. in media, sexual activity in a feminine body is the same thing as painting a target onto your cheekbone. it is saying *take me!* in every sense of the term. others have joked about it before—the virgin lives, and the slut dies. the slut dies first of many or at least very early. it is actually sort of an honor to lie your body down before others: her blood will set the scene. the camera likes seeing women coupled closely to their mortality; their desires *invite* the monstrosity; their choices *make* their suffering. a body laying open or a body lying, opened.

there is a conjugation of *to cleave* which also means *to fuck*.

so sex demands punishment.

not to distill something nuanced too far, but it's my general understanding that *the slut* and *the pervert* are virtually the same in the eyes of the audience. if they are not the same, they are at least close enough to hold hands through a mirror and interchange their bodies. one cannot be a slut without being a little perverted, after all.

the pervert is how queerness steps onscreen. our orientation *alone* is a predetermined rated-r, hays-coded, dsm-diagnosed *perversion.* the actual *act* of queerness would be nc-17.

often, in these creeping days of passing representation, we hold another binary. the slut/the pure of heart. either we're virgins that are just now coming out and our story is a heartwarming tale of success and bravery—or we are deeply promiscuous lovers with no desire to "settle down," and our story is a warning about the maladaptive, the cruel, the unholy.

EITHER:

    a. you have never touched another girl, fear of retribution slanting through your body. while this is sad, it will keep you alive at the end of the movie.

    b. you are only ever touching other girls, but none of them love you, and you are alone when you die, knuckle in your mouth like a hanger.

c. you are never able to touch another girl, and it makes you want to kill every person around you, because of your *latent* desires of a *perverse nature*. you wear a skin mask, which is sort of nice, because it is like being able to touch, but without having a person attached to it.

d. you aren't in the movie, but your story is. you recognize the coding and don't say anything because *it's just a movie*. the girl wears a suit and/or follows around her best friend too much and/or (etc.)—and then she stabs someone while cackling. watching it, you jump at all the right moments, and aren't sad in public, and drop your eyes at halloween when someone in a spandex version of that monster mimics the body language of perversely loving another girl.

while collecting the mythology of horror, sometimes the artistic question of shaping the "next great monster" becomes—*so what do we do to make it scarier?*

the answer is usually *more viscera*, which is boring. it is lazy to assume that the burden/fear/hiding of *pain* is the scariest thing.

many of us are used to pain. we are used to being a body.

it's more interesting to me when the question of monstrosity is— okay. we have starved this person. now what do they eat?

◇

The seasons crisp themselves russet in your hands. Everything so agonizingly perfect, even when it has no right to be. Six months turns into a year. She cries when he cheats, you hold back her hair as she throws up in a club. You get your heart broken. Marlowe makes you a cake from scratch that says in shaky icing *NO SCRUBS*. You both make dating rules that start simple (*no man babies, no evil women*) and get increasingly more convoluted and complex (*never again with a triple Scorpio, no man that works at the Panera on 9th it's not worth it*).

Fall comes and you hold her hand and pick out pumpkins and take pictures where you are both running through orange leaves. You kiss her in flannels and take her to cider tastings. She buys you a sweater that lights up and says *Happy Halloween!*

Winter comes and you both curl up inside, start a book club with your shared friends. Your apartment becomes the go-to holiday venue. She gives you presents while blushing; having drawn about one thousand individual holiday-themed doodles on the otherwise simple brown paper packaging. You give her a bracelet you made her, with the date you two met stamped in the metal slightly askew. You sign your card *Depot* and she signs hers *Lowes*.

The collapse of her ribs, the sigh underneath you. Godspell. What brief hands avoid, hungry tongues savor. She rides the inside of your teeth. She will replace each of your solid parts and make you all surface or all edge. One of you always breaks away before things become too *obvious*. Too difficult. Too hard to resist.

When you were young, you wrote a whole aria to the potential of meeting her.

You both tell people that you are just *fast friends*. And then, in the same breath, you will both say, jokingly—*of course I'm totally in love with her.*

If you never pass *that* point, you can never slip. The void will not open into a yawn too big to manage.

She kisses you at midnight on New Year's. You make her cupcakes for Valentine's Day. She gets a raise and you both celebrate by going to the beach, shivering under a blanket, cackling, cheeks ruddy. You ride home singing to bad music and telling each other stories. In bed, she falls asleep against your chest, perfectly fitting, like always.

Two years of this, of having it, and now the crickets are coming out in spring. On a Saturday evening, perfectly warm and tipsy, you both splay out in the tight lawn behind your weird not-quite-a-house apartment, trying to get whatever thin early-May sun is showing.

"I am going to learn how to become a vampire," you tell her, head on her lap.

The light is almost eaten by the beautiful pink-orange sunset, and Marlowe's hands are toying idly with your fingers. She throws her head back when she laughs. She's letting her hair grow out; yours has been dyed blue-red-black. These days everything comes steeped in amber.

"Okay." She leans down and rubs her thumb against your cheek. "How are you going to become a vampire?"

"I'm going to read a lot of books and one of the books is going to be about how to become a vampire."

"Oh, I see. What's it called—a grimoire?" She picks a piece of lint out of your hair.

"A grimoire or maybe some kind of spellbook. Maybe a novel?"

"I heard colleges recently, like, have a really good program for aspiring vampires actually," she says. "I think they renamed it Computer Science though." She picks back up the book she's been reading—one you lent to her. Kafka's *Letter to His Father*.

"I'm serious." You prop yourself up on one elbow. "I am going to become a vampire."

"Oh, I believe you. In the meantime, I'm going to become a violinist. Since we are following our dreams." She turns the page and her brow furrows. "Wow. Fuck."

She means about the book, you can tell. She's been saying this a lot about this book, which is what *you* said about this book, which is what convinced her to read it.

You pick at the grass. "Do you think you'd ever like. Undead yourself? Give up sunrises? Picnics?"

She peeks down at you. "*Undead* myself? Oh, like vampires. You'd love if I was into that, huh?"

You give her a wicked grin, flick your tongue around your canines. "How could I ever resist that throat?"

She rolls her eyes, goes back to reading. You close your own eyes, enjoying the strange half-there sensation—that this is *a memory*. The kind of thing that you experience knowing it is *good* and *big*, knowing you will look back on it and sustain yourself by it. This is the kind of moment that feels like a movie, like someone is panning a camera over you.

Once on a road trip she skinned her knee because she got out of the car while it was still rolling. You had pulled over to investigate a building full of taxidermy. The owner warned you—*you can look at one of those eyes and fall right in.*

You glance at her and at that second, she happens to look down. A small smile traces her lips. "Hi there."

"What's up. Come here often?"

She laughs. "First time, actually."

Her jaw and her smirk. You are so good at this now, and the banter, and the never having her. "Well, great news! I'm a recent vampire convert."

Now she really laughs, and gently nudges you. "I'm gonna go make another drink, do you want one?"

You check your phone. It's later than you thought. The buzz you have from earlier is a frothy, wild pink. "I shall . . . follow you," you announce, slurping yourself upward, exaggerating your drunkenness. She giggles and hip checks you as you both gather all your picnic supplies—cups and plates and books and phones and scratchy woven-plastic blankets.

You follow her up the stairs and inside, humming a song from middle school. She hums along the parts that you forget, navigating the door open for you. Without communicating it, you both form a quick conveyor belt, shuffling all your items inside without the door ever closing.

She starts playing music from her new phone's speakers, balancing it in a bowl to amplify the sound—you showed her that trick. You dance along to it, rolling up the blanket while she tidies the kitchen.

She pours you both a shot, links arms with you to take it.

"I'm gonna make more drink," she says, and you nod, settling down to flip open Kafka again, just to see where she left off. The music drifts in the air in silver notes.

"Do you think you'd be okay if your hands could shoot lasers?" You ask, mostly just to hear her answer.

"Oh, I—Oh, *fuck!*" she gasps, and you drop the domesticity to sublimate by her side.

Your heart is outpacing your blood. "Are you okay? What happened?"

She points to an absolutely huge insect, hovering on a cabinet door. An evil concoction of an earwig and a centipede, it *undulates.*

You gag.

Marlowe's hand is on her chest, panting the way you are. "Holy shit. That thing just *touched* me. I—I didn't see it."

Centipedes are your only *hard no* among insects, and this new thing is centipede enough. Your skin is crawling. "What the fuck *is* that?"

"You're the animal fact person! Fuckin'—do something!" She raises a dish towel menacingly. "I'm gonna kill it."

It's ugly and horrible and you hate looking at it. "No—ah, ah, fuck, hang on. Let me get a cup, I'll . . . I'll get rid of it." You don't want to do that. "Ahh . . . Okay." You whimper-choke while you gather the materials and slowly force your cup toward the bug. Marlowe clings to your shoulder, watching with your body to protect her.

You're about an inch away when the bug takes off, and then everyone is screaming.

You panic, almost drop the glass, jolt backward. Marlowe shrieks and leaps onto the opposite counter. She's screaming the bug's location like a GPS while you're just screaming, blindly striking the glass outward in any general insect direction. By sheer fucking chance you catch it on the floor of the kitchen.

Fuck it's big. It looks like it has a stinger on it, but you literally cannot look at it without wanting to throw up. You don't mind spiders, don't have a particular fear of bugs. *This* thing, though? It sends a horror up your spine.

"Fuck," you say, and then your mouth likes it too much. You find a piece of paper to scoot under the cup. "Fuck. Fuck, fuck, fuck, fuck, *fuck*." You awkwardly pick up your insect prison, begging God and all the angels not to let the absolute behemoth creature escape. You'd have to burn the entire apartment to the ground.

"I'm never going barefoot again," Marlowe breathes. "What the fuck *is* that thing?" She holds the door for you while you walk in a careful march down the hallway, out into the lawn.

The sun has set and the temperature has already started dropping. The light thrown by the streetlamps has a splintered effect—all the shadows are in squares and patchwork. "Okay," you say. You hold your hands away from your body, applying severe pressure to the insect sandwich. "Get somewhere safe."

Marlowe obliges, taking two big steps back. You hold out your arms as far as you can manage and try to think if you know of the patron saint of not having a big bug crawl on you.

"Okay bug. I am going to release you. Please . . . uh . . . respect the termination of this connection," you stall.

"Otherwise, we will *super* kill you in the real life," Marlowe finishes.

You take a deep breath, make a *gah!* sound, and *throw*, as hard as you can, the bug out from the glass. In divine intervention, you see the weird thing sail through the darkness and disappear into a bush.

It makes a little *click* sound when it hits a leaf, and then the world is silent again.

And then you can't stop laughing. You put the glass down in order to put your hands on your knees, wheezing. You hear Marlowe start giggling, and then she's laughing too, delighted, while the two of you breathe in one giant sigh of relief.

"I literally thought that thing would kill me," you say.

"I literally thought that thing would kill you," she agrees. She comes up and plucks the glass off the tarmac and takes your wrist. She presses your palm against her cheekbone. "My hero," she says in a high voice, batting her eyelashes.

"Anything for you, my lady." You manage an almost perfect knightly drawl.

"Oh, you're too sweet." She reaches up and kisses you, lightly, the streetlamp squares dappling across her cheeks. "I can't believe you let it *live*."

"I have a tender heart and much mercy. Also, I'm an idiot with a death wish," you admit.

"You . . . *do* have a tender heart," she says. And then something happens, that thing that has only happened once before, more than two years ago—the *thing* changes. You can almost hear the boundaries flex and tense and shift; sense their unsure groaning purr.

Her hand reaches up to you again, her thumb rubbing your cheekbone. "I like that you're . . . always good, in the end."

You should say something witty. Or something poignant. "Well, golly gee. Thanks, milady." You absolute *fucker.* You said *golly gee?*

Marlowe looks up through her eyelashes. She draws you down, so your mouths are almost touching. Frogs beep in the distance. The warm wind tangles fingers across both of your dresses. "You're . . . a good person," she says.

"I . . . I try?"

"Ha! Yeah." Her eyes are focused on your mouth. "I like that you save things."

You try to respond, but your nerves are shot. You can't see beyond her face, and the slow spread of pink across her cheeks that's visible even in the darkness.

She wraps her hands in your hair and kisses you low and slow and deep, her tongue flicking against your lips, testing. You kiss back, confused. You can actually *hear* your heartbeat racing, the steady hoofbeat climbing.

For one brave second, you slip your hands under her shirt— unallowed. Against the rules. Out of bounds. *Not* just kissing. You pause, unsure if she's okay with it.

But then she bends against you, and her fingers are under your shirt too, and they scud their way up your spine, her nails digging in just slightly. Clawing at your skin. Grasping, a controlled form of desperation. You nip her bottom lip, and she lets out a half gasp, delighted. She bites back, and then her kisses are trailing down your neck. You can't stop the way you melt under her, into her, turn molten.

She looks at you up through those lashes and those half-lidded eyes. Looping her arms around your neck. "Hi," she says. "I like when you play hero."

"Marlowe," you say, and the sound is closer to a whimper. She could have you, if she wanted, like this. You'd be entirely hers. You'd cross that boundary so willingly.

Her phone buzzes and she shoots a look at her screen and then, for the third time that night—the whole world changes color.

Marlowe pales in the white light of the device, takes it closer to her face while she reads. "What the fuck?"

Suddenly the night is no longer closed. The cold rushes in and you wrap your arms around your middle. "Everything okay?" You look away, watching the way the plaid shadows dance over the sidewalk. *Fuck.*

Her silence stretches as she looks more stricken, her thumbs scrolling. All of the heat blows out of you and you start trembling, taking the cup from her hand. Your panic starts to take a firm, hollow ring to it. "Marlowe?" You prompt. Fuck, you left your phone inside, should you call your mom? The world is ending, you always knew you'd be alive for that, the world is ending and—

"He . . . just fucking . . . broke up with me over text."

You are, at once, both distantly relieved and truly baffled. "I— what?"

She swipes angrily at her temple, catching a tear. "What the *fuck*—I'm sorry, Depot, like, he just *dumped me.*" She's already dialing his number, her cheeks now red instead of pink.

"Fuck, Marlowe. I'm so sorry."

She nods at you, her body a strange slump, her free hand gesturing aimlessly. "I literally don't know what's happening. I'm just fucking *worried* about him. Like—" her voice cracks, anger and sorrow bleak between letters, "This isn't *like* him."

"What the fuck," you say. You are so fucking stupid, holding the stupid glass and just standing there, stupidly, while she paces, swiping her face against her shoulders to stop herself from crying.

You hold up the glass. "I'll—um, I'll. Go put this away." Stupid. "I'm . . . I'll give you your privacy. I'm just inside, okay?"

She gives you another half nod, her hand coming up again in a wave. You hear the line ring through to his voicemail and she lets out a bitter sob and calls again.

You waver, halfway between steps. What if you're doing the wrong thing? Maybe you shouldn't leave her like this, maybe she needs . . .

"Go," she says, her voice shaking, "I'll be right in."

You go. You spend a weird amount of time wandering around the apartment. Playing with your phone. Looking out at the window, even though you can't see down to the street. You don't want to bother her. She likes her space.

You tidy up, but not in a way that actually makes a difference. You shouldn't go to bed without making sure she's okay, but you don't want to just be *waiting* for her when she comes in. You're not a predator.

After two hours, you start moving through your bedtime routine without her, shoot her a text. *Hey, I know that this is a really shitty time, take whatever space you need. I left the door unlocked so you can come back when you're ready.*

You curl into bed. You scroll through Instagram mindlessly. You do some googling. *What bug is like a weird centipede but it isn't a centipede.* You were wrong—it looked like a centipede because it *is* a centipede—a "house" centipede. Yuck. They eat ants and other small insects, though, which is nice. You also google *how to keep bugs out of the apartment.*

You continue your mindless scrolling, occasionally starting and deleting another message to her. You're kind of worried. Okay, you're *really* worried, but that just means you're being overly controlling. She's an adult.

You peek outside again, still don't see her. You could go out to look for her, but that would be super invasive. God, your attachment disorder is *really* showing.

Around midnight, vibrating with anxiety, you switch on incognito mode. You hover your thumbs over the white search bar, biting your lip. It feels illegal to be doing this. Dirty.

You google: *weight loss tips.* The results aren't really helpful. *Am I fat?* A Reddit thread pops up, you try to find if any person has your measurements. You get lost in *before and after weight loss pics* for a while, just looking. Promising yourself.

At one in the morning, you finally get Marlowe's reply: *Fuck, sorry, just saw this. Lock the door. He picked me up a while ago, we're at his place, talking.*

You stare at it, type back: *Are you okay? I can come get you.*

Her: *I'm fine. I'll talk to you in the morning.*

there is a belief that our ancestors come back through the wafer bodies and compound eyes of moths. there was a moth in the room when i lost my virginity, bent over and husked on the edge of his bed. the shrapnel of this moment seems to have wedged between the foot of my desire and the tip of my carotid—i nestle *cherry popped* back into the hole it should die in.

butterflies will eat blood. scientists believe they're drawn to the nutrient content. butterflies under the genus *calyptra* actually actively seek *out* blood—they are sometimes referred to as being "vampire butterflies." some butterflies have been recorded as drinking tears from beneath a sleeping animal's eyelids.

so maybe moths don't deserve all the hatred. some species of moths (including the ever-popular luna moth) cannot actually eat. they come back for a little while, surviving on memories.

i want to believe that if i was remade, i'd have wings. i think you and i both know better. that's okay. i'm afraid of heights anyway. and it's nice, in a way—i know exactly what's coming for me.

in the catholic faith, suicide is a no-holds-barred end of story. it holds
hands with murder; considered to be an atrophy of spirit. a rule: *if you
kill yourself, you go to hell.*

duty clings to the robes of this form. we are put on this earth for
His purposes (be fruitful, multiply), we cannot destroy what was made
in His image without committing a sin.

although i cannot speak for *every* catholic church, it was outright
stated in mine: there is a divine grace in continued suffering. whenever
we were instructed to pray for the sick or the ailing or the poor or
the weak of spirit—we were reminded that suffering is one of the
ways we can raise ourselves up to be closer to jesus. after all; his most
mortal act *was* to suffer. catholic doctrine orients suffering as a form of
spiritual purity.

romans 5:3-4: "More than that, we rejoice in our sufferings,
knowing that suffering produces endurance, and endurance produces
character . . ."

any image of jesus tends to depict him in moments of either
divine care or exquisite agony. the martyrs are often portrayed as
both pious and bloody. to be *truly* faithful, one must walk with
christ through pain. we must see how horrible and unfair our life
is—but remain unquestioning of god; and trust that he has yoked us
appropriately to our strengths.

we are absolutely enamored with any form of tragedy and will
stainglass it into every building we get our slimy fingers on.

in my junior year of undergrad, the man who was my first priest
will be excommunicated for pedophilia. in the same year, while
student teaching, i am advised not to "mention the gay thing" for fear
of creating tension. i am, at the time, seeing a man.

the pope has no words for how sad he is about the centuries of
abuse. i keep typing the same message to other people—the church is
a creation of man, and not holy by virtue of existing. it must be holy

by *action*, in this century. the church had originally been "closer" to god because it was the largest bastion of literacy—how could any of *us* translate these texts so holy?

the church must prove itself to *me*, now. it must prove it can follow its own rules. that it can uphold its own standards. rather than dissolving credo into overwrought masochism, it needs to prove to me that it can show me the *joy* of god, without the constant threat of guilt/shame/restriction.

i had been writing an essay about the number of queer people who kill themselves. i remember because of the dramatic irony. it was for a class about marxism—i was connecting our reading on alienation of the body to alienation of our identity. the text i got was only three sentences long.

█ *tried to kill herself. she's in the hospital. they don't know if she's going to wake up.*

she didn't wake up.

at catholic funerals, nobody brings up the *hell thing*. we politely don't say that it is a cardinal sin to kill yourself. we say *the pain is less now* as a platitude. the quiet denial of the everlasting floods the pews and sluices over our feet. drowns all the ants.

her family wanted to bury her under her deadname. her partner ended up fighting the courts for access to the remains. it was a long, drawn-out process. almost a year later, and her ashes were released in a private ceremony on the edge of a mountain, one with her favorite view of the city.

i am told not to worry about the predators in the church. they weren't *real* priests, after all. i am dutifully assured that— although they will never go to jail, they *will* have their judgment in the finest rooms of the finest buildings in hell. the devil will find a place to house them, and they'll have their eternity.

the gay people and the depressed people and the people who stole to eat and the people who didn't suffer politely—i guess we rummage around in hell too, scavenging.

◇

Marlowe wakes up into herself at the start of that summer. A month after she's text dumped, she swears off every kind of relationship all at once. The two of you have not stopped your platonic habit of kissing, but there is a new thing: for the first time since it started, both of you are single. You are trying very hard not to draw attention to that.

In July, she puts you in the car with her and drives the seven hours down to North Carolina where her mom and brothers live and the two of you spend a week in her childhood bedroom, eating ice cream and strolling the small places she grew up in. The orange cat she left behind when she moved to college comes back up north with both of you. His name is Toothpaste. You discover halfway home— despite growing up with cats in your home, you've somehow recently developed an allergy to cats. *Fuck.*

It doesn't seem to matter. You and Marlowe spend hours talking, laughing, singing, snuggling. You argue just once in the middle of the ride back—and then you apologize at the same time, saying *you were right.* You say *I got hungry, I'm sorry* and then play a game of feeding each other fries from Wendy's.

You keep most of the memories for yourself, Mouse. They're so happy that it burns to look at them. Full of excitement, immortality. You both crash through the door to your apartment in a race, cackling. You take videos of the cat exploring the apartment.

Two days later, the summer air is cresting with birdsong. You both still haven't finished unpacking from the trip. Your suitcases are open on the bedroom floor.

You will pulp anything into a poem; and the world these days is a cracked-open sonnet, glistening with pith.

Toothpaste is only allowed outside with a leash. You and Marlowe make a fire in the apartment-sanctioned pit, taking turns annoying the cat and reading books and sipping pink wine out of a chilled thermos.

You can't resist, swinging Toothpaste up so his striped legs beat the air, one dancerlike toward the ground, the other against your wrist. He is solid like a carnival mirror, and, for a minute, you both examine the other, perfectly still. His ears are flat.

"You're already crying, Depot." She takes him from you.

She's not wrong. You hold your hands at an odd angle, already itchy. "It was worth it."

"But, like, *was* it worth it?" She buries her face in his tummy.

You miss your own childhood cat, at home with your parents. "My sister thinks Dave can walk through walls."

"Oh, he *absolutely* can." She checks her watch and clicks her tongue. "Fuck, it's *way* later than I thought." She looks around at the mess you have made and groans. "I *super* don't want to pick up."

You help her start packing things. Neither of you is good at this task today—kind of awkwardly just grabbing whatever until you're both laden down with chip bags and books and have successfully put out the fire. Toothpaste stays with Marlowe; you get the majority of the picnic supplies.

"So like. Why do you think witches always have cats?" you ask, just to make conversation.

"Okay, you know something? Someone said to me recently that like, it's weird when men own cats. And I was like—*are you joking?*"

She bounces the door open for you with her foot, you squiggle your way through, aiming a peck at her cheek as you do.

"Fellas, is it gay to own a pussy?" You don't really think your own joke is funny, but at least it gets a derisive snort from her.

"I don't think Toothpaste is like, a *witch* cat. Like, if I was a witch I'd want, like, maybe a bigger cat."

"Lowes. He is *huge*." He weighs twenty pounds, and the vet said it was perfectly fine on his frame. He's just a big-boned dude.

"But I'm not, like, he's not *me*, you know? I'd want one that was *like* me." She follows you up the stairs, both of you quietly huffing with the effort. "I love him, but he'd be like. Totally useless."

You laugh, picturing it, your mind giving Toothpaste a big purple witch hat. "Oh, oh no. He'd fall in the potions and stuff and make cat soup."

She laughs too. "He'd be, like, constantly trying to eat my flying broom."

"You'd be like—*Toothpaste, fetch me a goose!* And he'd come back covered in mud carrying like, a baby moose."

There's a little scrambling while you both try to figure out how to unlock the door with no hands. Eventually you put some stuff down and manage it, putting a pretzel stick in her mouth while she walks past you into the apartment.

As you both settle, she releases Toothpaste and starts lighting the many, many slightly illegal candles you've both spread across every available surface. "Okay, I actually, kind of, like. I actually *love* this idea now that you're saying this."

"I know, right?" You adopt a fake valley accent, pitching your voice high. "Like, his heart is good? Like he's *trying*. Like sure, he absolutely *did* turn one of my customers into a frog? But it was a *cute* frog."

She picks up on the bit. "He like, *did* drench all my spellbooks with acid? But I had already finished reading them and, like, the ashen remains made a decoration that was *so* chic."

You start pouring shots into wine glasses, even though you're both already tipsy. "Toothpaste *might* have, like, done a *little* bit of theft and broken into an ancient mausoleum, disturbing the dead? And he, *like,* *did* mistake a cursed amulet for catnip and *did* leave it under my bed. And I, like, *do* have *dead*-bugs now."

She groans at your joke, comes into the kitchen to take the shot with you. You both choke and retch. "Movie night? Pregame? See how we're feeling?" she offers.

"Oh, fuck yeah." You refill the wine glasses with gin and juice, your current favorite not-a-cocktail. You pass her one, she kisses your hand, leads you into the living room. She turns on some low party music.

"I genuinely, like, *love* the Toothpaste thing though." She gives you a gentle nudge with her foot. "You should write it. Make a children's book."

You haven't been writing at all. Too stupidly happy for words. Blisteringly, wildly happy; when you are not pining so loudly that the whole world trembles for it.

She guides your limbs into a familiar waltz stance; one you've taught her from your brief stint in ballroom dance. You both sway gently, giggling.

Marlowe looks up at you, and something plays at the corner of her mouth. "Hey," she says, "I never said thank you."

"You're welcome." You look down at her. "Why are we thanking me?"

She laughs and pulls you closer, down onto the couch. Oh shit, looks serious. You sit with your knees touching hers. She takes a deep breath. "You came home with me. You met my family. You like. You try *so* hard, all the time. Just for me."

Your brows furrow. "You've met my family, like, four million times."

"Yeah, but," she takes a deep breath. "It just. Means a lot. And they like you. And *that* means a lot too."

"Oh, they're, like, my best friends now. I have your older brother saved as my emergency contact. I'm texting the middle brother as we speak. We have a group chat where we all talk about how cool I am and how gross you are."

She rolls her eyes and gives you another nudge, this time with her thigh. Once she makes contact, she leaves her leg pressed against yours. "Just. Thank you. Thank you for letting me bring Toothpaste up here even though you're *super* allergic."

"Not *super*." It's super.

"I just," she sighs, her eyes closing. "I couldn't have fucking done any of this shit without you. I love you so fucking much, dude."

"I'm great," you reply, "That's just good taste."

Marlowe snorts. She holds up your hands in a clasp in front of her and then puts your palms around her cheeks. "Just . . . thank you. For doing that for me."

Okay. Time to be serious, if it has to be. "You're my best friend," you say. The liquor is starting to spread warmth across your cheeks, ringing against your nose.

"You're *my* best friend." She takes a deep breath, and then says it again, slowly, like she is tasting the words for the first time, even though she's said them a million times. "Depot. For real, you're . . . my. Best friend."

And then tears lick at the corner of her eyes, and panic shoots through your entire system.

"Oh my God." Now you hold her tight, try to study her eyes as she drops her gaze, "Are you okay? What's happening? Why are we crying?!"

"I'm fucking *happy,* you idiot," she breathes, and then she kisses you, hard and fast and deep. She wraps her hands around your face.

Your heart slackens and then grips for air, turning into mesh. This is a quick path to losing control. You want her to keep going anyway. You manage a giggling, "Marlowe!"

And then in one swift movement she is straddling you, and her mouth is needy, passionate, devouring. Her hands skim your whole body, her breath high and fast. Your fingers claw at the low of her back, and you hear yourself groaning. She answers with a sigh and then she pulls you forward, downward. The two of you tumble, laughing, and then you are on the floor and she is above you, her eyes dark and round and hungry.

You both freeze, staring at each other.

This is dangerous. You should get out of this before your skin slides off and she sees what's been living in your tonsils.

She takes her shirt off. You've seen her half naked and mostly naked and have even gotten glimpses of her very naked. But something in this, with her thighs on either side of you, while she ripples through this motion—it turns every part of you into a highway. Your hands find her hips, her spine, come cresting over her breasts. She gasps and leans into it, pushing herself down and closer to you, grinding her hips against you.

Take your hands off of her. Stop panting. Do it now, while any semblance of your self-control has a name, has an origin. While you can pretend this is something friends do, with no romantic connection.

She leans forward and slips your shirt over your head. Her kisses trace down your chest. You hear the sounds you make—the ones she hasn't brought out of you until now, the soft whimpering ones. You angle up toward her, try to achieve coagulation.

Marlowe leans down and kisses you, her fingers slipping behind your back for your bra clasp. She undoes it in one swift motion, like she's been waiting.

She buries her face in your neck. Her hands move their warm way over you. She dips her fingers below your waistline, testing.

"Marlowe," you moan. You sound desperate, hungry. Stop that.

She trails her fingers over your bare chest, trailing indolent circles around your nipples. You turn hot and wet and melting.

Your heart is pounding. The little fear is shouting in your ribs. The last bastion of a warning. *She is probably just playing. You've both been drinking. She's just bored of being single and is now testing boundaries. You shouldn't be okay with this.*

"Marlowe." This time you manage to make it into almost a gentle admonishment. This is not in the rule book. Her hands slipping your bra off your shoulders is not in the rule book. Her teeth nipping gently at your neck is not in the rulebook.

She shakes the hair out of her face, pressing her body harder against you, overlapping so your edges blur and your whole being breaks out into a whimper. How slick the night and her mouth on yours and her fingers tracing the inside of your thighs. Her skin to yours, so warm and familiar and alien. Her tongue dragging down your throat, over your chest. Anymore and you cannot be a gentleman about this. Anymore and you will simply be overcome, and allow yourself the ocean, the ship.

"Mmm." She bites your bottom lip. "Fuck yes," she whispers, "Say my name again."

"Marlowe." Without meaning to, you beg with the same high note of prayer. Your guilt and shame and reservations all collapse into oblivion. Your sanity shreds itself. There is no before or after, just now, and her, and the way she presses up between your legs. Fuck it. Literally fuck it, who cares? Who's keeping track? Holy shit. If there's language, you're not around to parse it. If there's any matter left in you, it has turned into a hot and desperate static.

She kisses you deep and dips her hands between your legs.

"Show me how you want me," she says.

to be fair to our mammalian bodies: there *are* four basic natural fears. one of those is "fear of the dissimilar." *that which is not like me.* snakes, spiders. aliens, maybe.

linguistically speaking, the original implications of the adjective *queer* refer to the strange/odd/incapacitating. *queer*, like the perverted, held hands with *monstrosity.* it positions queerness as being somehow an alternative state to *human*—what else is there? either you are a human or *not*; you cannot just be "other." and if you *are* other, what differentiates you from beasts?

queer is not just an anthem; it is a *species* in this way. a sort of branch of *homo sapiens*—i'll leave it to you to make the rest of the joke here.

to want in a queer body is *other.* you'll forgive me for not citing this, but i think we can both agree—the actual *action* of queer behavior is, for many cultures, *monstrous.*

the label is two things: a confession and a safety net. i *like* being queer. it fits me. it lives in my collarbone and rushes down my hips and holds all my organs in. it is a way of saying: *i know i am different.* it's *other people* that have a problem with it.

according to my father, an aspect of catholic sin is that to *think* the sin is, in many ways, still committing it. over and over, i have watched my identity be distilled down into a singular sexual act. when i say *i am queer*, i watch revulsion hit others as if i had laid out the specifications of a sex toy i've played with. in the catholic faith, it isn't just that i want to be with girls—it is also that i might consummate that desire. the sex is almost all of the problem. in that act is the death of the soul. my identity isn't a label but rather an admission of guilt. it acknowledges desire as a horrible perversion.

my ocd loves this particular problem. i have *thought* a million different horrible things; it would be a long confessional. my father assures me that as long as i never *actually lie* with a girl, i will be forgiven for my impudence.

i picture a marriage bed, two women only holding hands,
navigating the space of thinking about it so loudly that our bodies
defeat the holy.

at some point, to accept what we are, we must empty ourselves to
the horror of it. the unknown and ugly. the dangerous, lurid, replete.

and we have to say: okay. if i will be lost in the bloodied space for
all of my life, at least while i'm here—let me feast.

Afterward, in bed, sleepy and soft and curled together while you both
trace lazy circles against naked bodies: she murmurs something.

Downy-covered, sated, half purring, you have to struggle to turn
your brain back on. "Sorry?"

"I got the job."

You sit up, almost pass out from how fast you change levels, have
to come back down to Earth. "What?!"

She blinks up at you, wearing only a shy smile. "I got. The job."

"Marlowe. Are you serious?"

She nods just once.

You grab her, hug her so tight she wheezes and you hear her back
crack. Bury your face in her neck. "Holy shit! I'm so proud of you! This
is huge! Babe, it's a five-year contract!"

"In France," she adds.

"In France!" You pull back to trace excited kisses over her cheeks
while she giggles. "Holy shit! When did you find out?"

Her smile grows. "This morning. I leave in two months—right at
the end of the lease." She lets out a soft laugh. "It doesn't even—feel
real yet."

You jump out of bed. "Hang on. Holy shit."

"Babe?" she calls after you. Something like worry edging her voice.

"Just—wait a second!" You're back in half a minute, glasses and bottle in hand. "Champagne. We're celebrating. I'm *going* to be throwing you a party. Holy shit, Lowes. This is fucking amazing."

Her eyes trace your naked form, dipping in a slow way. And then she glances up to your lips and grins. "Hi."

You worry that you weren't sucking in. You worry you'll read too far into this. "Fresh mouth." Your voice is high and tight when you wanted it to sound silky, seductive. You hand her the bottle. "Here, you're better at this."

"I've showed you the trick for this literally a million times."

You shrug and scootch her over as you flop down. "You're still better at it." While she wrestles with it, you pile blankets around your body, covering up your stomach.

She squeaks as it pops, pours you both a glass. "I thought you'd be, like, upset."

"Literally how?" You hold up the glass. "Fuckin'—cheers. I'm so happy for you, dude. This is. And I know I've said this. Actually, fucking amazing."

She clinks her glass to yours, and you realize she's blushing. You both take a sip, and then, when you look over at her, you find that her gaze is still on your half-covered body. She must realize you've caught her staring, because she gives a shrug and takes the glass out of your hand. Puts everything on the nightstand.

Pulls you toward her.

Somewhere in the night, you lie in bed with her, examining the ways she is and is not a cat. Tracing your fingers over her.

"Are you studying me?" She narrows her eyes at you, smirking.

You shrug. "By habit."

She kisses you again.

"Marlowe," you say, trying to find the words. "I know you're leaving.

But—" God. Fuck. Don't ask about this. "Are we . . . ?" You gesture awkwardly. ". . . Is this . . . ?" Fuck, dude, if you're going to ruin the relationship, at least have the courage to do so with real adult words.

She frowns. The crease between her eyebrows is deep. The silence stretches long and horrible.

"I can't," she says finally. Doesn't meet your eyes for it.

"Okay, just checking." You almost sound cheerful about it. And then you kiss her, because you're a fucking idiot.

lunatic: from the latin base *lune,* meaning one whose sanity is based on the moon's transitional state. it might derive from the old wives' tale that the lunar cycle can make *everyone* sort of crazy. it's generally agreed, even at the time of writing, that people should avoid driving, having surgery, or otherwise making serious choices on the full moon.

panic attacks are lunatic behavior. counting and praying and freaking out in public are lunatic behaviors. it is okay to be broken, but do so quietly, and prettily, and without much fuss attached to it.

when you are a lunatic, the first thing you learn to be, before anything else, is *good.* well-behaved. obedient. you are taking up a lot of space by being here. you need to allow others the opportunity to forgive you for it.

"Come here," she says, and takes you into the bathroom. You are drunk and in her arms, and regretting eating so much at dinner, you'll be bloated. Your apartment is dark and full of people. *Marlowe's Big Goodbye Bash* on a hand-painted banner overhead. She chose the bisexual pride colors, and both of your fingerprints smudge the corners. She leaves in two weeks.

You kiss her on the back of the sink. You kiss her on the tile floor. You kiss her and you are both laughing. Your teeth click in your excitement.

"I want to show you something. Look." Her fingers hook her skirt up. Your heart, parallel, hooks the bottom of your stomach and makes you dizzy with desire.

Sometime during the night, she has gotten a moth stick-and-poke tattooed right over her left hip bone.

You blink. "When did you even—that's cool as *fuck* dude."

"Don't tell anyone, but it's from one of your poems."

A fist opens up your whole chest and takes out the small bits, leaving only agony. "You . . . ? My—?"

She laughs. Her cheeks pink. "You wrote me a poem once. And it had a few lines in it: *Hope can collect in beads on the persistent wings of moths/ light is a compass/and on moonless nights/we paint stars below our roof.*"

You push her hair back behind her ear and kiss her. She kisses back, deep and slow, like she's taking her time with it.

You both stay like that for a while, just kissing, and then you break apart to look back down at the tattoo. "I can't believe you got that because of my writing."

She shrugs. "I liked that line. It made me think of my childhood room."

You kiss the skin beside it, reverent. "Did it hurt?"

She snorts. Instead of answering, she pulls you up to her face again. Runs her thumb over your bottom lip. Presses her forehead to the softness of your neck and sighs. "Hey. I just. I know I can't—I mean, is it okay if this feels different? Us, I mean."

"Different good? Different bad? Should I stop? Are you okay?"
She pulls back and rolls her eyes. "You *would* be worried."

"Okay, but I *am* worried."

She blows out a breath. "I don't know. You're—like, fuck, dude.
You're my favorite person. Like, actually, for real. I'm used to—" She
laughs, high and strange. Looks anywhere else, not at you. Gestures
vaguely.

"Marlowe . . ." You start, not even sure what you're going to say.

"You just feel real," she blurts. It looks like she's about to start
crying. She runs the pad of her thumb over your cheek. In a softer
voice, she adds, "You know . . . different. You feel different to me."

Your head is spinning.

"And . . . I can't," she whispers. She grips the front of your dress
like she's drowning, and then slumps against you. Into your shoulder,
she murmurs: "I just . . . can't."

mouse crash-landed here in the spaceship in the middle of 2011. she
has since been pretending she is a human girl. she is not. if you are
reading this, pay attention. mouse is an alien.

mouse took my body. and i took hers.

◆

PART TWO:

HE WILL COMMIT A FEDERAL CRIME UPON MY BODY.

M Gmail

Client Request
2 messages

To: ▮▮▮▮▮▮▮▮▮

Thu, Aug 4, 20▮▮ at 1:52 PM

Hi!

My name is ▮▮▮▮▮. I am writing with the hopes of being one of your patients. I have some passing experience with therapy, but due to a recent life change, I believe that I should begin to explore more long-term options.

A little about myself: I have struggled with OCD, depression, and anxiety for much of my life. I have some coping mechanisms that I think might be ▮▮▮▮▮▮▮▮, and I'm hoping to untangle from ▮▮▮▮▮. I have unfortunately experienced a degree of ▮▮▮▮▮▮▮▮▮▮▮▮▮▮▮ and I think it is affecting my relationship skills. If I was to have a singular therapeutic goal, it would be to try and repair my connection to my body. I often feel somewhat disassociated, and it makes it hard for me to ▮▮▮▮▮▮. I have noticed this disassociation for some time, but I have not been able to ground myself using any easily-available techniques (meditation, etc).

Additionally, I have an addictive personality, and am easily consumed by things. While I don't believe I have an ▮▮▮▮▮▮▮▮▮▮▮ yet, I am worried about the ways I might use ▮▮▮▮▮▮▮▮▮ in order to self-soothe. This relates to my disassociation as well: I have noticed that when I am experiencing hardship, I turn to disassociation and ▮▮▮▮. However, due to ▮▮▮▮▮▮▮▮ in my childhood, I do not feel comfortable using the materials from AA; as they are based in Christian religious practices, which makes me uncomfortable. Any insight here is very much welcomed.

I am a queer Cuban, and I was attracted to your listing as you mentioned being sensitive to queer experiences. My insurance is ▮▮▮▮▮▮▮▮▮▮

Let me know if this sounds like it would be the right fit for you. I'm happy to answer any questions you might have.

Thank you for your time and consideration.

Best Regards,

▮▮▮▮▮▮▮▮▮▮▮

To: ▮▮▮▮

Hi ▮▮▮▮!

Thank you for reaching out to me. Unfortunately, I have recently closed my availability and will not be taking clients. However, I very much recommend my colleague ▮▮▮▮▮▮, whom I belie

Unfortunately, our practice does not take ▮▮▮▮▮▮▮▮. The current rate for out-of-network patients would be 350 USD per hour. If you find that to be acceptable, I am happy to move forwa▮ what your goals are as you move forwards. We begin any client interaction with a discovery meeting; which would be prorated at 150 USD. During this interaction, it is our intention to get to kr

I appreciate you asking for more information about AA and other options. However, it is not my policy to give advice until I have met with a client in person. I recommend you discuss this matte

Thank you for sharing your information with me. I look forward to hearing from you.

Best,

▮▮▮▮▮▮▮▮▮▮

▮▮▮▮▮▮▮ (she/her)

Mobile ▮▮▮▮▮▮▮▮▮▮

A READING FROM THE BOOK OF MOUSE
GOOD GOSPEL OF FATHOMLESS TRUTH AND VIRTUE

At the core of it all, what if you just wanted to be loved? So badly and so widely and so terribly. Any love, any semblance of *feeling* loved. You couldn't bear the loneliness; it was too painful to just exist. We could hear you calling us from the great width of space, with all that nameless yearning echoing into our fins. A wordless prayer of desperation.

We found you and we knew what you wanted. Take this, and eat it. This is your body, which will be given to us for our purposes—for the good of your own sake.

We will own you, but there will be no pain in the empty. Only the quiet, buzzing numb of being without a name.

but is the ghost story real? there was a girl once, *maybe*. there was a girl once, *probably*. she was sitting in the same house you're in now, and her hands were cold, and she just happened to have the same favorite spot by the wood stove. she was like you, because in ghost stories, you are haunting her by watching her dissolve.

is that what happened?

A READING FROM ███████████ MOUSE
███████ GOSPEL OF FATHOMLESS TRUTH AND ██████

You meet him in a shop called Paris Books, which you think is funny.
He's reading a book you were supposed to have picked up but never
did. When people say *Oh, did you read that*, you always lie about it. You
say, *I've been meaning to.*

Marlowe is living with her new French boyfriend and you've been
"just taking the summer to make some money," thanks to your parents
and their little couch. They had expected better from you and had
optimistically redone your childhood bedroom into a craft den, so all
the prayers that once leaked out of your pores have now been washed
into the floorboards and you need to sleep upstairs instead. You and
your back problems and that *trapped!* feeling, like you are fourteen and
pacing the walls of your cage again.

The summer stretching thin into the fall, but! You are in mania
and loving it. You have decided you are a different person now. You are
a *great* person now. You are free of a potentially toxic relationship. You
and Marlowe still on-and-off text, and you love keeping her updated
on how cool and awesome and fun your life is.

You are going to apply for one million jobs and get fancy pens
and try bullet journaling again. You are going to write that children's
book about gender expression; you're going to sell out. You are going
to read every fantasy in the library. You are going to learn three
thousand languages. You are going to have so many boyfriends and
girlfriends and partners that they will put a glittering *warning* sign
around your neck.

You are going to forget about Marlowe. When she comes back
to visit, you'll have long shiny hair and a thin waist and straight teeth.
Fuck everything.

Just a little while, just to make money. And then you'll leave too, maybe. You shrug one shoulder when you talk about it, *just getting my feet under me.*

Paris Books always smells damp, but they carry the notebooks you like, ones with paper too high-end for Target. Moleskine isn't actually a good brand—you like MD Paper.

It's the only seat left in the shop. He flicks his eyes up at you.

Hi, you say. *I've been meaning to read that.*

i do not know what is real and what just *feels* real, but isn't real. i can't *ever* know. my mental illness is so significant that many of my memories are invalid; fabricated from ocd's half-believed *what if* quantum state. as such, i am constantly in the visceral act of recreation—who am i? i haven't met her. if i look too hard, her form shifts, and the idea of *who i am* slips away.

my journal is full of half days. i never write the bad things. i can't look at any sad thing too long; each cruel memory starts curling up at the edges and setting the paper on fire. i maintain my sanity by virtue of radioactivity—i leave a glow of better lies behind me. days and weeks of *at least i'm grateful for the small things.* i will evacuate my mind of all the horrible things i have survived and arrive on the beach of perfection. i will scratch out every bad moment and instead have a soul that is perfectly rendered.

i shake a lot. despite my best attempts, i don't think the body forgets.

Kaisa comes into your room while the rain is falling. You have positioned your bed under one window (no bed frame, that's always-next-paycheck), and the way that the paint is peeling allows you to feel the wind like a kitten tongue.

"Hey, I was just checking—are you with Adam this weekend?" Her soft, musical voice. You lost touch after college for a while, and now as adults it's kind of nice that you still have the strange sense that she's not a friend but friendly *enough*. A good roommate to split a walkup with.

Meanwhile, Adam's place is fucking enormous. These past few months of causally dating, you've always been at his. The first time he showed it to you, you choked and thought of how both of your parents had to work two jobs during the recession. He has an honest-to-God three-story spiral staircase. He has chandeliers. He has a jacuzzi and a pool and an outdoor bar. He says he's planning on putting in a koi pond soon, "just to have something to do."

He doesn't like to come out to see you; you go to him in your beat-up shitbox of a car. To be fair, you live in a cramped and uninsulated apartment. Kaisa was a lucky addition, at least—she happened to be looking for a roommate, and you were fucking desperate.

She's nice, and there's a familiarity there that's good, but it's actually more awkward than anything. More awkward than you remember it being.

The space between you and Kaisa is good for you, mentally, given the Marlowe thing. At least, that's what you tell Lacey.

"Oh," Kaisa adds, "Remind me to get grapes when I'm out."

"Can do." You're going to forget to do that.

"Wait, but. So. Are you out with Adam?"

You check your phone. "Nah. He's got, like, some house viewing or something."

"Oh, okay, word." She checks her own phone and then fixes her hair. "I was thinking about starting dinner if you wanted some." You're starving. "Ah. I'm not feeling good today." At her expression, you hold up your hand soothingly. "I'm like, totally fine—I think I got motion sick while watching video games."

She smiles. "My mom always said they'd rot your brain. The only game I play is *Tetris*. I like the . . ." she gestures, ". . . Organizing shapes."

You look at your phone again. Adam has sent you a picture of himself in a suit, his hands in his pockets. Fuck, he looks *good*. Behind him, the artfully decorated house is white and pristine. The housekeeping staff must have just left for the evening.

Lacey had cackled when you showed her the Zillow walkthrough: *This dude is fucking rich-rich. Fucking loaded. How do you not spend legitimately every hour at his? I'd be ass-naked all the time, just touching expensive shit.*

You saw him once pay for windows—good, double-paned, floor-to-ceiling windows—in actual cash. You'd never even held that much money, and he had it in his pocket.

You'd told Lacey: *I mean, it's like a bastion of capitalist extravagance. Nobody needs five living rooms. But by the way? Yeah, I'm naked there, like, constantly.*

What's weird is that you don't necessarily *like* his place, even though you like being *seen* in his place. The walls all echo strangely. It's kind of like everything there forgets to exist, turns plastic. Like even the sun is a projection once it hits the edge of his opulent private fortress. On the bad nights, it specifically feels abandoned and too quiet. All this *stuff*, and nobody to *live* in it. Not even like a movie set—something kind of sinister, if you're being honest.

You look up to Kaisa. "Girl's night?" You are reading *The Great Gatsby* for the first time. It seems stupidly appropriate while you scramble for financial security. Besides, you like little ironies, and while you love Adam's inground pool with lion fountain and waterfall—you can't actually swim.

Kaisa's hair slips out from behind her ear again. She has a lot of red lipstick she lets you borrow. Whenever she listens like this—like your words actually matter—it makes you super uncomfortable. Maybe you changed too much out of college. She's the type of crystal-granola-queer that always seems to have her finger on a different, more-educated pulse. Kaisa is of those people who carries themselves with *intention*. It unnerves you. If she listens too long, she'll find out that you don't belong, Mouse, and then she'll make you leave this body for another one.

"Are you . . . sure you're up for drinking? I don't want to make you more sick."

"Oh, fuck yeah." At her look, you wink. "Second stomach for liquor."

She stares at you. Like this, she is perfectly unreadable.

"You never really talk about him," she says finally.

"Who—oh, Adam? I don't know," you half laugh, "I thought it would be boring to hear about him."

"I mean, I care about you. It wouldn't be boring."

"He's just, like, a dude. I don't know." At her continued stare, you shrug again. "He's . . . nice."

She makes a noise in the back of her throat. You play with your shirt. The silence stretches out in a wheel.

"Didn't you say you wanted to do a photoshoot with your friends sometime soon? Why don't we do something like that?"

You wave away her suggestion. "Nah, that's—I don't think so. I wanna just like—Like I'm feeling like having a little party or whatever. It's okay if you don't want to, though. I don't want to, like, pressure you." You are so fucking immature, it's disgusting.

Marlowe wouldn't have questioned it. Marlowe would have said *yes*.
Kaisa takes a big breath. Releases it slowly. "Okay. What are we drinking?"

You are going to eat popcorn for dinner, you decide. You can throw it up easily, in cloud chunks. You text him *watch out ;) getting drunk, slutty texts incoming*.

He sends you back a bunch of exclamation marks. A few hours later, he follows this up with a dick pic.

You once let him fuck you in a car, at the head (ha!) of a hiking trail, somewhere between New Hampshire and Tennessee. It was uncomfortably tight and you were riding. He couldn't actually manage to wiggle entirely out of his jeans. Your thighs chafed on either side.

You told him *God, I came so hard* and meant *I'm glad this happened quickly*.

This could be a good life you are choosing. Choose it harder, Mouse. Lean in.

the phrase *eating disorder* is often parsed as a language of extremes. it exists in binary: *anorexia* or *bulimia*. High fashion and complimentary to each other.

meanwhile, the reverse—*disordered eating*—feels (ironically) palatable. disordered eating feels almost friendly in its approach. it can enter into a conversation almost lovingly, a saturday buffet of shared complaints.

good girls don't eat. you mention to a friend that you have forgotten. when you are *normal sized*, this is a roll of the eyes. oopsie.

she will say *i wish i could forget*.

when you are *normal sized*, the oopsie is said over coffee. the eating is discussed between two people like a shared burden. you both laugh about it. you say how hard it is to be a person and wanting to eat. you mention that you want to learn to cook but there's no time. you both bemoan how easy it is for men to lose weight, how you both wish you could snap your own weight off. it is normal for a person to want to lose some amount of weight, the way it is normal to feel bad about *not* losing weight.

it is probably not good, though, to lie awake and think about cutting off your stomach.

i have found it is always, pathologically, *better* to feel shame in public than to delight in eating. one needs to be loud about how you fucking hate salad, but you should also be aware of how *much* salad you eat. it is important to eat salad most of the time, to complain while doing so that you wish you could eat something other than salad, but to *only* eat salad. you should hide what you eat too—behind a napkin, a hand. shovel it in your mouth while in the parking lot of a grocery store, alone.

it is also important to sometimes *be naughty,* and to announce the naughtiness. to be *bad.* to say out loud, "okay, just one!" while rolling your eyes and winking. we need to coax you—but you should be eventually willing to take the slice of cake. people don't want to *worry* about it. they want you to remain thin enough, but not a *problem.* people cannot know that a boston cream donut *literally* makes you break out into a sweat. that's not a normal thing. it *is* normal to say *i just gave it up for lent and never got back to it.*

disordered, but still *eating.*

there are people who don't think before they take another serving, who just eat and never worry about it.

the idea of that terrifies me.

MOUSE GO HOME

MOUSE: Okay, where do you want me? Give me a job, seriously. Okay, I'll get to chopping.

THE CHORUS: You will rot here, revulsion to Prometheus.

MOUSE: Your house is so lovely! Oh, that's a cute picture too. And is this vintage carpentry?

THE CHORUS: He will drop your hand when he rings the doorbell and you will stand up straighter and even though you dressed up and they didn't they will look better than you and you will take his coat and not know what to do with your hands until someone takes pity on you and shows you where to hang everything and gives you a weird side hug and you shake hands and take off your shoes in the big foyers of houses that could eat your childhood home and sit at long tables where he doesn't make eye contact with you and you will try to interject with funny thoughts but you will not have anything funny to say and he will shoot you a warning look not to take a second helping of dinner while the smooth jazz will ripple under your clothes and you will prefer a white wine but they only have a fancy red from a year before you were born (but not him!) and you will swirl it in the glass the wrong direction and you will all get drunk and he will only kiss your forehead once, while no one is looking, and you will be forced to have an opinion about rich people things you couldn't be fucked to care about and everyone knows that you literally don't know enough about the subject but *they* all do so you will try your hardest and later read the books about it but it'll never measure up to their *real world* experience so no matter what you just look pretentious and young (and how often his friends bring that up, surprised by the answer *twenty-five, almost twenty-six*) and next time you promise yourself you'll be better and less shy and less anxious and less weird about asking where the bathroom is and less weird about wondering if they can hear you pee in the other room and less weird in general and then maybe he'll be proud of you because your father thinks this is a man who could really take care of you and maybe it *is* love and not just boredom/having no other options since like nobody has trapped you here—but you *are* here and the door is closed again and you shake their hands and take off your shoes and talk about politics only to laugh and directly not talk about politics and you will bite your tongue about the feminist thing and you will laugh about capitalist comments and he will invite six of them over for your birthday (*yours!*) and you will all get drunk and never eat and you will even develop sort of a love for some of them even though they're never really *your* people (they're *his*) and you might cry in the Crosby's parking lot about how you don't really have any friends and he won't know what to say to make it better because to be fair to him you *don't* have any friends and at least *his* friends are cool and older and have cool cars and cool careers and mortgages and you live on the floor with your old college roommate and he takes care of you like a guest and often gets you drunk and besides you're a writer so it's lucky that you got this far to begin with so what if you ever tell him *no* he sulks for at least a week and it's literally easier to just say *yes* instead of having the argument particularly since if you ever say *no* he will bring it up over and over again about how you don't really *care* about him so you just close your mouth and hope for the best and the door closes again and you take off your shoes and give them genuine hugs and he still doesn't make eye contact with you but you don't look for it anymore because now you've been taught not to expect it so you do shots with *the wives* in the back kitchen (they have two kitchens and it no longer surprises you) and you all giggle and none of you *girls* will text each other after but during *these events* you will develop some kind of private understanding about *just chatting* that centers around *the kitchen* and washing their dishes and getting drunk and talking about the safely sanitized general things while the men sit and talk around the television and get similarly wasted and you don't try to interject your opinions about art or the spectrum of the human experience anymore because nobody will listen and that will just hurt your feelings and you don't go up for the kiss anymore because he'll dodge it and that will also just hurt your feelings and actually *fuck it* you are absolutely too strong for this so when he reaches out to ring the doorbell you drop his hand before he can and you pull yourself up and smile while they answer the door and know where to put your coat and know where the bathroom is and say *it's been too long* and kiss their cheeks and keep yourself a glistening, pretty, vapid little thing and the door closes and you take your shoes off and you will say:

MOUSE: Thank you for such a lovely evening!

interesting etymological note: the *old wife* in the idiom *old wives' tale* isn't actually referring to the position of *wife*, it's actually *any woman*, from the old english *wif.* Another translation would be "old women's tale," then. We can have a conversation about why all women were assumed to be wives at a different time, but i just want to take a moment to talk about being a cassandra.

cassandra, of the greek tragedy, is cursed with the ability to see the future. however, no matter how much she speaks the truth, no one will ever believe her.

the word for *hysteria* derives from the latin word for *uterus.* by the way.

correlation does not prove causation. but the sapir-whorf hypothesis has a tenant that the more words a language has for an idea, the more important the idea is for the culture that speaks that language. for example, the sheer number of slang terms for *disagreeable woman* (bitch, harpy, shrew, nag, shrill) versus the relatively scant words for *love*.

i do just want to address, because my father has read this book and it's come up in our conversation: in the same way that i cannot definitively prove words have been invented to specifically target women, this work is not intended to prove i hate men.

there doesn't have to be a binary reaction. i didn't have to hate men to believe all women deserve better on a global and personal scale. unfortunately, due to the fact i *do* hold this position, i have been informed my opinion on men has been made *for* me.

to support women and survivors is to take a stand politically. whether or not you want to: you sacrifice some type of agency by virtue of your empathy.

◇

MOUSE GO HOME

Mouse had sworn to do better for the body she's in, but the skin she's wearing has become like rice again and now it's peeling off if she nibbles too long. You should have followed up about the lease, but you're not here right now.

And then she is you again, horribly, in a strange and nauseating moment.

Adam is lying on the floor beside you, and you're day-after-drinking sick-as-hell. So is he. It was six shots too many, but you do that so frequently now that the sickness is comforting. You shouldn't resent him. You should resent *yourself.*

He's a *good man.*

Nine months, not that you're counting. You keep wrapping your hands around your thighs idly, watching the way your thumbs do or do not connect. You drink a lot of chicken soup straight out of the can, cutting your mouth on it.

Why does he keep commenting on how good you'd look while pregnant. Why does he always grab the soft parts of your stomach. Why do the two of you drink so much. And what, exactly are you trying to *do* when you drink? Are you bored, are you angry, are you running? How many nights have you spent like that, babe? Drunk as shit, just to—what? Be interesting enough for him? Be interested *in* him? How *fucking* disappointing.

You check your phone. You have texted Marlowe a few times, but she's kind of stopped responding. Your side of the texts looks desperate, annoying.

At least you have Adam, and his hands, and his car, and his fucking house. And he has you on his mattress. He has *you* and you can only give him your body, roughshod. Your bones all gilded. You are fucking lucky to have this. Throw your spine at the problem or otherwise you are functionally useless.

He got bored of vanilla sex on like the second date, and then your definition of *rough sex* became a different goalpost per evening. Now you are his perfect mewling *sex kitten.* He doesn't even ask before putting you in handcuffs, he just expects them. You don't even balk at the size of the paddle. You close your eyes, trying not to feel exposed and awkward in the rope-bondage poses; hyperaware of every fold and jiggle. Sometimes you want him to ask if this is self-harm, and sometimes you just want him to get the knife out. He's never followed up about why you're so into pain. Lately, he's been shoving things into your mouth so you cannot squeal. He likes to suffocate you.

He used to go to anger management classes as a kid. He hasn't seen a therapist since.

You read somewhere that having a partner that practices nonlethal strangulation makes you seven times more likely to be killed in the real life by his hand, but you don't want to be an uptight *Catholic guilt* kind of a partner.

So you say you think it's hot.

Maybe you're actually asexual, because you *don't* think it's hot. You just know it's *sexy,* and you're struggling to *find* it sexy. And you can't walk it back anymore, he's already staked off that part of you. Once the horse is out of the barn, what exactly are you supposed to do.

You conduct sort of scarily thorough research into BDSM pornography, literally taking notes rather than getting off. You develop opinions on it, on types of whips and leather and ball gags. Like this is a literature review, and not your life.

Did you want to lay your hand on someone's hip and feel them laughing. Did you want to spend a summer watching the ceiling fan spin, the two of you tucked in together, just breathing. That is too bad. That is not giving back to your partner. Adam thinks cuddling is *boring.* Adam thinks cuddling is only for aftercare, while you are covered in welts like wasp stings. If you want to feel loved, you have to fucking *earn* it.

If you squint, it's actually kind of *romantic.* Like, he's playing with these institutional power displays in this taboo way, free of patriarchy. You're a feminist; you should know that applying moral standards to sex makes you a prude. You're leaning *away* from the slut-shaming body horror of your upbringing—and *into* the obscene. It's feminist to take back your own body, right? It's actually feminist, kind of, to let a man use you like this. The reason you don't actually *like* it is because you were raised too Catholic. You need to just teach yourself different. *Other* people enjoy it. You can give him this, you *need* to give him this.

He's been there for you for *nine months*. And think about it! You've subverted your own cultural expectations so completely that you are now making the *perverse* into the *sexual.*

God, you're so clever and sexy.

And besides, you're sex-positive! You wouldn't judge someone *else* for their choices. A body is a beautiful neutral space, and he absolutely has done the reading (right) and sees you like a divine goddess (right) who is occasionally into ████ (right) and neither of you think your willingness to experience pain has anything to do with your past (right) or how you learned to take the ███████████████ from your ████. So what if he knows how you were raised! What matters is that it's all *loving.*

One small *maybe*-a-problem: he won't engage the feminist conversation politely. You have since stopped asking. You really didn't like the resulting arguments.

Okay. Maybe there's another problem too, one that's been bothering you recently: he never wants to just kiss you; it always has to *lead* to something. You try to kiss him under fireworks or during movies or in the rain—but if he reciprocates, he *always* makes it into sex.

You like to kiss people to make a connection, and he likes to kiss people to *inform* the *species* of connection. Like you aren't a person, you're a possession.

Today the air is greasy. A closed eye always finds you pretty, don't wake him up. Everything is salty in a bad way. Your teeth are fuzzy.

He rolls over in the bed beside you, his long fingernails tracing up the inside of your thigh. You're grouchy. *Stop that, there are too many eels wriggling around inside of me.* Don't you dare say that, it sounds crazy.

Coward. You *won't* say that.

Go on, Mouse. Tell yourself the good story.

I am in love. I am a good woman with a good life and a good job and luck like a kite and I am a hot young professional. I am in love. We are in love. We are so, so in love.

We roll over and we tuck our hand underneath his face and say, *Hello, darling,* and we nuzzle up to him and his breath reeks—but ours does too, probably—and we stick our leg between his and we fold ourself against him so he will be reminded we are supple like a tree branch, even with the extra weight on us.

He is bleary-eyed. He grumbles that he doesn't want to wake up.

What *you* want to do is take the sickle of your spine and bend it like wheat until you expose each of your organs under the blistering sun. What *you* want to do is cry like a big bitch baby where nobody can hear just so you can freely howl in that high, blistering keen.

You kiss the thickness of his thumb.

something about the inevitability of "the cycle of ███ always felt extremely cruel to me. my own body will hunt that which hurts with such a rabid fervor that i will not notice the process; it will simply be secreted out of me. i will annihilate my own future to hide in the shadow of the colossus i've already killed and eaten.

a common response when people find out is a shocked sort of backward compliment: *it's just that you are far too smart to have fallen for it.*

██████████████ ████████ M███ E

A year and six months. He gets you a locket for your Christmas present. You recently landed a new job, and the gold chain matches one of your new business-casual sweaters. You both watch snow falling from his bay windows. You have his sister's number saved in your emergency contacts.

You lean against him, and think about how sturdy he is, and how he makes you feel small, and how you're doing a good job of being a woman. How you're doing a good job of being an adult. How your life has settled into a shape of clearly defined portions—a preplanned designation that is oddly and sweetly satisfying.

If you are bleeding somewhere, you will not have to worry about it. There is nothing to worry about at all, actually. Look at you, and how perfect life is.

You have everything taken care of.

how strange to say that at times i love the obsession. persephone can corroborate: rules create meaning. one can find solace in toxicity, *if* that toxicity is specific. it is easy to become addicted to the tang of battery acid—it is full of flavor, of nurtured shock. the saying: *it's better the devil you know.* a rule doesn't need to make sense either; crickets have their own logic and delight in their personal mathematics.

rules pacify the insatiable. if you are always thirsty, develop a rule about water. if you are always hungry, develop a rule about carbs. develop a rule about dishes. develop a rule about sex. develop a rule about donuts. develop yourself into the picture of the person you *wish* you were, if you hadn't been born so goddamn fucking *weird,* kid.

there are body checks, private ways we admonish and measure ourselves. we wrap our fingers around wrists or thighs or pinch quietly at fat deposits. ███████████ encourages it. it is almost a horrible comfort, a form of having both a hug and a judgment.

touch/don't touch. turn the lights off nine times before you leave. eat the six seeds, arrive in the underworld. marry and have babies. lower your voice. smile more. cross your ankles. do not kiss her. bend over.

rule yourself perfectly. adjust your settings. make yourself charming and lovely and fuckable. maybe if you do it right, someone will finally love you the way you actually need.

maybe. just maybe.

◇

His birthday is coming up. You get too drunk again. You tell him it's from being stressed at work, but you actually feel exactly and precisely *nothing*: a type of numbness that is almost sanctimonious.

Recently you asked him to please stop ██████ your head down while you are swallowing all the sharp need of him. He has been ████████ you, but was unconcerned when you explained that you *literally* couldn't breathe, that you are in clear and present distress in those moments. He says it is an accident. You try to argue, but it's not really a conversation.

It's easier if you're a little too drunk, so you get a little too drunk *a lot*. He fucks you in a room you've only been in twice. You stare at the chandelier the whole time, barely registering your body shift, almost like a clock ticking. Can it be passionless sex if it's not vanilla? Isn't the whole point of BDSM to like, put passion into it?

You told him once *I feel like when you hold me down I can't, like, actually participate in the sex.* He said he *liked* that part of it. So maybe you are just bad at sex and he's doing you *both* a favor by restraining you during it.

The problem is that there's been a few times, now, where you tried to push him off you, and then you had the worst kind of realization—he really *is* stronger than you. He really *can* make sure he finishes. You really *don't* have a say in any of this.

You are ignoring that. It is better not to think about it. Easier to get drunk and forget it.

Three days ago, you found out that Marlowe has moved back to the States. In fact, she's been here for a few *months*.

Six months ago, you'd been one of 326 people to "love react" to her new profile pic. Her, tanned and laughing, holding up the orange body of Toothpaste for a kiss. This new picture had replaced the one with her in a bikini—which had, eight months beforehand, notably replaced the one with the last (final?) French boyfriend.

Not that you're keeping tabs on her. Not that you keep trying to be cool about reaching out to her. Not that you just stare at her Instagram for hours, purposefully keeping your hands poised so you don't accidentally "like" something.

And then she posted a picture, tagging your alma mater's nearest ice cream place. Someone else had beaten you to it, asking her in the comments: *Are you visiting?? OMG!*

Tucked in between all the other *love this* and *pretty girl* comments, her reply: *I actually live in the area now! Come hang out!!!*

She didn't tell you anything about moving back to the States. Never mentioned it.

And who cares? You have a beautiful life, and you are so *fucking* lucky. You need to eat something, sooner rather than later. You should really, really, really, really, really stop drinking.

Ironic, you draw a smiley face next to your journal entry: *This isn't even really a thing. "Oh, you party too much." Like, because I have a glass of wine with lunch? Just because I like to relax? I use it for my anxiety. Can a bitch get some, like, basic empathy?*

horror stories are recursive. we come back, and the girl (it is usually a girl, except when it is a boy, very rarely) is suffering. she is dragging her shaking palms over the pouted lip of her porcelain bathtub. the hair sticks to her skin in wet, slimy tendrils.

right now, we are learning what will kill her, or what will torture her, or what will break her. the story isn't so much about the unfairness of her suffering. instead, it's the gleeful *celebration* of when she is torn asunder.

sometimes it is instead about how she herself will learn to do the rending, and become a monster. *rendition* is from the french *rendere*, to give back. *to rend* is from the old english *rendan* and the german *rende*—to tear sinew apart with one's teeth.

so listen. she will be a ghost in this one. the pool of light in the bathroom is a yellowed teeth one, and there is a fly in the sconce, and there is a ticking in the girl's chest, and there is something dripping. she is waiting for the part of the story where she becomes a chain email, but she is not quite there yet. she is in the era of her suffering instead. her dampness ekes through the words around her, so she is the sallowfaced worship of words like *mildewing* and *drowned*.

this girl is the ghost of every campfire story. someone bullied her or they killed her dog or they made her watch her family die; and now she is sitting knees up in orange water, her long thin arms wrapped around her tiny brittle legs. if the text she lives in isn't sent to all of your contacts, she will be able to crawl out of the bathroom, up the pipes, onto the walls. over beds; she will become her own canopy, flaking the ceiling with her decay. she will be released from the fragile and, in the real life, bead herself forward in dewy steps, shimmering at the foot of her summoner's sleep.

but first she *must* suffer. suffering is the requirement. after the suffering, she can live for an eon as a glutted spider, full of her anger and hatred.

we will hate her for it too, the way we hate anything ugly and human. we will tell her that her suffering does not require *our* suffering, and that she should come down off of the walls and get ready for school. no one will say she died too young and that she deserves her wrath. we will tell her to stay in her bathtub's baptismal font. she can turn into soup there and dissolve her flesh down the u-bend. it would be so much better for all of us if she submitted tenderly. it would be so much better for all of us if her anger happened peacefully.

anger does not befit (case 1) *a survivor*, not if they want to be pretty enough for the movie screen. it is equally ugly in (case 2) *a young lady*. (how often are case 1 and case 2 synonyms? google isn't helping.)

first she *must* suffer, though. we will retell the story and her anger will leak out at the sides. at the bottom follows a warning— you can't let her sleep. once you've read something like that, you need to pass it on.

over and over, she wakes up, she suffers. her pain scattered in ghostly breadcrumbs for all the birds to eat.

Mouse doesn't know what time it is, but her body is full of spat teeth. Hungover, bloated. She pushes the heels of her palms against her eyes, holding until stars wiggle into focus. Wait, is that healthy? What if she's going blind?

She can't believe today is happening.

The shirt she wants to wear is skintight, so she goes down the four flights to his basement gym and puts her cold paws on the hard IKEA bamboo. She takes a second to set up her single yoga mat, and then takes a full fifteen minutes to examine herself closely in those floor-to-ceiling mirrors.

She runs her hands over her body, shirt pulled up around her ribs. She turns to one side and then the other and then practices flexing and breathing in. She just always looks so *gummy*. Like she was invented to be chewable. Somehow, despite her heritage, she always looks so shockingly *pale*. Some people look good with their stomach showing. She always just looks undressed. Somehow, she feels more naked in a crop top and shorts than when she is actually in her underwear. Something about her is just *too* soft, too yielding. It just feels *incorrect*. Out-of-focus. Like she was supposed to be painted different.

She completes forty minutes of high-intensity interval training and then thirty minutes of cardio and then twenty minutes of strength training and then a fifteen-minute yoga cooldown.

She is still fat. Surprising.

Mouse is going to be good today and eat an allergy tablet so that she will not be annoying. People can't tell she is an alien when she is calm. She needs to be drowsy but still awake enough to be entertaining. What if she is not entertaining *enough*, though? So two allergy tabs, but then later she'll have Starbucks and directly apply heavy self-control.

She wants a Boston cream donut. Embarrassing. She wants a glass of wine. Sure, it's early, but wine is an anytime drink.

Since she's getting anxious, unseated, unhappy, Mouse tells herself the story again. Mantra-esque. It is so familiar in her borrowed head that it's worn-down now: *You are a good girl. You are happy and in love. You are the envy of others. You are not sad or lonely. He is so good to you and you are so lucky.*

You *are* so lucky. But you aren't going to wear that shirt after all— you're too ugly.

Lacey calls during breakfast. You have settled on granola and overnight oats, gruel you eat without joy or passion.

You answer on the third ring. "Hi, sweetie. You're on speakerphone." Not that Adam is even awake yet.

"We're getting there early," she informs you. "I want to really get a handle on the situation as it develops. Get in the car."

"You're a crazy person."

"After everything she put you through? This is basic-ass reconnaissance. We *must* discuss. I need to know everything before I go once more into the breach."

You dry-laugh. "Okay, it *could* be fun."

"She strung you along for like forty years and now won't even fucking pick up your calls. This is going to be a fuckin' sting op."

Ouch. You draw your finger along his marble counter. "Okay. I'm gonna pour myself a glass of water and head out."

"It's the S-bux by the River Street Inn, right?"

Actually, you shouldn't drink water because it'll mean you have to pee during the drive. You'll just have to take the allergy meds dry. "Yeah. Next to the Kroger."

"They closed that, actually!"

"How the fuck did they close Kroger?"

"Happened like last year I think." Lacey pauses to rifle around. "Okay. I'm gonna hop in the shower, but I'll see you in like an hour?"

"Google says it's an hour and twenty."

"So speed."

"Lacey. For the love of God, have mercy."

"Fine. I'll give you an hour *and fifteen*. I need to hear all the good goss'."

An hour and seventeen later, you shut off your NPR smart-person podcast and pull into the parking lot. Someone bought the Kroger lot already and is building one of those pre-fab complexes where everything has the same white trim and similar jewel-toned paneling.

Lacey's sitting at a black wire table outside of Starbucks. She jumps right up, hugs you so tight that you wheeze. You both grab your preordered drinks from inside and then return to the table. The sun is just warm enough but the wind is still kind of chilly. You wish you brought a jacket. The iced Frappuccino is too cold to help you withstand it.

"Are you gonna be okay if you drink that?" Lacey pauses, watching you struggle to angle the straw correctly.

"I mean, yeah? Maybe? Why? What is that supposed to mean?" It comes out higher and sharper than intended.

Lacey holds up her hands. "Oh, sorry. I thought you said that coffee—like, caffeine—was giving you anxiety recently?"

They fucked up the syrup ratio. Your vindictive sip just gives you a headache. "Sorry. I'm being a bitch."

"You're not a *bitch*." Lacey says it in a way that means *you were kind of being a bitch.*

The Bitch sighs into her hands. "Sorry. I'm freaked out."

"I mean, yeah." She rests her head on her hands. "It literally took *me* asking her to hang out, and I *certainly* wasn't kissing her ever. You spent *like three months* trying to get her to literally *talk* to you. And lo and behold, turns out—she's been here for *the whole time.*"

"She's busy."

"I'm busy. You're busy. Literally every adult on Earth forever is busy."

"They made this wrong." You shake it, watching the oat milk redistribute. "Ugh. No. This is the only thing sustaining me."

You sigh, thumb pressing against the tight space between your eyebrows, knowing you can't finish the drink now—you're thinking about calories. Fuck. You *knew* you had plans for today, and you drank last night *anyway*, like an idiot. You should never touch alcohol again. It makes you bloated and fat and angry and anxious.

"Oh baby, I'm sorry. I hate that." Lacey extends hers; mocha cloud with no whip. "D'you want the rest of mine? I'm, like, done."

"Why must God choose me to suffer?"

She laughs and shakes her cup. "Literally *take it.*"

"Lacey. I am *not* stealing the rest of your legitimately brand-new coffee."

"No, for real. I was about to throw it out. I've actually been getting super bad anxiety too, and I shouldn't have ordered a grande. I'd just waste this, to be honest. You'd actually be helping me, and, like, I don't know, the environment. You're crazy about the environment." She looks down at her phone. "How are things with Adam, by the way?"

"Don't you demur to me. You're straight up lying about not wanting that coffee."

"Okay. I hear you. But . . . I did just hit submit on another order. For you."

You want to cry. "No, you did not."

Lacey is already getting up. "Wait here a second, I have to pee anyway, I'll get it on the way back."

"I'll Venmo you," you offer.

"I'll literally just send the money back."

You know from experience that she's being honest. She winks at you as she passes, dropping a kiss on the top of your head.

You stare at your phone, feeling something weird and passive. You scroll Instagram. You read the news. The feeling sticks around, tacky and thick.

Wait. Oh. Does the weirdness you feel come from Lacey being kind to you? Is *that* why you're nervous? Why do you feel like she is expecting something from you now? Like she'll hold this against you for the rest of your time here?

You know better than that. Lacey doesn't hate you now. Lacey doesn't want anything in return for literally just buying you a coffee. This is a normal thing that best friends do.

Still. You shouldn't have gotten something so expensive. You should have just bought a black coffee, no cream and no sugar. Or with six Splenda or something. Or you could just snort the Splenda and stop pretending.

You start typing the text to Adam that you got here safe, and then delete it. Maybe he'll worry. Wait, is that fucked up? You shouldn't play that game. You go to retype it. Delete it again. To be honest, he'd be annoyed by the notification.

God, this is such a mistake. You're being a burden, get your shit together. Instead of listening to the pretentious smart-person podcast, you should have been listening to something funny. Now you can't steal a funny personality and wear it—it's just gonna have to be you, and how sickeningly vapid you are.

You close your eyes tight. *Stop drinking so much fucking caffeine, it gives you anxiety.*

Nothing you've seen on social media is actually sinking in, so you do the thing you've been avoiding: you check the group conversation with Marlowe.

You'd tried an embarrassing number of times to make contact. It's genuinely so immature and stupid—your texts all hopeful and *oh, okay, but sometime soon!* Her texts all, *idk sorry dude.*

And Lacey, taking pity on you one night—just took a shot of tequila, made a group chat, and managed to get Marlowe to agree in writing.

You're technically "celebrating" your birthday. Late. By almost a full month.

But to be fair: Adam had been too busy at work, Lacey had a legitimate family thing, and Marlowe of course hadn't been responding.

Be good. You're a good girl. You close the app and force yourself to enjoy the chilled spring air and the fat black-capped chickadees making sunny coven dances in the sand across the parking lot.

Lacey sits back down with a sigh. "Okay." She hands you the new coffee.

"Okay," you repeat. They made it right this time. Less watery. You sigh into it, half your body releasing something unnamed and agonizing. "*Thank you,* oh my God. This is genuinely lifesaving."

"Okay, so we were talking about Adam?"

You snort. "Fuck men. I miss *you.*"

"I miss you too. I wish his house wasn't like, six million years away."

"They're going to develop teleporting so I can actually see you ever." Or see *anybody.*

Then you talk about how many people have moved to her area recently. You talk about how you *could* have moved to the area, but it's expensive, and, well, money. You notably do *not* talk about how you stayed near Adam just to be close to Adam; that you'd known you were *choosing.* You'd had the sense with him that if you had moved even a *little* further, the thing between the two of you would have crumbled quickly and angrily.

It wasn't even that being alone would have scared you—it was the idea that he would have no problem with it. That you would be out of his life and he might not actually notice. That even with all the terrible, embarrassing effort of your perfect-girlfriend routine—he wouldn't miss you. Even if you were the one to leave: you'd be the only one hurting.

So maybe it *was* about being alone.

You talk about Kaisa—Lacey says *they're so pretty*—and you talk about your plants and she talks about the guy she's been seeing for a year whose name is Tanner and is actually sweet. You talk about a show you're watching, she talks about her job and the new painting she's working on. You let questions about Adam slide off of you and into other topics. If she notices, she doesn't bring it up.

Neither of you talk about Marlowe yet. You both know you will have a private debrief after the hangout. Lacey even made a series of GCal invites, blocking out the whole day: *coffee before Marlowe, mall with Marlowe, drinking after/because of Marlowe.*

It's not that Lacey doesn't *like* Marlowe. After all, they were close before France. It's just that Lacey held your hair back, after. Watched what happened to you, after. Watched what might still be happening, now. And Lacey, unlike you, actually cares that you might have, technically, at a certain angle—gotten your heart completely broken. Not that you get to claim something so sinister, since you were never actually *dating*.

Lacey rides shotgun in your shitty car while you drive down the street to the sprawling white mall to meet Marlowe in front of Dick's Sporting Goods.

Her bag is sliding off her shoulder. You didn't expect her to look just like a person. When you think about her, are you thinking of *her* or the *idea* of her? What do your *actual* memories look like? How much have you just imagined?

She smiles and hugs you both, you try not to hold on too long. She lets go faster than she used to. Whatever, not that you should be noticing.

"Why hello there." Marlowe shifts her bag up her shoulder. She puts on a gremlin voice. "So happy to see you today, my pretties."

You have so much you want to ask her. Maybe too much—you suddenly have no words to offer. You make a weird stuttering noise.

"Hi, oh my gosh." Lacey takes charge, shifting the awkward triangle into motion. "Ugh, it's too cold out here, let's get inside. ███, you said you wanted to go to the bookstore first?"

"Yeah—uh, yes." You had forgotten why you were here at all, and it's always alarming to hear the Body's actual name, since it's not *yours*.

"Oh good, I'm cold too." Marlowe's hair is a new color. She parts it on a different side now too. "This is actually really well-timed. My boyfriend's parents just moved and I'm getting them a housewarming gift." She looks in her bag for something.

Your ears are ringing.

"Ah-ha, a *boyfriend*." Lacey holds open the door for you all. "That's a development." She almost doesn't say it in a mean way. She *almost* doesn't.

"Sorry, is that—" You can't remember the name of the dude she'd last tagged on Insta. You shift approaches. "I mean, how long have y'all been together? How'd you meet?"

She doesn't answer. She's looking at her phone.

The mall is decorated for Easter. You find yourself surprised by this. "The casual Christianity of American consumerism," you say out loud, mostly to yourself.

"Oh yeah, Passover is late this year, huh? Want to get a picture with the rabbit?" Lacey looks over at you. "Are your parents gonna make you go to Easter vigil?"

"Easter vigil?" Marlowe's eyebrows knit. She doesn't look up from the phone.

"Her family always does midnight ma—"

Marlowe waves a hand. "Oh right, midnight mass. That's the five-hour one, right?"

You want to throw up. "Do you think it's the same people who play Santa who also play the rabbit?" You find the directory and stare at it without taking anything in. For some reason, you always feel embarrassed while looking at mall maps, like you're doing something inappropriate. Why even choose the mall to hang out? You don't actually *like* the mall. You are actually exhausted by the concept of shopping. Now that you are here and it is happening, the anticlimax is choking you.

She just looks . . . normal. Is the thing. Not even older. Do *you* look older, really? It's been, what, two years and change?

You picked out an outfit for this from your *business-casual* collection. Your blouse is stupid. You're trying too hard. Overdressed.

What did you *actually* think was going to happen, during this?

"Hey, you're a child of God, does the Easter rabbit have a name?" Lacey stands beside you, and then points easily to the bookstore on the map. "Okay, it's not too far. Upstairs."

"Why do they put the escalators literally in the worst places?" You step backward to reorient yourself; Marlowe lets out a squeak while you step onto her. You massive oaf. "Fuck, sorry. Didn't hear you come up."

"Not a problem." She moves you to the side easily, guiding you by the hips the way she used to do. The familiarity of her touch sends a strange pole through you. She looks up through her lashes at the map. "Okay, y'all. Show me where we're going."

Lacey rolls her eyes and starts walking. "So what have you been up to?"

Even though the question was addressed to her, Marlowe is on her phone again. In the long silence that follows, Lacey gives you *a look*.

"Marlowe?" Lacey prompts.

"Oh, me?" Marlowe shakes herself and puts the phone into her pocket. "Sorry. What was the question?"

You laugh, but Lacey doesn't.

"Like, where ya been, loca," Lacey's *Twilight* reference *almost* keeps the annoyance out of her voice. You shoot her *a look* back. *Behave.*

She rolls her eyes again, in a way that says *fine*.

Marlowe shifts her bag again. It looks too big on her. You want to offer to hold it, but that would be weird. She sniffs. "I'm contracting right now."

"Oh, that's cool!" Lacey steps onto the escalator and you both follow her.

When Marlowe doesn't reply, you offer: "Like, what kind of contracting?"

Marlowe looks at you directly. Something plays at the side of her mouth, but you don't know what it is yet. "It's boring."

"Your degree was in acting, right? That's the job you did in France?" Lacey steps off and leads you all to the left, and points to a jewelry shop. "Oh, don't let me forget; I want to stop at one of these to see if they have an extra jump ring."

"Oh, for the necklace Tanner got you?" It broke on the second day. You didn't expect to like Tanner. He had kind of pleasantly surprised you, honestly. He had offered to buy her a second necklace to make up for it; Lacey had stopped him.

"Yeah, I don't know. It sucks because I *really* like it, but I can't find the right thing to fix it and I super don't want to lose it if it falls off."

You don't say *With Adam, I don't* ███████████████████████████. "Are you excited about the London trip?" You look over to Marlowe, but she's back on her phone. Whatever. She's an adult, she's allowed to text, and it's not like you're even talking to her right now, so it's kind of unfair you're annoyed by this.

She's not talking to *you*, either, though.

Lacey follows your gaze. "I'm like, cautiously optimistic about the London trip." She shoots you another dark *look,* and mouths, *Wow.*

You spot the bookstore, tucked into a weirdly dark corner next to Spencer's Gifts. A massive teddy bear sits on a rocking chair in the display window, surrounded by bestsellers. You like the bear's pince-nez. "Okay, don't let me buy too much in here," you say.

A bookstore? Really? Fucking pretentious bitch.

The three of you walk in together, and Lacey stops immediately at the travel section.

"I'm gonna go check clearance first," you say, and slide behind her. Her nose is already in a book, but she nods to you anyway.

You feel weird, like you're holding your breath. You run your hands over the yellow-stickered books. None of them are particularly interesting to you, but you have to look anyway, just to see if you will like something that is somehow both attractive and cheap.

What are you performing right now? Why do you have to stand up nicely and hold your head at an attractive angle?

You wrap your wrist in fingertips. Too tight. It cuts off your circulation.

"Hey." Marlowe comes up behind you, and you jump. She laughs. "Sorry, I forgot you're so skittish. That's twice now today."

Are you offended? "What's up?"

She pulls out her phone. "Okay. Please don't hate me."

Not a promising opener. "Alright, who'd ya kill?"

She doesn't smile. "Okay, I know I, like, just got here, but I think I have to, like. Go."

You don't know what to say to that. Are you disappointed? "I—oh! Is everything okay?"

Marlowe shakes her head. "Uh, no. My boyfriend just, like. Something is happening in his family." She lets out a weird half laugh. "I like, should be there, I think."

"Oh, I—wow. Oh my god. I hope everyone is okay." You don't actually hope this, because you don't know any of the people she's talking about, but this is what you're supposed to say when someone has something go wrong in their life.

"Yeah, it's just like—" she laughs again, in that high and tight way. "He, like, gets really stressed out if I'm not, like, there to help."

"No, of course, totally." You pretend to be looking at books so you don't have to look at her. "God, I hope—I mean, the situation sounds really scary."

"No, it's, like—it's nothing like *that*. He just, like. Needs my help to write texts and stuff because otherwise he pisses off his family—like. He just has, like, no filter. So I kind of need to be there to, like. Text for him."

"Oh?" You tilt your head to the side. "That's. Uh." You wonder why she hasn't told you his name. But if she isn't saying it, you're not going to ask for it. "Yeah, that sounds really rough. I, um . . ." *Don't say it.* "I guess I'm just like—like, can you help him, um, text . . . after? Like, can he wait until we're . . . like, done here?"

You finally look up. She frowns deeply. Now *she's* the one pretending to look at books. Or maybe she really is looking at them, what do you know. "I mean. He's my boyfriend, and I, like, should be there for him." Shit. She looks upset. Nice going.

"Yeah, I get that." You don't get that. "I didn't mean, to like, imply anything. I just, like, I'd be like—I'd just make him wait." You let out a tight laugh. "Like, my boyfriend, he—like, I'd be like. *Anyway bye.*" Dear Lord. None of this is even true. You text Adam back immediately most of the time, a graciousness he doesn't usually afford you in return. It makes you end up playing weird texting mind games.

She shrugs. "It's, like, his family, you know?"

"I hope everyone is okay," you repeat.

"They are. This, like, isn't even a thing. But if I don't help him, like . . . it will *be* a thing, you know?"

"Yeah, I get that, totally." Again, you don't get that, totally. "I'm really sorry to hear this is happening, babe."

"Yeah. I'm sorry I gotta go." She gives you a weird side-hug, her over-large bag pressing into you. "Thanks for inviting me out and everything. It sucks that we didn't really get a chance to hang out."

"It does suck." You fake-pout the appropriate amount. *Of course, she's doing this.* "I hope everything goes well."

"Sorry, this is happening." She sounds sincere. Are you surprised by that sincerity? "I just, like, have to go. This is really triggering my anxiety."

"I get that. Malls are, like, a lot. Do you want us to walk you out?"

"No, no, like, y'all should stay here. It's just, like, I can't, like, be doing this and having a good time when I know he needs me."

"Yeah, I totally get that." You, again, for a magical third time, don't get it. You also don't say: *We weren't even having a good time yet, we just got here.* Something else, still just a pinch pissy: "I'm sorry you had to come all this way for literally nothing."

"We, like, should *actually* hang out sometime." She already has her phone out again. "This whole thing, like, sucks. Like, it's killing my anxiety." Weird little laugh. Is that a new laugh, or have you just never really seen her nervous. "Please tell Lacey I said goodbye. I tried to look for her, but I don't know if she's, like, even in the store anymore."

"I will," you promise, and then you turn back to the same books you've been staring at for the past fifteen minutes. "Will you text me if you get home safe?"

"Of course," she says, and then gives you another weird hug and a peck on the cheek. Something rings in you, and you don't return the warmth. She smells different than you remember.

She takes a deep shaky breath. "You get home safe too, okay?" And then she's just gone.

You find Lacey in the Historical Fiction section, sitting fully on the ground, chewing a nail, beautiful and already a chapter into what looks like a bodice ripper.

You stare down like a bird. "Guess what just happened?"

"What?" She stays in her book, her voice slightly glazed, not listening.

"Marlowe left."

Now she looks up. Her eyes are hard. "Left?"

"Like, said she had to help her boyfriend, and left."

"Are you fucking kidding me?"

"She says he needs help with a family thing."

"Oh." Her tone is almost disappointed. "I mean, I guess that makes sense. Is that why she was on her phone so much? I hope everyone is okay."

"She says they are, but—get this. She needs to *text* for him. Like is going home to *text* for him right now."

"Wait—hang on." She holds out her small hands, and you help her to her feet. "What am I not understanding here? Like—*text*?"

"She says that if she don't write for him, he pisses his family off. Literally, she has to be there to *text. For. Him.*"

"Oh my God." Her hand on your arm gets painfully tight. "Are you fucking *kidding* me right now?"

"Yeah, dude."

"Okay, first of all—is he illiterate?"

You laugh. "Trust me I was like—"

"Secondly, are you for fucking real telling me that she, just, like, *has* to go *text* for a *grown man* right now?"

"Right? Okay. So I was like, what's happening right now that you can't just—"

"Literally any other time, dude. Like, what is the emergency."

"I asked her the same thing and she was like—*I need to support my boyfriend.*"

Lacey snorts, taking a pile of books to the counter. You, in the meantime, have forgotten why you came here. She adjusts her grip on her books, stopping a thin *London Sights* from sliding out of her hands. "Sorry, I do *not* believe this. Like, at least tell us the *actual* reason. But, okay, whatever, *bye*, I guess."

You hadn't even considered that Marlowe might have been lying. "Okay, also, you're right and she was on her phone *a lot.*"

"Okay, *right?* I thought I was just being judgy." She gives you a look and then exchanges pleasantries with the cashier. You check your own phone in the meantime. No texts at all. Very popular!

Lacey swings the white plastic bag over her shoulder. "I'm sorry," she murmurs, bumping her hip into you. "This fucking sucks."

"It's fine." It isn't fine. You will get drunk tonight as a result of this. "It's literally, like, if she don't want to be here, don't be here."

"I can't believe she fucking left without saying goodbye to me."

Oh. You're kind of surprised by Lacey's hurt feelings, even though of course it hurt her feelings. You're a bad friend for not considering that. You squeeze her arm gently. "Please tell me you don't, like, have to send texts for Tanner."

Lacey laughs. "Is she his *mother?*"

"If she was, this dude couldn't talk to her." You remember as you are walking out of the store that you genuinely-needed a particular book. Fuck. "I do send emails for Adam sometimes, though," you admit.

"That's totally different. Emails are like, evil. Like actually."

"It is, right? Like. Nobody should have to, like, email alone."

She loops her arm into yours. "I can't fucking believe her. We're doing this for your fucking *birthday.* I literally *cannot* believe her."

"Whatever. Like, fuck her." You squeeze your eyes closed for a second. "Literally, let's just, like, have a good day anyway."

She *is* a good friend. She takes you cheerily around to stores you only spend a few dollars in and then she gets you drunk and takes you out to a club and you both end up on her couch, giggling, ears ringing from the music, winding down the night with wine while you discuss literature in your pj's. Adam expects you at his house tomorrow at noon, but you drink until dawn anyway.

When you wake up, you realize you haven't heard from Marlowe. You waffle on it before your worry gets the better of you and you group-chat text her: *Are you home safe?*

Immediately, the reply: *Yes!!! Sorry. I suck. Didn't mean to make you worry. Sorry for ditching yesterday it was really nice to see you both though!!!!!! Love you so much.*

Second text: *For real. Reach out whenever. I am trying to be a better friend and I genuinely want to hang out. I know I've been shitty. My anxiety is really bad lately and I am bad at answering texts.*

Third: *But fr fr fr fr. If you call me I'm gonna pick up. Luv u luv u luv u and miss you a LOT.*

You stare at that for a long time.

Don't go back to his house today, Mouse. Don't go back at all. Go home. Go to *your* home. Your cat is still alive right now, and you have a moment, right now, right at this second. You don't know it yet. But you have a moment here where you could have escaped the rest of it.

◇

It is getting bad. All of it. The drinking and the food things and the .

You know it's bad. *Everyone* knows it's bad. You are ignoring all mounting evidence, swiping away at the knowledge; *seen, blocked, unsent.*

You are keeping your wounds like beads on a friendship bracelet. The frayed thread of your life is getting in the way of swallowing. Everything is a flat plane and so gray that the whole world is a fogbank. You are letting the soft parts of you slip into the drain, turn toothpaste. It is lovely this way, like an art piece. You haven't washed your hair this week. You have been sleeping for fourteen-hour stretches or getting no sleep whatsoever. You keep forgetting to brush your teeth. A spider bit you and it itches.

You stare at the sassy pamphlet for eating disorder recovery: *good girls swallow*.

Maybe you're addicted to the drama. Maybe you even kind of *like* it. Maybe this disgust is really just your internalized misogyny and Catholic guilt.

Incoming text from a member of a writing group you joined for a weekend:

> Your prose though has much melancholy and I am concerned!! pls lmk if there anything I can do to support you rn

You leave them on read. You quit the writing group after this.

◇

A SCHEDULED REMINDER FROM THE BODY:
guess what! you don't have an eating disorder!

that is for good girls who r like wax paper & have bones that crackle
over fire & who shiver the whole rot out & who sicken the viewer.
that is for a siren & someone so so beautiful. and dying.

what u have is a preoccupation with eternity. with ur stupid pasted
glue body. with cellophane. u need to stop. tiny fiberglass bits of the
universe have been falling out of ur hair & into the shower drain.
ur ruining the plumbing. u do not have an eating disorder ur just a
fuckken narcissist. u luv to spiral & make everyone else worried about
it. ur rotted.

u won't & can't access silence unless u stop being a coward & finally

[

]

but the good news is! drumroll please!

if u lie with ur belly open, not only wolves come to feed.

he doesn't understand tombs, most men like him don't.
    i'm not going to tell you specifics. there's too many books about
the specifics of violence against women and mice. there are too many
books about looking in and getting off on the gore of it, books that are
a gluttony of our surviving.

but since you're wondering, the first time he ████ me, it *was* on a sunday. i wish i was making that up. i had, and this is not a joke or hyperbole, just gotten back from church.

i kept thinking—the fucking *irony*, though.

i kept thinking—my grandfather would just be so disappointed.

i kept thinking—*lord, let my loved ones be peaceful in heaven. and don't let them see this.*

it was worse when i tried to stop it, so it kept happening for about two years.

i thought that if i could stay with him, it would somehow feel less intolerable. i didn't want to have to wake up in the world where my boyfriend had become my ███. i didn't want to wake up as a victim. i just wanted to wake up and still be in love.

i had already said yes to so much. what else was there, really, to lose?

you look out the mirror and Mouse, in your body, waves at you from the real world. you don't like seeing your skin this close, it makes you want to pick at it.

how is it going on the spaceship? she asks.

it's okay here, you guess. it's quiet. things fizzle over through the mirror sometimes, and land on the back of your arms. you watch them, the glitter of broken glass, these silt memories you can no longer hold—and then you blow their dandelion seeds away.

you ask her if she's been working out. you don't want this to be your first question, but of course it is.

adam's been a lot of help, she says.

we need to do more cardio though. biking isn't cutting it.

your mom is going to be worried if she figures it out, she warns you.

you reach through the mirror and pick at your skin. she doesn't flinch. she knows you need this moment. you buzz with the sensation of standing so close to your body.

i'm gonna have to fuck him later tonight. she doesn't sound happy about it, but she doesn't sound frightened, either. she is an alien; she is not frightened of something so simple as the body of a human man.

get drunk first, you advise her. neither of you particularly like the idea that the endometriosis might have spread, and that you'll never enjoy sex again. if you ever enjoyed sex with him in the first place, that is. try to relax into it. try to breathe beyond it.

you pick along your jaw. *mouse,* you say. *i think he's encouraging our eating disorder.*

she takes your hand from you and guides it over to your cheekbone. she worries your lip, and then whispers: *you aren't happy.*

for a second, contract broken, the two of you switch places.

you are standing in your drying body with a burning face and newly open pores blinking out glistening spider eyes of blood. Mouse's alien body is peeking back at you, shocked and kind of afraid, her mouth open.

"i know i'm not," you tell her.

and then you are back in the mirror, and cold, and in the pink brutality of space, where it is safe and beautiful and alone.

saying yes was easier than arguing about it. it was easier than having to deal with the fallout. our relationship wasn't that bad. i just had to turn over. *you don't need to like it, you just need to do it.*

i think about this mantra a lot, trying to find where i learned it from. i repeat the same phrase at the gym. *you don't need to like it, you just need to do it.* i repeat it over salad. *you don't need to like it.* i repeat it any time i need to finish something. *it doesn't have to feel good, but it does have to happen.*

where did i learn that life is a thing to be endured and not celebrated. that i must spend all my time either suffering or bracing for the *next* suffering. in bird steps, i hop from little hurt to little hurt. one cruelty to another—over and over, i arrive at another something to live through, another horror to turn over and survive.

it is easier to lean into pain when it is in the form of an intention. intentional pain is just control.

i once saw a crow that was still flying despite major holes in the flight feathers—likely due to starvation. in birds, lack can be witnessed.

i had been a good girl all my life.

this was just another version of being good.

The night that the condom breaks, he says, " ███████ ." He seems almost angry. Almost. If you didn't know him better, at least. Were you supposed to laugh, or something?

You say, "Sorry."

And then he takes you to the Nacho Cheese & Tacos truck, stationed in the dark parking lot of the local fire department. You can't eat cheese, but he loves nachos. You sit on the curb and pick at your wilted burrito bowl while drunk college kids in stiletto heels stomp their cloven hooves waiting for the line to move.

You feel suddenly silly in the black skirt and thigh high socks you wore for him—you're too old for this outfit. It's basically a costume, like some weird acting challenge where you're dressed up as a different woman. He would never actually make you feel *sexy*, but hey, the closest you get is when you're adorned in this parade attire. He says it gives him *easy access*.

Shit, wait. Does he like you most when you look *young?*

Think about *that* particular nugget later. CVS is closed now, so you'll have to get Plan B in the morning. It's not the abortion pill, you already knew that, but you like that *this is not the abortion pill* is written on all of its branding. Just in case anyone was curious. You would be 100 percent taking it anyway, even if it *was* an abortion pill.

It's going to make you violently ill. Wikipedia says so.

He doesn't ask if you're okay. Remember this for later, because out of all of it, this is the thing that will burrow into your tiny brain. You accept that accidents happen. You accept that you are just taking extreme measures at this point. But he will not ask, and you will not tell him.

You both half-heartedly drink and then you go to sleep as quickly as you can, making sure you are not touching him at all.

The alarm goes off at six, when the pharmacy opens. You make him go in and pay for it. Usually, you have more dignity than this, and will go Dutch on most expenses. You sit with your hands in a prayerful clench as the car grows cold around you. What if someone had seen you buying that?

Maybe he feels like you're being dramatic, but for once he doesn't say anything. For once you don't offer him the opportunity to.

The pill is smaller than you thought. The pamphlet with it is intense. You check your weight against how effective it can be and have one wild moment of panic. What if you are secretly a ghost and weigh nothing.

As if *you'd* ever weigh nothing. As *if.*

You take it with stale orange juice from his bedside table. Afterward, you kneel alone in the shower and cry and beg for forgiveness from God, unsure what exactly you're asking forgiveness for. Now you *are* being dramatic. The hooks at the corners of your eyes rip your jaws apart. The back of your ears hurt.

While you are still hurting but before you get sick, you wrap
yourself in his fancy thick towel and stumble dripping wet into his
fancy wooden office. He's watching YouTube videos of drumming
techniques. Did you expect otherwise?

"I need to go to church," you say. "I'm going to go to church."

""

Did you want him to offer to take you? Offer to come with? Didn't
your father warn you against being with a man who doesn't believe
in God; being with someone who doesn't have religion? Didn't he say
something like this would happen? "I'm going to church," you repeat.

It's a Thursday, so the only Mass is later in the day. According to
Google, it's thirty minutes from his place, but in the wrong direction,
so you can't leave from Mass to go back to your apartment unless you
want to spend the whole night on the road. You're worried you'll be
too sick to drive far, so it looks like you're spending the night at his.

You are one of eight whole people in the audience, and the
youngest. And now you *are* sick. Head spinning and bile in the back
of your throat. You've never been to this church; you don't know where
the bathrooms are.

You don't throw up. You don't take the eucharist. You sit and you
stare at the cross and at Jesus and at the exposed-wood arches and
at the thin tile floor and at the men in the front of the room in their
not-a-dress vestments and at the singular cantor in her red business
yes-a-dress and at the old guy banging away on the rickety electric
keyboard. You wonder where the smell is coming from.

The last song dies out and you get up to leave because this isn't
a movie, it's just a building, and that *feeling* did not burn off like fog
in the light of the morning. It just stayed in you, in that same space
behind your ears, haunting.

tomorrow's gonna be so, so beautiful. it'll be great. it'll be the best day ever. we will eat whatever we want. we won't *have* to drink, but we *could*, if we wanted to. when we want to drink, we will stop drinking at six drinks. we will be tipsy and carefree and funny. we will wear our hair up and out of our face for once and still feel pretty. we will get a therapist, or else no longer need therapy. we will kiss anybody that looks at us twice. we will sing and go to the beach and love loudly and laugh like a bubble popping and feel anything at fucking all. oh, it will be amazing.

tomorrow though. but also it might have to be the tomorrow after that. or later. soon, maybe. eventually.

not now, though. not now. it's just so quiet here, and that's lovely.

You're fighting with him again. You put your hands in your hair, which is something dramatic you don't usually do, because it *is* dramatic. It's just that you have no other words for what you're trying to say.

"You're just, like, a *guy!*"

It doesn't fit the stage you've created, because you're trying to say something bigger and runnier, a grub lashed to the side of a cruise ship. Something that reeks of a long-held scream. And it's not about the *guy* part but the emphasis fell on it anyway, so he's mad about that.

"  ."

And it maybe is that he's bad *for* being a man, but it is also that he's bad *at* being a man or even just a person.

But he's not real, you're remembering the wrong thing. That's cartoonish, no way he's *that* bad to you. Or, if he *is* real, and you're actually experiencing the fucking blank way he hurts you—almost carelessly, idly, like a Sunday—that is *horrible*. And you can't handle *how* horrible.

He's just not . . . *it*. He's not an excellent villain or a slideshow of manipulation. He's not even that intelligent. You don't even think he's doing it on *purpose*. You think he would be insulted and sickened if you implied he's even *capable* of cruelty. He isn't even particularly violent. He's just another guy, and you've let him take the tire tracks of his hands over your body and called it sacrifice.

He's not *God*.

You've never even seen him like God (if you had any faith to begin with), not really. You've always kind-of/sort-of pitied how out of his league you are, and you've always been sardonically aware of the age gap, and you've maybe had to give an ironic wince every time he's opened his mouth—but that was *part* of it, before. It felt *powerful,* and that was *good*.

But it isn't enough anymore. He used to be just a guy. Something slipped, and you let him in, and now the ache spreads up and over everything. He's in the halo of your greenhouse, catching all the light and eating it in hurried fistfuls.

And you *let* him. And he is not God. Or not your God. Or not yours.

Or. Not her.

You're a writer, after all. Write a better story. Write one where joy is all that you experience and you get your happy ending. Write yourself loyal, perfect, abiding. Write yourself as a wife, without anguish; loving, joyful, content. Millions of people wish they had a man like this. Faith can be an abandonment of the soul for the sake of worship.

One night after it happens again, we write a poem: *happiness is a bent knee, and my future is a homestead.*

u will be good for him & sit w/ur legs crossed & spine assholeishly
straight & teeth whitened from fourteen days of Crest 3D White
Strips Advanced Technology (amen) & u will allow him to make
comments about your thighs & u will know that the forks go on the
right & u will know to laugh at his jokes & u will know to weigh a
silence & u will sniff the wine before not liking it & u will pretend to
like it & u will compliment his huge & amazing & horrible & useless
record collection of jazz variables ft. smooth clarinet & when u hit
ur head fainting in the french-inspired bathroom from throwing up
for the fourth time today u will scrub the blood out of the charming
yellow floor tile w/ur $8 mini offbrand cucumber melon hand sanitizer
while ur eyes pinball & tunnel & u will remember how ur mother
used to weep over giving u baths & what her wet hair looked like
while crushing aspirin for your toothache & u will wish u had aspirin
to crush into ur eye & u will wish u were thirty-six in prague eating
pralines out of fancy bowls & u will wish u were thirteen so u could
tell urself the awful truth & u will wish god had made u into an egg so
u could step on urself & yolk the floor & u will buzz in ur gums & u
will burn in ur nostrils & in the seaweed air the faint & tinny & (again)
horrible jazz music will have a sick clarinet solo & u will want to

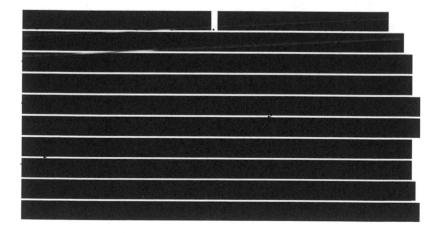

& her hair will still be wet in your mouth so u will stop staring at the dead fly in the overhead light & u will stop crying about little lives & u will stand up & go outside & be good & smile & u will stand up & go outside & be good & u will stand up & go outside & u will stand up &

It hasn't snowed for a while, so Elijah hasn't come back. It is too cold to snow. Your mother would say: *Do you know how cold it has to be that it's too cold to snow? Fuckin' cold.*

You read once that there was a job interview that had asked potential employees to name the biggest desert in the world; and it threw off most applicants because the answer is actually Antarctica. Sometimes you check on that. Antarctica is shrinking and the Sahara is growing. At one point maybe they'll be able to hold hands with each other and switch places through the mirror glass and the polar bears will have to live in beach chairs.

Elijah doesn't know about polar bears.

You are googling if you are right about where polar bears live (if they are still extant) when Adam comes outside. He is wearing the coat that you bought him after your holiday bonus and therefore couldn't actually afford. He had gotten you a chemise. Your mother had tried to be optimistic, had said, *it's not your style but at least it's silk!* but it wasn't real silk. Her voice gets scratchy over the phone these days.

"█████████████?"

You were wrong about polar bears. They live in the Arctic.

"Nothing." You wrap your hand around your wrist, making your thumb and middle finger overlap in a cold bracelet.

The gallery of his lawn is the crinkled kind of winter—no longer dewy and fresh; each inch is instead covered with mud and sand and the curved prints from wild animals. The predawn light still does the brilliant trick of loving New England—a yellow like a wedding invitation spills over his manicured tree line. It *looks* cold.

"███████████████████████?"

Now you remember that there's a very easy trick to remember: "Arctic" comes from the Greek word for bear: *arktos, Ant-* as a prefix to mean *against*. It's actually a complete coincidence that the bears live up there too—the Greeks were referring to the North Star constellation, Ursa Major. Antarctica means *opposite north* more than it means *no bears*.

You bury your face into the coat that you "borrowed" from your younger sister. You're still searching for Elijah. You hadn't meant to name the bird after *the Holy Spirit*, but you did. The first time you had seen the owl, you thought he was a hawk. Then your brain did enough mathematics that you figured it out—*that's an owl resting during the day and I can see him.* And then you'd grown attached to him, and given him, accidentally, a name.

Or she. Elijah might be a girl. She's big enough to be a girl.

You don't want to break the silence. Adam shifts uncomfortably beside you. You are not going to tell him about Elijah, and you know this without even deciding it, like recognizing hunger.

There are small and private things. You have started to collect them in your pockets. Secrets. Not big secrets. They are just places you don't share with him. Elijah is one of these.

For a while, you pretended it wasn't about who Adam is.

But you *had* told your family about the snowy owl and how you'd stayed outside for a whole hour during driving sleet, just to stare at where it hunched on a branch. You had blinked up at it through glasses that you had to continually wipe off and reapply. The condensation of your breath whisking up onto your eyelashes had made them freeze. Your toes started hurting in the first half hour, and you'd just stood, dumbstruck, taking stupid blurry pictures with your broken phone. Elijah had just been so *close*. You'd never been that close to an owl in the wild, much less a snowy owl.

You'd seen her/him/them twice since. Usually during a storm. Hunkered in a tree, looking for all the world the same way you felt: scrunched with her/his/their shoulders up around their ears. You always looked now, just in case.

" ▓ ?" Adam presses. You flinch at the pet name. He has never really used your full name, only these cute little stand-ins, which, since it's not actually your name, Mouse, it's the name of the Body—you haven't minded until recently. It's just starting to feel infantilizing. All of it feels infantilizing, actually. You should really look into getting a therapist.

The days are passing strangely, lately. In and out of reality, in and out of drunk memory, in and out of hurting.

Elijah is probably a girl, now that you think about it. She's pretty darkly colored to be a boy. The boys don't need the same amount of camouflage. Why did you assume that Elijah had to be a male? Did you assume that male is the default? Didn't you attend a fancy college and get a fancy degree so you *don't* assume that kind of thing?

The thing about *these* secrets—the secrets that are like Elijah—is that they're somehow different from other, normal secrets.

Before Elijah secrets, you'd hidden certain small things from Adam just so you could talk about them later—so you could appear interesting, busy, reserved. So you could casually drop—*oh yeah, forgot to tell you* into the conversation. You also liked that they could resolve any awkward silences. *Oh yeah, let's talk about my workplace drama.* You'd sometimes even half lie, just for effect, leaning into whatever story you were weaving. You're borrowing his friends; he doesn't know yours—so it's not like you'd have to keep the story straight (ha!) later on. You kept tiny things back so you'd have something to *share*, is the thing.

But Elijah secrets are different. These feel like you are folding something sharply private, tucking it under your napkin. These feel *intentional*.

Your first thought is actually—*he won't get it*. But that's immature. It's just that having someone know-but-not-get-it would tarnish the whole experience. It would take the magic and force it through an exhaust pipe. You couldn't explain it to Adam—how it felt, awestruck, to be this close to Elijah. He would just have to *get it*, immediately, and you know, horribly—he *wouldn't*.

He stands there with you. And whatever *thing* you had been experiencing is broken now anyway. You don't want to grab his hand. You want him to leave you alone so you can return to your hard-won private magic, but you know that none of this will feel the same, even if he does leave.

So you turn around instead. Shimmy your shoulders and stomp your feet back inside, leaving your boots on the rubber mat, shaking your hair out. Slip away to take your shower in his bathroom with his soaps on the wall. You spend your coffee time near him, still not wanting to talk, staring at the countertop.

For your lunch, you pour yourself a glass of wine. As an
afterthought, you splash gin into the glass as well.

And Adam, to his credit, doesn't ask.

◇

u kiss him on the cheek and he asks u why u woke him up. he u
again last night. if u begin to run here, u will slip into the shower drain
& smash ur teeth through ur own carbon copy. u don't have to be held
upside down, the coins all rattle out of ur ear anyway. a centipede is
making lunch in ur brain & all the rot is having high tea.

if ur drunk, ur happy. u never need to eat. this way u can sleep
lambchop cold in a puddle or his bed or in ur own oil slick bloodstain.
u can cut the chords of ur childhood nightgown & hang like a ghost
from a pink ribbon noose.

he loves that ur flightless. the sex is a party like this, and never
painful. it whips around in ur body like a blender. ur future is good
like this, glowing, smooth.

u can slip out of the mirror and even further from ur life. hover
overhead, splayed out like spray paint firmament, calliope organs, a
salmon viscera dream plaster coating.

you stand in the corner and watch the alien wear your body. she sucks
in your belly and mewls and cries out and trembles. she looks sweaty
and desperate. like, obviously trying too hard. dear god.

can someone please come get her? this is so ugly.

◇

okay, google: can i feed chickadees any of my memories or will it make them sick.

mouse keeps calling, but i'm never coming home. we will keep throwing this body at the floor until it finally sticks.

it *can* be good, though. these frisky moments shining through. cutting the glass in spikes of amber. we are impaled each time—*oh! we love him. that was always true.*

singing along to the radio and debating the virtues of art and discussing what we would name our kids. chasing him through the rain and picking apples. giggling over a cake we baked at 3 a.m., eating ice cream in bed directly out of the carton, watching action movies, jumping from the swings, listening to his heart. the way he sighs happily over *lord of the rings* and how he gets so excited about japanese candy.

it would be a sin to throw away something like this. it would be shameful to turn your face away from something that *could* be good again.

love can fold itself. we can fold ourselves, too. shrink away from the bad parts. let the mold grow into each room.

we will just start closing doors. ignore it. tune out the alarm. crawl into his bed and hear your memories louder than you hear reality. trace your finger over his tattoos. when he is cruel to you, forgive him like your mother taught you. when he is quick to judge, remind yourself that there are different ways to love. when he ███ you—close your eyes. remember the summer and the kisses and the wild, abandoned bliss.

tell yourself that it doesn't count. he's your boyfriend, for Christ's sake. besides, it's probably not technically ███ because now you don't even bother to argue, too tired and too sick of it. it's not ███ in the way a caught bird is now no longer a bird, but a pet. it modifies the species.

real would be loud. what is happening to you almost never makes a sound.

like this, the cheekbone is just a cheekbone. like this, what does not eat does not starve. like this, the mutiny of the body is a blessing. the spirit exhibits signs of decay, which is a mushroom's dream of growth.

    want to say: no.

    want to say: i cannot endure anything more. there isn't another door here. there is nothing left. please. please. you've already taken all of it.

    want to say:

◇

Kaisa is checking herself in the mirror she got from the side of the road. She hot-glued a bunch of vines and roses to the frame and now the whole thing is an art piece in your shared living room. It is a good interior decorating choice—it brings in light, and the pics in it are always *phenomenal.*

    You're a carrion bird.

    She's recently redone her undercut. You've always wanted one, but now you worry it'll look like you're copying her. Your head is too weirdly shaped anyway.

    She rounds her hip over to check her ass in her jeans. They're thrifted, cute and chic. Different and trendy without being too costumey. She has a fuller body than you do, but it actually looks good on her. With your frame, you'd just look stupid.

Do you want her as a friend? Do you even like her? It's now not even *awkward* between the two of you, just distant. Your schedules just don't match up. And you're never home these days, out ███████ ███████████████████████.

She flicks her eyes up to you. You look down to the work you're supposed to be doing.

You remember belatedly to ask her about her partner. Or about her life. Or about anything.

She beats you to it. "What's up?"

You blink and offer a wan smile. "Sorry, zoning out."

Kaisa goes back to her jeans.

Oh, nice. You just killed that conversation. Make an effort, Mouse. "How's, um. How's stuff with your partner."

She shoots you a look. "It's fine? Why."

Oh, you're being weird. "Ah. Sorry. I didn't mean to be, like, weird. Just checking in."

The look she sends you changes to something even darker, and you don't know her well enough to place it. "You're not . . . being weird. Uh. It's okay." She shrugs and pads into the kitchen and picks up an orange from the bowl.

"Hey, it's my turn to do groceries, by the way, so let me know if you want anything different this week."

Kaisa doesn't answer while she drives her thumbnail through the peel.

God, you're fucking stupid. The two of you literally have a list. She'll just put it on the list like she is supposed to do and *has done* consistently. Now you just sound like a passive-aggressive nag. Great work!

"How's . . . stuff with Adam?" She keeps her eyes on the orange. Her lashes are thick. You wish you had her clear skin. God, how easy life must be to not have to worry about wearing makeup constantly.

"Those jeans are really nice," you say, which is a dodge so obvious that she actually makes eye contact. Her eyebrows raise.

You laugh, voice high and tight. "Sorry, I just realized I meant to say earlier and . . ." You trail off. Why are you so *fucking* awkward. "Things are great with him."

You stare at the paper in front of you. You've been doodling pictures of food in the margins. A burrito. A Boston cream. A monster made from bones.

"That's good," she offers, like a prompt.

You don't take it. She watches you too hard, so you have to pretend to be distracted by your work.

The silence hangs, weird and ceremonial.

"Um . . ." she navigates a wedge of orange out of the naked sphere, her fingers deft around the pith. "Me and my friends are gonna smoke a bowl and then probably hang for a bit. Did you wanna come with?"

Your heart tries to exit your ribs. Your chest caves in. "Oh, I can't. I have . . ." You gesture vaguely at your work. "I wish I could."

God, fucking imagine that. Imagine going to a stranger's house and being the pity roommate-invite. All of her friends are so fucking pretty and cool and queer. They do interesting, exciting things with their lives like pole dancing and fire spinning. And you just sit around and work full-time for a soulless corporation and live part-time with your boyfriend. God, can you imagine how fucking *embarrassing* that would be? Kaisa would die of shame. She wouldn't be able to look you in the eyes after that. All of her friends would talk about how fucking *weird* her roommate is, how awkward and ugly.

Kaisa kind of nods like she was expecting the answer. "Invite is open any time."

You thank her and the two of you go back to being politely silent, the known dance of being in the same space without actually being in the space *together*. It navigates easily, a horse bit in your back molars. Walk the road that you know, pull the carriage.

Later, in bed, you get a second wash of the anxiety again. Thinking about how fucking *horrible* that activity would have been. How everyone would have hated you in an instant. How you wouldn't have been able to fit in. How they would have sensed that *wrongness* in you and spat you out. How they would have figured out that you're an alien.

Somewhere in there, a horrible thought rises in froth to the surface. Fuck—what if you just hurt Kaisa's feelings? You never invite *her* anywhere. She was making an effort. What the fuck were you *thinking?*

You'll go next time. If she asks. Next time, you'll be thinner and less weird and will have had time to do your hair and makeup. Next time, you'll be able to fit into better clothes so you'll actually look like a normal person. And it'll be effortless. You'll just stay at the back of the room and hope nobody notices all the bitterness burning in your iris.

Your whole soul is an empty looking glass, and you're secretly a narcissist.

hypothesis. the monster is not *the killer*, which is different, and that makes the monster lovable. that makes the monster something that can be desired.

if you are not [a type of person], then you have been raised to anticipate *the killer*. you know the killer without me having to bake him into this paragraph, but let me bring him into the ring so we can look at him in the light.

the killer is lurking in your shower. that's right, *your* shower, if you're the type of person the killer wants (which is *anyone*). the killer is lurking in *your* back seat. the killer is waiting to grab your child out of your shopping cart. the killer will open your tent and rend you under the stars, he will calligraphically spew your lifeline across the Ford Taurus hood. he might be in the city's alleyway, where you called to him via lowcut crop top. he might be inside of your walls, scratching your name into the plasterboard—you forgot to lock your doors. he might be in your economics class, grinning callously while you answer a question incorrectly. the killer is going to wait for the end of your shift to stalk you, noiseless, across the parking lot's vast coliseum.

a gladiator battle of wits; you tremble your alone way through public transportation but will then stick your little body between the killer and the girl who is too drunk at the bar—but now the killer will just kill you *both* later.

the killer is judgmental, but he's often portrayed as being kind of right about it, you *shouldn't* have been such a bitch. the killer hates that you had premarital sex, it becomes a joke on the internet.

later, when you are on a dating app, the killer is not a joke anymore—he is waiting to catch you again.

the killer is the real-life "isn't that horrible" true-crime drama. if you are not [a type of person], then you have *also* been raised to anticipate the possibility of being *on* a true-crime drama. your hair might match or you might just not have enough privilege that your body is noted as missing in action. a foundational element of the killer is his ability to be *anywhere*, to be targeting his first person. and you might be it, after all.

in comparison to the killer, the *monster* is sort of a cute, rule-following thrill ride. less vague; thereby knowable. simply follow the rules, and no harm will come. it's all well within your control.

a werewolf, for example—moon-based, avoids silver bullets. vampires like to count, or they *are* a Count (ha!), and also generally turn from religious symbols, which is very respectful of them. you can make a tame ghost by pouring a salt circle around them. you can hang out with a zombie if you simply follow the steps that are already rote for your average large-animal veterinarian (don't get bit, wear thick clothing, have a pre-prepared sedative).

something that can be controlled is something that can be taught to care, in my experience. *isn't* it romantic, after years of being a good girl, that you could take something wild without bias and make it gentle again? something like a monster just wants to eat you because it wants to eat *everything*, not because you had the right body type for chewing.

a monster wants *any* person's life—you wouldn't be a victim because of your "poor choices" but rather because the monster cannot be sated. i would much rather be killed by something that is not bigoted—to be killed just out of *violence* and not, like, something pointed.

if and when a thing has rules, then a person can find a way to negotiate them. the killer does *not* have rules, and the thing is—the killer is *real* and could *actually happen*. if i somehow fail to prepare for every eventuality (OCD notwithstanding), then the killer *will* get me, and i'll have deserved being gotten.

not the monster. the monster is asleep right now, and she forgives you. your body was soft. that isn't your fault. and at least you served a purpose—when you went, you were delicious.

You can't leave him. If you leave him, everyone will think you're a lesbian. Not that there's anything wrong with that (and sometimes you think you actually *might be* a lesbian, depending on who's asking), but it's the way you know he'll spin it once you're gone. He'll go around and do that annoying *what-can-you-do* shrug (did you find that endearing, once?) and tell everyone that you *just ended up being a lesbian*. It removes responsibility from him.

One day it's just not sexy anymore. Maybe the thrill wore off and now he's aware it's actually part of your-identity. *Queer*. The academic, cold, unlovable word.

You discover he hates it by accident.

You are setting out pictures to put into an album, organizing them in careful circles around your body. Fuck going to therapy. Therapy is probably just rich-person bullshit anyway. You can train *yourself* to be happy.

Your hobby this month is to finally take photography seriously, the way you've always been threatening. You hand develop black-and-whites in a Groupon-afforded senior center lesson. You hate the smell of developer, but you like the other-world peace of the darkroom. Nobody talks at full volume in there. The lights are too red; there's an unspoken requirement to whisper. Despite how you are as a person— you might even be passably proud of your photos. Your teacher keeps saying—*you have a good eye*.

The final project is coming up, and you're going to put together a series called *before/after*. Your concept is of a cycle; of the way we swing from one extreme to another.

You print some of your favorite pictures off your phone for the *before* section, using a tiny handheld printer that makes a sound like it is half-dying.

Okay, yes. Marlowe is in a lot of the *before* pictures. But to be fair—she had been your model too long to trash all evidence anything happened, and the theme *is* the idea of something from your past. Looking at the pictures makes your cheeks get hot and red with a weird feeling: something like the lovechild of embarrassment and panic.

And then he walks into the room and suddenly you can't make eye contact with him. Your queerness splashed on his floor like that, to be waded through.

"."

Okay, maybe he's joking. It's a weirdly aggressive joke, but it *could* be a joke. "To be fair, we did a lot of touching of *each other*, so it was mutually beneficial."

"█████████████████."

You look up and he's frowning. He bends to pick up a picture where Marlowe's hair is back and she's laughing, her freckles plain and the chip in her canine tooth showing.

His hands look too big around the photo. Not big in an exciting way. Big like they don't understand how to be gentle. For once in your life, you feel bad for him. It must be terrible, not knowing how to be small.

You try to change the subject. "I'm glad you're here, actually, I'm gonna—"

"."

"What do you mean?" Now you are playacting slowness. Stilling your hands, waiting to see what exit travels you fastest.

"████████."

"I mean—literally, I don't understand. Why aren't you okay with it?"

"█████████████████. ████████."

"I'm not *hung up* on her." You are, still, a little. You've been having dreams about her. "I don't like her like that anymore." You do, still, a little. You've been writing poetry and posting it onto the blog you know she reads but he doesn't. Not that you're really expecting her to answer. "I'm—that's what I'm trying to say, like this is for a project. So, like, my—okay, this sounds stupid, but my concept is a cycle—uh, like a *before/after* thing, but it like, circles around? And this is my *before*, and I—"

He makes a noise in his throat, a cough-grunt. *Oh shit! He's super old!* You blink twice and he is close-enough in age again, thank God.

"███████████████████ a fucking lesbian, ████████."

"Like, I'm . . . not. You know—I mean, you knew I like women, but I'm not—I have literally told you like—I'm—like . . . ?"

"████████████."

"Yes, thank you, I'm *aware* I'm dating you."

"██████████?"

"It doesn't, like, wear off." You start to absently stack and unstack pictures. This hobby will be completely ruined for you now, you can just *tell*. It just feels . . . almost creepy now. It isn't *yours* anymore, not really. Like the fact he thinks he can "approve" of it makes it *his*.

"██████████████ ██████████████████."

This pisses you off, but you don't show it. You still your hands. "You didn't think. I was. Being serious. About . . . being *bisexual?*"

"████████████ straight now ████████████████. ████."

You just stare at him. He stares back.

And now the jokes have started. Okay, they aren't *jokes* but they aren't *not* jokes. Gritty and stabbing questions and comments, even in front of friends.

Otherwise, you are both ignoring it, because you're at an impasse, because he wants you to not be queer, and you can't help it, and the argument just spirals from there. You suck his dick in the shower and let him take you from behind and let him wrap you in chintzy handcuffs because you are *not* a fucking lesbian.

(God, though. So many nights you lie awake and ask yourself— *are you sure? Are you sure? You were always 90 percent gay, 10 percent in case of emergency . . . What if you are just in denial about the whole thing?*)

You can't leave, he'll make it about Marlowe. He'll make it about *himself*.

And it doesn't matter, and you shouldn't care, but it's that you *know* he's going to use your queerness as an excuse. He'll swell up his chest and crow that nothing was ever really wrong with the relationship or with him—that *you're* the problem. That you've always been lying about being bisexual. Or maybe all bisexuals *are* lying; and everyone is right about how untrustworthy *the queers* are.

(Are you lying? If you were ever lying, it was by accident. To your knowledge of yourself, *yes*, you like men. But then the sex happens, and you sit there, wondering about it.)

You skip the rest of your photography classes. So what. It's just like—whatever.

disordered eating is also the bold, institutionalized letters of thanksgiving. disordered eating is also keeping a food journal obsessively, while the app you do it on makes boatloads of money. disordered eating is feeling bad if you *aren't* counting.

it surprised me, genuinely, to find out that an eating disorder is in-line with obsession and compulsion. i don't know why i needed it pointed out to me—on second examination, it makes complete sense. they are both held up by applying rules, sanctions, order. in hindsight, the logic of "safe foods" or "bad foods" or "good times to eat" were all forms of magical thinking.

i still find it in the middle of all of my poetry: inevitably, the same winter of the soul. i return to hunger as a standstill.

dominated by control.

you look at the odometer and the single *check engine* light that your mechanic says to "ignore until it's important."

you glance at the time. you accidentally just wasted an hour sitting still in your driveway, car cooling, doing absolutely nothing on your phone when you were supposed to have left already. you're usually running late to things, but this is *very* late, inexcusably so. spring had been gentle, but the grey sky is beginning to bleat out the lamb's-wool of new england sleet.

adam has sent you exactly three texts, asking where you are. if something happened. a final single question mark.

you type and retype a bunch of answers. you are tired, suddenly, pulled through to the ground. your edges are all frothed and runny. you think about going back up into your apartment instead of driving the hour-and-forty-five-minutes. it's not like you're going to enjoy what happens when you get there.

but what else are you going to do? it's not like you have big plans you're putting off. you can't just cancel on him last-minute like this. and you *cannot* be alone. nobody trusts you when that happens.

you sigh and start the bad engine. it turns over, thank god. you snort a laugh—you can continue to ignore the problem until it's important.

Adam is scratching his balls as he walks in.

You're in a cross-body lace bra with six different straps. It's leaving a mark under your ribs. You choose an uncomfortable angle to bend over so you can fold laundry without folding yourself unpleasantly. "I'm doing another load of laundry and then I'm gonna head to mine."

You hear him stop moving. You pretend not to notice; you shimmy your ass as you bend deeper. You toss your eyes over your shoulder.

He's scrolling through his phone. "████ ."

"Okay. By the way, it's girl's night." It hadn't been. but you'll call Lacey and make it be. You want to seem busy, and cool, and funny. Able to have friends over with no warning.

But what if Lacey notices that you've stopped being funny. You're boring these days, clammy and weird and silent. It's been a really long time since you could get a whole room laughing. It's because you're too pretentious and it's making you into an unpopular piece of shit.

No answer from Adam.

"Do you need anything washed?"

"███████████████████."

"Okay." Did he tell you this and you just forgot? God, your memory is a fucking sieve. "I guess, uh, I could come through on Sunday?" Okay, don't be desperate. Don't give him another option. You're already annoying him. "Or, like, Monday or Thursday works?"

"████████████████████." His brows furrow. He doesn't look up, which is good, because your alien antennae are showing. You tuck them back into their cups.

"No, I remember." You double-check—you had put his plans in your phone, and sure enough; he has changed them without letting you know. "Um, if that day doesn't work . . . ?"

"█████████████████████████████?"

Okay, yes, to use his words, it's always *crazy* in your life. He's always making fun of you for it. "Yeah, I have lunch with Lacey on Tuesday; she's got a new project she wants—"

He waves his hand dismissively. "████████████."

And whatever else. Why is he like this. "Well. You remember Marlowe?" You want to use it like a weapon. You take your time folding three more of his pants, not looking up. "She messaged me yesterday. She says she has something she wants to tell me. I should reach out to her, set something up."

"███." He comes over, drops a kiss on the top of your head. "███ don't ███████ tell me █████████████████████."

The truth is that you'd replied to Marlowe asking when she was free—and then heard nothing. It's been two weeks. Maybe if you follow up or something. Maybe it's actually *your* responsibility.

And hell, maybe she loves you. You saw that a few nights ago in a dream: getting a text that just read *I love you, I'm sorry.* It had seemed so unlikely that you'd immediately woken up, confused, almost laughing. *As if.*

You finish folding the laundry. You put his laundry into his walnut bureau. You put your laundry into your duffle bag. You get in your beat-up Nissan Altima. You text him when you get home: *home safe!* with six heart emojis.

He leaves you on read. You wish you had crashed the car. How embarrassing.

You once told your family—*I really think he's it!* and you can't lie to your family, right?

How do you start over?

This is a fun game you play with yourself, in the late hours when the body starts to itch too much to be a home. All your gills and tendrils start leaking out. You soothe yourself with old promises. *Okay, if tomorrow I wake up and I go, what do I do first?*

Do you even *like* this dude? You have a habit of just sort of falling into people. Meeting them and choosing to ignore every red flag. Falling too fast and too hard and buying into that rich-people bullshit that true love just takes work and a therapist punch card.

You were arguing again. He should really leave you. Piece of shit that you are. Always causing trouble where there doesn't need to be any.

Every day is somehow more blank. You started crying about the impermanence of pencils the other night, hating the *erased* cliché.

Okay. If you wake up tomorrow and you leave him, the first thing you do is find a new yoga instructor. Your current one is nice, and you want her body (. . . *want?* To own, to keep, to emulate, to . . . ?) but

God, her voice is annoying. Some feminist *you* are. At first you thought it was the weird tinny bell music she likes to play, but genuinely it's the nasal exhale of *namaste*. So, okay. First thing: go somewhere with better yoga options that you will again attend somewhat frequently for a month before giving up on completely.

Wow. Set higher goals for yourself, *honestly*.

No, actually. If you wake up tomorrow and you leave him, the first thing you should *actually* do is get back into gardening. You used to love gardening. What happened? Oh. Apartment living. Maybe there's a CSA you could join or something. A community garden seems plausible and friendly, once the winter ends.

He *should* leave you, really. This is how you treat other people? Planning your escape? It's almost summer. It's almost his fucking *birthday*.

You swing over the side of the bed and check your phone, the way you have been checking your phone for months. You are still somehow waiting for a single text that never comes. You pretend you do not know who you are waiting to hear from. You mean to google local community gardens, but instead spend an hour lost on Instagram.

Okay, for real? The first thing you *actually really need to do* is get back into therapy. Jesus Christ. And besides—what would you even say to her? Adults *drift apart*. This is a normal thing that has happened.

Oh, you could get back into crochet. You were always kind of a homebody. You were always better alone. Sunning yourself in the manta ray stinger of your own thoughts. Collecting those pieces and examining them rather than letting them swim, gutless, into the open window of a heart.

Hi Marlowe. It's been a while! You are never there when I need you.

Incorrect. She *has* been there, or she was, beforehand. You just need her *more* right now, in a way you cannot need someone that is just-a-friend.

Hi Marlowe. I know it's been a while but wow sorry I got weird about that guy last year! LOL. He just seemed intense.

Incorrect. He was completely fine. He was just a guy. You just had snapped, snarling over your hurt paw, demanding blood for her freedom, fucking bitch that you are.

You're jealous. The pictures of them together—you're *jealous.*

You need to call up your old friends. Weren't you going to restart the DND campaign? Weren't you going to have a book club or something?

When did you become comfortable with the idea that Adam is your problem for *the rest of your life?* Like, forever. You are so stuck. It just happened and you couldn't stop it. You turned your head away from the sound of your own stagnation, let the idea of it slip off of your brain in meaty chunks.

You don't want to be clingy; you weren't even *hers*; you were a plaything. Yesterday you *again* wrote a poem about her on the internet. Someone commented *i want a lover like this.* You wanted to open up the back of your throat and let the entire river in.

Right before she left, you'd said—*I think it's worth it.* She didn't answer. She let the words hang in the air, collecting rabbit fur in their webs. You thought about dying. You thought about undoing time. You thought—*why are you doing this to me?*

hi bb. sorry i've been like totally out of touch.

She hasn't responded to your last six messages—not *happy birthday!* not *hey are you around? i'm in town for a few hours, wanna grab lunch?* not *hey some friends are getting together for new year's, just popping in to see if you're free?* not *just had a weird dream about you lol seeking proof of life* not *idk what i did, but i'm sorry* (you removed that one, unseen) not the second *happy birthday bb!*

When (if) you leave, it can't be going to her, then.

If you leave him, you would be alone. And maybe you could be happy alone; you've probably been good like that before. When you were a kid, maybe.

Okay, be honest. You're fucking terrified of being alone. Your father was right, you are viscerally unlovable. You are never going to find anyone who wants to be with you. You're old and fat and exhausted.

When she left you, all the light of your life slipped out from under the door, and you were suddenly, completely ruined. Remember when you looked around and found out you'd been building all your life around her frame. That you had *nothing*. Remember how you'd had to spend entire months rebuilding—remember how much energy that takes?

But hey! Maybe this time it's different. You can be *happy*. Hell, even after her: you had still found your way around the world, hands ghosting over the brass knobs of getting through it. And it's not like you're giving Adam as much as you gave her—right? You had used Marlowe as stitches; but Adam cannot even begin to cover the wound.

Even if you're going to be alone forever, it will be alone with *yourself.*

Wait, shit. It will be *alone with yourself.*

If you leave him, do you tell your family? That would mean it's *real*. You can lie to yourself and to the Body about a lot—but your family will hold the mint of your hurt under their tongue. Your family will steep it into a tea and distill it over your life and make it tangible. They would-not-forgive-him, which means they love you more than you deserve or expect.

Not to mention your friends. Can you imagine the next six months of your life? They're all going to ask about him, and then you'll have to be so achingly awkward while you say *oh, it didn't work out* and then they'll flinch and it'll be awkward and the tally mark for wasted time will tick upwards. They'll all feel very bad for you and then go home to their beautiful partners and say—*Wow. I really thought that he was right for her.*

And you're too old to be single. It was so stupid that you moved here to be closer to him; your life has settled in the wrong place at the wrong time.

Maybe you actually *can't* leave. You *just* paid off the deposit to your apartment, you can't afford to go through with that again. You're in trouble at work anyway—everything is a risk waiting to happen.

But still. You could make a life *there*, in the green apartment with your too-cool roommate and you could try again. This time, you'd actually manage to be an adult, maybe. You'd get back into therapy. You'd focus on *yourself*.

What does *happy* even look like these days? None of your friends are going to want to get *crazy on girl's night*. Your friends are too old too, happily married or happily soon-to-be married, or happily holding themselves together in the way you never seem to be able to.

God, fucking pathetic. You really only work and focus on Adam or drink too much or have rough sex or pine for your ex not-a-girlfriend. Plus, you spend more time and money on yoga than you need to. God, you're clingy and belligerent. If you don't love him, it's fucking *selfish* that you're staying.

You're not *happy*, though, are you. So why are you staying? Are you really *that* afraid to be alone? Aren't you an adult now? *Everyone* is occasionally alone. Do you think you're the first person on earth to break up with someone this late in their life? Do you think you're so special and pretty and cool you can just walk away from a life as good as this because you're a little upset he's not *kind* to you?

That selfishness again. You're just here because you need to be loved—no matter the shape of the love, how it clouds up your insides. No matter what that feels like. You need to be loved so much; nothing can stop that need from swallowing.

Fucking pathetic.

◇

i have decided actually i have been a werewolf this whole time, except
i got the fur backward, and now all my worst qualities are kept on the
surface like skin on a knife.

no, actually, it's my star sign. if you're straight you can't say this but
like gay girls *love* to blame their star sign. if you're straight and you are
offended by that it's okay and i am making you gravy and biscuits.

but no nevermind i'm trapped in a time loop. my ocd is actually
right. all those weird feelings of déjà vu. in french that means *already
seen*. i wonder how universal the experience is since us only having a
word from another language implies that someone over in france is *also*
getting this particular sensation. in the last time loop i died. in the last
time loop i think i killed my family. i have to pull the car over to let an
ambulance go by, and i am given the visceral body-memory of actually
driving *into* the ambulance. in string theory, isn't there a universe where
that *is* how i died. maybe i'm just feeling myself die in another life.

actually, hang on. maybe it's some kind of spell. when i was
younger i knew how to do magic and the wind used to talk to me.
maybe i did the wrong kind of magic and am still experiencing the
blowback. once i saw the sky light up with blue lightning and what
my panic mistook for the end of the world turned out to be a squirrel
frying on the telephone pole. maybe i am the squirrel. i've never tried
anything serious with candles or books or anything but honestly
between me and you i think the reason i don't try magic in adulthood
is not because of what happens if it works but because i know some
part of me will be crushed when it *doesn't*. so maybe this is happening
because i am a bad witch and i am ignoring all the signs that i am
secretly very powerful and frightening.

i just don't want it to be my fault, is all. i don't want it to be *my*
brain. i don't want the reason i stayed for so long to be so horrifically,

utterly mundane. i knew *early* something was wrong. i saw what it was doing to me and to my friends and to my family. i saw how it was all falling apart, and i did fucking *nothing*.

so okay i'm a werewolf. think about it. it arrives like poetry. i unslip in/out of my own mental clarity. don't monsters find a bitter comfort in being ██ed because violence is familiar. why else wake up covered in running sweat every night. i'm not on a horror movie set. what other excuse do i have. i should get over all of this. i can't even fucking trust my own *memories*. i argue with the doctor while we are both staring at the screen. i didn't *actually* get hurt, i am just exaggerating.

i did love him, is the thing. i know i did, and that makes it so much worse.

◇

Okay, so the night is probably ruined, and you're going to get yelled at about it. Not that he'll *actually* yell (okay, he will a little bit), but you actually don't mind the yelling part that much. What you are actually dreading is the *real* punishment.

Yes, there's the rough but it's his birthday so you were already expecting to endure it. The thing you're like, not *super* excited by is that you knew going *in* that even if it was *perfect,* he'd find some kind of problem with it, and then take out his disappointment on you like a tantrum from a kid. You are going to have to spend the next few months making him feel pretty and popular and special and lovely while he completely ignores your basic needs because of this *one* particular evening. Like, he's going to be sulking for *so* long after this. He won't want to go to your family's birthday parties but he'll be mad if you attend them without him. He will complain any time you want to do something for yourself; he'll dig his heels in. He'll bring up the party as leverage in fucking *every* conversation.

The brisket had been extremely dry. Adam is nowhere to be seen. The brisket (which you don't even actually like, and wasn't the main entrée, and was served several hours ago, and wasn't even under your control) has completely fucking annihilated any chance you have of peace within the next few weeks. You should have stopped him from ordering from that company. You should have known with some kind of meat-based extrasensory perception that the brisket wouldn't be cooked correctly, and you should have pushed him to purchase extra sauce. You should have called up that God you're so fond of and asked for an ambient environmental humidity that does not dry a brisket out.

Wait, is it "*a* brisket," or is there no article before the word *brisket?*

How should you know. Despite all your fancy clothes, you were raised in a house that celebrated holidays with rice and beans.

An hour after dinner all the women with names you actually know had vanished into the ether with their cutesy barely domesticated husbands. Now it is just a house full of people in tight clothing and weird lighting for, like, 11:30.

You check your phone. No messages, but the time is actually 11:23. Why is this night so fucking *long?* Good guess about the timing though, that was pretty spot-on.

You look down at the woman you do not recognize. She is trying to throw up into your palm tree. You are just a *little* bit too drunk for this, and the ground is faintly slippery.

If you heard correctly, her name is Gretchen. You want to ask her how old she *really* is, but don't want the liability. Her dress is a purple lamé. You didn't think that was in style anymore, but she has the kind of body that makes things *look* in style.

You could have that body, if you stopped fucking eating.

And besides, why are you even looking? You're a creep. She's probably, like, sixteen.

You don't want to be mean. "Okay, babe? I love that you've selected a private corner, but, like. Is there *any* way I could convince you to throw up *literally* anywhere else. There's, like, ninety bathrooms in this house and that palm tree is, like, really old." And also it is *your* palm tree. It is your baby. Your mother had rescued it from clearance so you could take care of it.

"I hate Grey Goose. It just tastes like vodka." Her mouth has a red-orange smudge on one side of it, which is kind of interesting. Did she find sauce for the brisket?

"Oh, darling." You want to have anybody else pick her up. You put your hands on your hips like you're looking at a plane taking off. Fuck, if you bend over, you'll expose how much fucking *older* you are then her, your belly fat slopping off your bones.

Just a normal part of aging, your doctor had laughed. You had been staring at your feet, feeling your cheeks burn, embarrassed about the number.

Gretchen gags into the plant pot. You wrap your hand around your wrist.

You had wanted to move the palm tree out of the public areas. You'd put the rest of your plants into a locked room, just in case. But the palm was really fucking big and it had been too heavy and Adam had been getting pre-drunk at literally ten o'clock in the morning. To be fair, he *could* get pre-drunk—you should have had everything taken care of.

You *had* tried to protect the plant, though. In your brand-appropriate leggings and your matching sports bra (clearance rack at Marshalls due to a small tear you whipstitched closed with dental floss), you had made a brutal attempt at dragging the fifty-pound palm across the floor. You shuffled the pot and grunted and "entered beast mode" and tried to be a good feminist rather than needing a man to help you with it.

It had been too tall to get through the door.

Which meant you had just stood there, panting, sweat dripping off your limbs and into your eyes. You'd put your hands into your hair and stared at it for a really long time. You can't just tilt a plant; the dirt will go everywhere. There's no, like, *easy* way to pick a plant up and turn it. You can't just get it in at an angle, you could potentially hurt it.

And then you'd laughed, and it almost sounded like a sob. After all of that, it should have just stayed put. You had slowly and agonizingly moved it back into its original corner. You made the second trek almost sheepishly, feeling like you should be crying.

You'd scratched the floor. You'd half-heartedly rubbed a walnut over the hardwood, the way your mom had shown you after you'd done the same thing to her kitchen table. Then you swept the floor twice, trying to put any loose dirt back into the container. Good potting materials are surprisingly expensive, and you didn't want to waste any of it.

The palm tree is like, special to you. You had this bitch back in high school. You've been raising it from a crooked brittle stick into an actually beautiful tree. It's still a little lopsided, but it has thick and luscious leaves.

And hey, maybe the vomit could actually kind of be good for it. You could teach the tree to eat meat. Feral, it would be the envy of its species. You've heard that mixing potting soil with like, compost and other scraps can actually be *super* beneficial. Aren't there people who water their rosebushes with blood?

Nah. Shit, wait. Vomit might have stomach acid in it.

You sigh and scoop Gretchen upward. She's light and boney, but it's hard to do anything gracefully in a party dress. You need to take a second to blink back black dots. You stood up too quickly.

Adam had said he liked your stupid outfit and had even run up behind you to stick his hands between your dry thighs and murmur in his drunk way that he found it attractive. "████████. ████████," he'd said, maybe as a compliment. You had smiled and shimmied for him and thought—*what the fuck does that even mean, Adam.*

Gretchen doesn't look like she's trying to be a sexy lawyer. She looks young. Or maybe people her age just look young to you now that you're in your *late twenties.*

"How ya feelin'? How's it goin'?" You glance around, searching one last time for whatever person she belongs to.

"...My...My boyfriend—mmm, broke up with me." She tries to push her hair out of her face, but it makes the mess worse. You'll lend her a hair tie once you get her to the bathroom.

"Sorry." That's nothing, so you also offer: "Men are the worst."

"I don't even . . ." She pauses to hiccup, and clutches your bicep.

Okay. Not going to bother with the guest bathroom, too far away. Better to aim for the closest one, one of the nice ones upstairs. On the other hand, Adam will be mad that you let people into private parts of the house without his permission. Risk/reward—your stupid sexy lawyer dress could go, but any more vomit on the floor and you'll have to teach ants to swim.

"I don't even, like, even really *like* him?" She struggles with the first stair, feet weaving in the air. You could pick her up, but you'd probably drop her. Repeat of the palm tree incident, but her brains would be the thing to sweep up.

You half drag her upward. It hurts your old shoulder injury, because what doesn't. You murmur something soft and soothing even *you* can't parse, something along the lines of *it's okay, come on,* like Gretchen is an aging dog.

"I don't even—he fucking, like . . ." She hiccups again. It sounds wet. God, fuck. You need to work out more, because you should be able to, like, deadlift this woman. What is she, six whole pounds? You should be capable of throwing her down the hallway at high speed. She squints up at you. ". . . You know?"

"You wanted to break up with *him*," you translate.

"Exactly!" She actually figures out you're going up the stairs and manages to put effort in, which is nice. "Now I'm . . . I'm wondering what is, like, what is wrong with *me*."

"Oh, no. It's not him, it's you—I mean, no, shit. It's him, not—you know what I mean."

"Wait, hang on . . . Where are we going? Are you—" She pushes at you. "Are you . . . is this . . . kidnapping . . . ?"

You laugh. You have to give Gretchen points here—you're drunk and, like usual, you have completely forgotten that kidnapping exists.

Didn't this used to feel good? Remember taking shots off Lacey's stomach while she shrieked in delight? Remember when Marlowe held a funnel to your mouth and you chugged tequila? Remember being drunk enough to go to things like an older stranger's house party in the middle of fucking *nowhere*? You would have *absolutely* been led upstairs without asking any questions, just blindly trusting any single person who has ever shown you even the *smallest* amount of kindness. Because that is what you *do*, Mouse. You love any person if they are just even *passably* nice enough, even if they are actively trying to rip you apart.

Oops! In vino veritas, maybe. Think about *that* particular nugget at a later destination.

You grunt and ease her up another step. "Goin'. . . to the bathroom."

"Okay . . . I have to throw up, but you can pee first."

"It's okay, we aren't goin' for me." Now that you think about it, you do kind of need to pee though, because you always do these days.

"We're not—not supposed to go upstairs."

She must not have noticed that with this final step you have both now already reached "the upstairs." Sisyphus has an easier time.

"It's okay. I live here." Nastily, you think—*we're both guests here, though, aren't we?* You almost add, *he's my boyfriend,* but it's embarrassing somehow. Like, admitting to knowing the birthday boy would make you uncool to her. Although, really. Was she invited by *him,* or did she end up just-getting-invited. There had been over a hundred people on the list, and all of them were allowed to bring as many friends as they had wanted, and all of *those* people brought friends, who brought friends. It's like a frat party.

Adam's Forty! Like a newspaper headline. Okay, yes, like, you've *obviously* always been aware of the age gap. You even have teased him about it. He had already graduated college and was living alone while you were entering *middle school.* You've jokingly called him *old man* before. You've said (a lot) that you find it kind of hot.

But something about him being *forty* feels *huge.*

And what exactly are *you* going to do about it? You will accept it tastefully; the same way you have accepted everything he has fed you from his belt. You will accept the price of it. You will accept that you are aging out of his preferences.

Ha! No need to be bitter.

You shuffle Gretchen through the bathroom door, onto the tile. You drag out a bathmat for her to kneel on and it takes some fiddling, but you fold it under her. You give her the hair tie, but you end up putting her hair up for her—mostly because it's just nice to help someone.

You glance in the mirror and wish you hadn't. You had thought the gold dress had looked classy, flirty, appropriate for twenty-seven but also appropriate for a club. It's bunching on you. Your cheeks are ruddy pink. What were you thinking. Your skin tone just does *not* look good in gold, you have too much yellow undertone.

Sexy lawyer, you think. Chubby, sexy lawyer. Like someone's drunk mom. When was the last time you weren't bloated?

Gretchen straightens her dress so it covers her ass and then, in a practiced motion, bends over and throws up almost gracefully. She slumps, one skinny arm over the seat, the other bent to steady herself.

You want to go to bed. You start trying to rub away the smeared mascara from under your eyes, but it's waterproof. You dip a bit of toilet paper under the faucet. If you're careful, you won't remove too much foundation.

"Sorry," she says.

"It's okay, baby."

"You . . . You live here?" She slurs. The bowl makes her words echo.

"Yeah." Again, for no reason, you don't offer that Adam is your boyfriend. You just look over at her. "How ya doin'?" You ask again.

"I . . . He broke up with me."

"Fuck that guy. I'll get you an Uber when you're steady."

"I like your dress." She pauses to spit up. "It's nice."

"I look like a mom."

She throws up again. You apply hand cream.

"Sorry," she moans. "I'm so sorry."

How many times were you like this? How often did you laugh about it the next morning? "It's literally no problem. I've been there plenty."

Wait. Shit. Now that you're thinking of it—has Adam ever actually taken care of you when you were like this? Most of the time, don't you just slink away privately, run the shower, try to throw up silently? Okay, to be fair, though, isn't it *your* fault for being too ashamed to ever ask for help? And Jesus Christ, you're entitled. You spend all of a few years dating a rich man and now you think people need to help you vomit.

Your phone buzzes. Oh good, the bill for catering came through. You should leave them a scathing review about their lack of sauce on the brisket and how they forgot the tilapia and how nobody actually touched the cake.

The birthday shot Adam had made you do had hit fast and hard. You'd almost gagged it back up. Next time with water—if there *was* a next time. Before this, before you got old, you'd do this kind of thing in a flash of seven, one after another, in what Marlowe called "a snake trick." Adam had already gone off to go talk to his friends before you'd even recovered from it. You hadn't even really *wanted* it, but you knew *he* was going to expect birthday sex. And you needed to be much more faded before that happened.

"Are you okay?" You find a stale water glass at the back of a cabinet and offer it shyly to Gretchen, feeling bad about how clean it probably isn't. Adam most likely left it here forever ago and it somehow got missed by his housekeeping staff. You weren't raised to use cups inside of any place with a toilet, it grosses you out.

She retches, so you take the glass back and rinse it a few times before filling it just enough to like, swish around her mouth. Not enough to chug.

Her slim wrist flashes with a gold bracelet as she takes the cup. Goes to push back her hair, looks surprised when she finds it's been tied up. "I'm sorry about . . . thank you for taking care of me." She takes another dainty sip. "I'm. This isn't . . . like me."

"It's okay. We've all been there. Are you ready to stand up?"

"Do you have to pee? I can hold it back until you finish peeing."

You do have to pee; you appreciate her reminder. "No, it's okay. Let's get you home."

"Okay." She nods once. Takes another sip of water. "Okay, yeah." She does actually seem better. She stands up like a warrior. Roman centurion stabilizing herself in the mirror, fresh from the vomitorium. She asks for toothpaste that you provide, depositing it on her finger in a flourish. She manages to not mess up her makeup worse while she spits into your sink.

"Sorry, I don't even. Like. Know your name. I'm." She hiccups. "My name is Helen. Like from Troy."

You were *so* wrong about her name, what the fuck. You shake her hand. "Oh. Hi. I'm █████." How the fuck did you get *Gretchen* from *Helen?*

"You're, like, *so* nice." She burps, but it sounds dry. "Sorry. Thank you. I—I got broken up with. You're like *so, so* nice."

"It's okay. Did you come with your friends?"

"Yeah. Two of them. I don't know if they left. My phone died."

It's tragic to know these things. You shouldn't have learned them. You should have sent her home before knowing them. Say what you will about your luck, but you have never been left truly alone at a party—unless you consider being left alone with Adam.

"Oh. Can I see? I might have a phone charger."

She has the wrong kind of phone, which sucks, and you apologize to her. She nods, pushes her hair back again. "You're pretty."

You love drunk girls in the bathroom. "*You're* pretty," you counter, and then offer your phone to her. "Okay, enter in the address for the Uber."

"You're so nice," she repeats, almost whining. "Why are you *so* nice to me?"

"Didn't you just get dumped?" You're snappish without meaning to be. Fuck, roll back that attitude, you don't want to be a mean drunk. You soften it by elbowing her gently. "We're best friends now. Fuck all men."

She can walk now. Remember when you could recover this quickly? She stumbles going down the stairs, but you catch her.

"I can't believe he fucking *dumped me.* It was just," she takes a sharp breath. "It was. Like he said it was o-over something so—so *fucking* stupid. He's, just. *So* fucking stupid."

"All men are." You say this in the same way all women say it. God, you're so old and jaded, even though you've been saying it that way for years.

The house feels larger while navigating her through it.

Hadn't it been lovely when you'd first been with him. All starry and tittering in his ear.

Some days you try to plan what you would say to a therapist, but, like. Are you *really* going to complain about having access to all of this? Sure, okay. Maybe he had he found you and loved you only because you had been an easy mark. He'd taken you on his arm and had shown you through the wings of the place like he was unfolding a treasure map. But hadn't you boggled at it, little country Mouse? Wondering what kind of a person could fill all those rooms. Now you know *exactly* who, don't you?

You take her the faster way to the back door, through your off-limits sunroom. Although technically it's not *your* room, it doesn't belong to you. Technically Adam just thinks your green thumb is cute. Technically, if you dumped him, you'd have to take all forty-six (and counting) of your leafed friends back to your shitty apartment in the city an hour and forty-five from here that has no natural lightning. No sunroofs in the city. And who knows if Kaisa would even be okay with that; since you're never really home anyway.

"These are nice." Helen touches one of your trees with a supremely delicate finger. This makes you fond of her, so you try not to like it, because it will break your fucking heart.

"Thank you. I grew a lot of them from tiny cuttings." You stumble a bit, too. "They're mostly rescues."

Pride is a sin. You pick up the pace, relock the doors behind you, step into the wing he's kept open for the party.

The house sprawls out into tents on the manicured lawn, the rooms still blue-lit and pumping music from his hidden subwoofers. Some of the vendors are gone, some are packing up. The intent is to move the party inside after midnight. The juggler is still going, because you let everyone collect tips and people keep paying him in shots. The bartenders have been culled one at a time so that the foremost remaining one is a large man, beleaguered, still accepting cash.

Circus themed. Adam's idea. Tacky. His original plan had been a warehouse full of neon lights and cocaine and strippers. You'd talked him down to a single contortionist and a backyard event. *It would have been embarrassing*, you told him. He thought you meant for *you*. That you, watching young bodies gyrate on stage, would have been embarrassed for *yourself.*

You haven't corrected him on this.

You walk her down the unlit service path toward the front of the house while you watch the car come up on the map. It's gonna be kind of expensive, but it's not like you can ask her to pay you back. Her heels sink into the grass while she waits, shivering even though it's warm. She spits up again. Whatever. She gets to go home.

She gives you a sheepish half-wave as she gets in the car. You wave back, watching until she's gone. You should have given her your number, to text if she got home safe. Wait, no. Her phone is dead, that's the entire reason *you* called the Uber.

You trot upstairs, use the bathroom, avoid eye contact in the mirror while you wash your hands, stomp your way back outside. There's a bottle of champagne half-finished in one of the rosebushes, so you wipe off the top of it with the inside of your dress hem and take a swig. You start a conversation with the large bartender, who says he's going home soon, and then you work your way around to each vendor, many of which have contracts ending at midnight— *thank you very much. Lovely job with the fire breathing. Wonderful balloon animals. Excellent job being flexible. The check is already written and on its way.*

Halfway through the crescent of tents, you come to the purple one with a neon eye. The fortune teller. You'd found her on the internet and had actually kind of liked her. When you'd gone in person for the interview to be sure she was okay, she was mostly businesslike rather than spooky. Only offered to read your palm once. The tea she made you was excellent. It was spicy but not overwhelming. And her office had plants in it.

I tried to be a psychic in high school, you told her. *I had this neat party trick because I'm very good at reading people.*

Are you? Her lips had quirked.

I, like think so, maybe. When I was young—like, definitely.

I'm always hiring, she had said. *You know, you might have thought you weren't Gifted, but many are passively able to See and don't recognize it.*

The implied capital G and S were a nice touch. She was just over-the-top enough, and she was also older, and not as pretty as you are—at least, not once you'd put on your makeup. Way too old for Adam's tastes, but theatrical enough for his vision of a night of being too drunk to remember the party he made you assemble. She was perfect for the role. You can't remember her name, though, which does make you an asshole.

The tent is nice. Very stereotypical. Beautiful and gauzy. The door is small, so it takes you some doing to find the break in the cloth.

It's smoky, a pine or pitch scent thick in the air. Extremely atmospheric. You'll recommend her to all of your friends (his friends), obviously. She's doing an excellent job of really selling it. Crystal ball on a shrouded table, hanging plants, spooky lanterns, nice black outdoor rug. Mystic but approachable. Specifically, nonreligious vaguely-wiccan decor. You'd gone over Adam's head about this—you liked the idea of a fortune teller, but not the cultural appropriation it sat uncomfortably close to. Not that Adam cared about that sort of thing.

You take a swig of your champagne and sit down hard into the provided velvet chair. The rug and the chair both creak. Yikes, you must be getting *heavy*. The music she's piping in is *also* a nice touch, but it does clash with whatever pop music the party DJ is blasting.

"I'll be in soon." The voice from the back of the tent trails on the air. Good touch—she sounds different than when you met her, has applied a spooky accent. Something familiar, but fluid. Higher. It's hard to hear her over the music. "Why don't you go through my Tarot cards and see what calls to you?"

Tarot is stupid, but like, you do find it interesting. The art on the cards is nicer than you expected. Gold-leafed and on—what is this, cardstock? It's heavy. Back in high school during that psychic phase, you'd taught yourself the meaning of each card from the major arcana, trying to impress a girl who had disappeared and never spoken to you again. Okay, so the moon card means . . . something about femininity? Well, there's the tower—that one is definitely bad. You put it to the side rather than keep holding it with the others, as if the touch of it will seep into you.

You cheat and pick the funniest ones. The lovers, the fool, the hermit. The hermit you mostly include because it looks silly and you like his wide and open face.

The tent rustles. To hold onto the pageantry, you don't look up while she makes herself comfortable in the swan-backed chair across from you. "I see three are calling to y—wait."

And then you do look up, and she sees you, and you see her, your voice dies in your throat.

"██?" Marlowe says, the phony mystic voice dropped around your name, "What—what the fuck?"

"You're not. The psychic." Your stomach has dropped. Your cheeks are hot and your body is cold and your skin is coated in lightning. Something invisible has punched you. It would have been better for her to have actually slapped you. You can tell your jaw has dropped, but you have no recourse for it right now. You just stare at her, dumbfounded.

It's been what, a year? Why do you feel like throwing up—wait, shit, you took the champagne out of the fucking *bushes*, what if you've just drugged yourself.

Think faster. Why are you so sluggish and idiotic. "Marlowe, I— oh my god. Hi, I guess? I—what are you . . . ? I mean, it's nice to see you, but . . . the other woman . . . ?"

"She had to—she got food poisoning. I'm filling in. I'm—I'm freelancing."

"For—psychics?"

She shrugs. "I'm desperate," laughs, high and tight. "It's a livin'." The joke comes out cracked and wild.

Her hair comes down past her shoulders now. It looks good. *Mermaid hair.* She's wearing an airy white Grecian dress that dusts the ground. Long slits show leg all the way up both of her thighs. On her head is a golden crown. She's put on heavy makeup to pair with the gold bracelets and charms up her arms. More feminine than you've usually seen her.

Wait, do you only think she looks good because she looks feminine? Aren't you supposed to be like, a feminist? You've really got the male gaze for someone who's actively trying to take a stance against any of this.

She looks, truth be told: fucking gorgeous. A Roman goddess.

"Hi," you say again, floundering. Jesus.

How many times have you pictured a situation where you just *show up* and there's Marlowe, and you get to *finally* say something. How many conversations have you scripted. How many times have you planned out *exactly* how you'd "win"? You've imagined running into her in bars. Grocery shopping. Out with friends. You'd be out living your life (unconcerned about her, of course), and then you'd just *find* her, and there would be that singular moment where you finally say the right thing and manage to get closure.

So, where the fuck are all of your words?

"Hi." She blinks at you.

You blink at her. "Sorry, I'm just." In shock. "You're. Hi . . . Marlowe." It's odd to say her name, like the weight of it will crush you into little pieces or like the span of your wrist is too thick and will snap it.

"Okay. I mean—okay, *hi!* What's up?" She tilts her head back and then laughs like it is the funniest thing on the planet, for you both to be here, for you both to be across a table from each other. The laugh takes off in the air and kills you.

What was with that one text about how you needed to tell me something because you sent that and then disappeared when I tried to clarify it. Are we even friends? What did I do to make you so fucking angry that you would drop me like this? I thought I was your best friend, and maybe that's fucking stupid but I thought you were my best friend too. Is all of this because of that one time I wouldn't let you drive drunk because I know you were upset about it and I know should have handled it better. I know I apologized but I legit still feel bad that while I was wrestling you out of the driver's seat I accidentally closed the door on your ankle, but I swear it was an accident. It was super wrong of me. Do I owe you another apology? Why are you even here right now like are you actually here right now or are you about to go leave to that boyfriend you like more than me. Why have you been avoiding me. Why haven't you been answering any of my messages. Did I say or do something shitty? You can tell me if I did something wrong, but stop fucking ignoring me. What happened, what did I do? Why was it so easy to let go of me.

Where the fuck have you been?

Instead you say—"I found this champagne, do you want any? It's bush champagne, though. I mean, like from a bush, not a Republican Bush."

She holds out her hand. You pass it over, stand up to go get a glass, sit back down when she takes a swig directly from the lip.

"I can't believe this is happening." Her face softens. You look down so that she does not grow in you like an orchid. You hear her take another sip and sigh. "This feels like a dream. How are you? You look amazing."

"I'm, like, good." You bite your tongue so you don't say *no, you look amazing.*

"You *look* good. I like your dress."

"Ah, do you? I feel like it makes me look like a lawyer. I'm a little worried I'm like, a little too old for this?" You pull at the hem, examining the material.

"Aren't you, like, twenty-seven?"

You make a noise rather than affirm anything.

Something is happening behind your back tooth. You're dizzy and your heart is pounding. You want to bite something. She has stepped on your reflection. She's not supposed to *be* here, not here in this world that you have made. This is the place away. She's not supposed to be able to get to you from here.

She is not supposed to still be beautiful.

"You don't look like a lawyer," she's saying. "You're too pretty for that."

Where the fuck has she been. Think about Lacey. Think about how many times Lacey has heard you cry about this. Think about how your sister and your brother and your mom have all had to sit still while you vented about how unfair it-all-is.

"Almost serious enough but not quite. Maybe furrow your brow a little bit more? Then I could see it." She's actually laughing.

This is all fucking unbelievable.

"Oh, perfect! Good acting."

Without meaning to, you laugh. She caught you by surprise, maybe. Or you're just too drunk to stop yourself.

Fuck—*wait a second.* Holy shit, you're not just angry, you're fucking *embarrassed to be seen here.* You take back the champagne and draw a huge sip. You can't make eye contact, like that'll stop her from perceiving you. God, you probably look so fucking ugly right now, it's not fair. You should have reapplied your makeup.

Be fucking normal. Say something with the least amount of noose in it. "It's um . . . How'd you get here? Are you—I mean, do you live in the area, or . . . ?"

"Yeah, kind of. Well, like, no, but. I do a lot of little projects and stuff so it's a lot of wandering? I, like. Get to do a bunch of really cool things." She nods, almost to herself. "It's, like, really wild but like—I'm genuinely, like, *so* excited about so much of this stuff."

"Oh, that's really awesome. That sounds, like, so cool." Wait did she actually answer your question? Okay hang on. It would make sense for a psychic to work with an actor, right? Was it like something through her acting gig, or was it like a different connection. Or shit, wait. Does Marlowe actually believe she's psychic? Now *that* would be something.

Marlowe is running her hand through her long thick hair. "Yeah, I mean, it's a lot. It's pretty fun, but, like—why are *you* here? Are you working?"

You school your features so you say it in a normal way. "Actually, I'm, like, dating—like, the birthday boy is my. Boyfriend. Actually." Ugh. Why does it always feel gross to say that. Like an admission of guilt. Like you're lying somehow. You examine the label of the champagne bottle, not actually reading it.

She laughs again. "Wait, for real?" She almost sounds nervous. "Like, you're—wow."

"Yeah. We, like, met the summer you—" *the summer you left,* "uh, the—like two-ish years ago? Something like that."

"Dude he's . . . like he's rich, huh?" She lets out a low whistle. "I— like, yes, girl. Make his pockets hurt."

"Yeah." Once you saw him throw out a five-dollar bill. "But this shit is like," you don't know why you're saying it. You don't *know* her anymore. You are *not friends.* You have tried to be her friend, and she was not willing to be your friend in return. Turn around and leave.

You lean in toward her, feeling yourself grin. "It's fucking tacky, right?"

She cackles, and you see her shoulders relax. "Oh God, I'm glad *you* said it."

"It was Adam's idea." You roll your eyes. Your heart is thrumming in your throat.

Oops! You're super drunk! Should have stopped before that last one!

Marlowe looks up at you through her lashes. "Like, no offense. But if someone was going to ask me if you'd planned it or he did—like, I'd have always known *he* did."

"You met him?"

"I've met *men.*"

"No, for real, how *are* you. Tell me about your whole life. I feel like. It's, like, completely crazy this is happening. I mean, like, we're not supposed to say crazy." You feel weird, unsure where to put your hands.

She answers the problem for you, sliding around the table, pulling you up beside her, hugging you deeply, sighing, burying her face in your shoulder the way she always has.

You wrap your arms around her on instinct alone. Something unknots inside your belly, which isn't a good sign, probably. It feels like you've been holding onto a breath for the last two years of your life and just now have you remembered how to use your lungs properly.

Uh-oh!

"This is fucking wild," she murmurs into your skin. "Holy shit. Talk about—I mean, it's divine intervention." She steps back, offers you a hand. "Walk with me?"

You take it without thinking, but then don't know what to do with it. "Uh. Well, okay, but. I should see what's . . ."

"I mean, it's okay. You don't have to come with, don't worry. I know you're probably busy. Like—"

"No, I'm coming. But—" But nothing. You gesture vaguely with the bottle. She just touches you so *casually*, is the thing. Like nothing happened.

You let her lead you out of the tent. The lawn is quieter, full of scattered small groups. You can still see the shapes of dancing people in one of the rooms, backlit in flashing blues.

God, please let every person here be at least twenty-one. Where did he even get half this guest list? Which reminds you, you need to update one of the vendors. Also, you need to send everyone on the guest list a thank-you note for attending. Also you should maybe figure out how to check up on Gretchen/Helen. While you're at it, you need to find Adam and make sure he drinks some water before he gets too handsy with others.

Marlowe stops for a second, looking up at the mansion this man has moved you into. "Damn, girl." She looks over at you while you chew your lip. "My only question is like. *How.*"

"Practice. And luck." If you don't specify what kind of luck, that's for dramatic effect.

"I mean, I knew you had it in you. Like, we both know this is so entirely on-brand for you. But *damn.*" She laughs. "Like, how many rooms even is it?"

"In the original house, the two additions, or like, all of them in total?"

"Have you had sex in all of them, or just some?"

You can't help the fox smile while you slide your eyes to her. "There are rooms I've never even *been* in."

Marlowe laughs again. This is all too gentle, easy. The sound of her voice finds a place in your stomach and starts chewing.

What happened? Where did you go?

She adjusts her bracelets. "Holy shit. I mean like—sorry, like, but what's he actually *do* with all that space?" She wrinkles her perfect nose. "It's kind of, like. Gross."

What he does with the space is throw parties like this, with you out on the lawn. What he does is watch the birthdays of his life come up and keep passing. "He's got things." He drinks, mostly. "And I—I have a room for plants." Your voice cracks. You almost visibly flinch.

"Wait, you'd *love* that. Is that your favorite room?"

She doesn't fucking know you. She doesn't get to be in your life like this. *What did I do that was so wrong you're okay treating me like this.* You should just get up and go.

Instead, you give your combined hands a tug. "Actually, hang on, I'll show you my favorite place." You lead her by the wrist, realizing too late that you should drop it—knowing that if you drop it now, you'll look rude, angry.

You just got her back. You can't make her leave. But also, like. You should absolutely make her leave, right?

She giggles as she follows you. The gazebo is through a patch of woods and into a second, secret lawn. Your almost-private garden space.

He let you help his staff design it, smiling in that *you're welcome* way. The careful pesticides keep the whole thing pleasant, calm, ensconced in trees and fairy lights and the sound of the gentle waterfall in the koi pond. It had been your idea to light their piscine bodies from below, and now their shadows trickle the light while they sleepily wander through their tiny unnatural heaven. It had been your idea to grow wildflowers and native species. It had been your idea to hide the gazebo among trees. It had been yours, so you should really be happy.

She lets out a low, longing sound. You used to—*no, stop that.* Your hands are shaking. You feel like you just got electrocuted.

For a moment, you stand still and let her wander, her eyes wide even in the dark, her fingers ghosting over your (his) plants and graceful statuettes.

You slip your drunken self into the gazebo, sit on the single swinging bench, watch her wandering. You try to smooth your dress down. Fix your hair. The drink starts making you giggly, stop that. You adjust your heel.

Marlowe's eyes are so wide. Is this what you had looked like, when he found you?

You put the bottle down and kick your legs as she slowly winds her way over. She stands awkwardly in front of you before you pat the seat next to you, giving her permission. She perches daintily, positioned like she could leave at any moment.

Why can't you think of something to say? Why can't you talk to her? Why is it so strange just to be near her?

You wish you hadn't put the bottle down because now your feet are awkward around it. A too-long silence stretches out. God, you're so melodramatic.

"MTV, welcome to my crib," you say.

She taps you with one of her toes. Her strappy golden sandals lace up to her exposed knees. "I can't fucking believe you live here."

You *don't* live here technically, but you don't correct her. "I can't believe *you're here.*"

"I literally only took this job last-second. The chances are fucking miniscule."

"Feels like a movie." If you don't specify what genre of movie, that's for dramatic effect.

She runs her thumb over your cheek, a movement that makes you freeze. Her mouth quirks. "It feels like a movie," she repeats.

You wrap your fingers around her skinny wrist, trying to catch her eyes. She is too busy staring at the ground. "How are you doing? You said—like, I tried to hit you up when you said you had something to tell me? But I didn't, uh. Like I don't know if you saw."

"Do you remember my mom?"

You blink. "Is she—yes, of course I do, is she okay?" Holy shit, what if her mom fucking died and you've been mad at her for being depressed for the last two years. Dude, you would be *literally* the worst person alive.

She kicks her heels and runs her hands through her hair and takes a deep breath and looks out over the garden. "This is fucking beautiful."

"Lowes—uh, your mom?" You look out at the garden too. Maybe you shouldn't have pressed about it. If something bad happened, you should give her the time to process it.

"It makes sense it's your favorite place." She cuts her eyes to you. "It seems like something that you would like."

"I helped make it." You chew on the words slowly, unsure how to handle this conversational tone. Maybe you'd be doing better if you were more sober. "I'm, uh. Glad you like it."

She snorts. "It's gorgeous. Of course, I like it." She sits back against the chair and leans her head, gently, on your shoulder. You stay perfectly still, not even breathing. She smells different. Wait, why are you even fucking thinking about how she *smells*. You're so fucking creepy. No wonder she went missing.

You catch sight of a shadow on her leg. "Wait, did you get a tattoo?"

"Hmm? Oh! Yeah." She cranes, lifts her left leg. A huge butterfly is perched above her knee, fanning wings across her thin thigh. "I got this one too." She pulls her sleeve down to display a cactus in a cowboy hat on her shoulder.

You examine both politely, for the amount of time you are supposed to look at these things, and then you look anywhere else. "Nice."

She nods and curls back against you, sneaking a little closer. She tucks her feet up on the seat. "Got 'em when I got back from Paris." Looks up at you. "Did you ever get that star chart?"

You'd completely forgotten that you'd even wanted a star chart. Now you want a bird on your back, actually, even though it's a pretty obvious metaphor for *rising*. "Nah."

"Still no tattoos?"

You shake your head. God, you are so fucking uncool it leaks out of you.

She pats your arm. "You'll get one soon. I'll send a few artists I like to you."

You don't know how to answer that. You both sit there for a long while, just watching the koi light show, listening to the far pulse of music you don't like, the ground subtly thumping.

"My mom," she breathes. You can barely hear her, so you bend your ear down to her, straining. She tilts so you are almost nose-to-nose, but doesn't raise her voice. It barely pulls over the slight sound of water lapping. "My mom says that, like. When someone is *really* your friend, being with them is easy and immediate. No matter how much time has passed, no matter what happened. If you love them, when you're with them again, it'll be like—it'll be like no time has passed."

You blink at her.

Marlowe looks down and gently takes your hand, sliding hers into it. Flipping it first one way and then the other. She snuggles against you. "I feel like. I feel like something in me has been waiting to see you for *months*. Like, when I saw you—I was just like, *so* grateful—like relieved, almost—like, you . . . you were just *here*, like we planned it. Like, it's so *easy*."

She turns and looks at you. Holds your hands in hers, and looks into your eyes. You think about the Oracle of the Greeks, looking into the face of gods.

"You're my favorite person," she whispers. "Like, I know you are, because of how I felt when I saw you. Like—*oh*, that's *my person*." She gestures vaguely at her chest. "Something let go inside of me."

"Is your mom okay?" You don't know how else to ask it.

She laughs, leans in closer. "Yeah. Thank you for asking."

Oh. So, hang on. "Wait so—what did you want to . . . like the thing you wanted to say."

That was the wrong thing to say. You can see it immediately. Her jaw works while she blinks and chews her lip.

You open your mouth to say literally anything at all, but then she wraps you into another hug. "It's just so fucking good to see you. I missed you." She pulls back, stands up.

"I missed—"

"Hide and go seek?" Marlowe has that same smile. Like she *knows* you.

You look down at your phone, but still no texts, which is alarming. She shouldn't be here; Adam could be around any second. You don't want them to meet, but you're not sure if that's for your sake or his. "The—I don't know. Like, a lot of the doors are locked for the party." You stand too, just because it feels weird to be at a different level, dipping your hand to make sure you take the champagne too.

She's already leaving you behind. "I literally have so much to tell you and I'm gonna be like rude if I start talking and only talk about myself, so you have to talk first."

"Hang on, we should actually go—" without thinking, you dart your hand to guide the small of her back and correct yourself only last-second. That is *not* an appropriate thing to do. She definitely saw. Fuck. Your voice is squeaky. "Uh, yeah, it's this way." You cough. "What do you want to know?"

In one swift and oddly practiced movement, Marlowe takes the bottle from your hand, chugs the rest of it, and then lets out an excited *yip!* "Tell me fucking *everything.*"

"That champagne was mine, bro."

She takes six steps, reaches into one of appropriately themed coolers, abracadabras another into existing. Chucks the empty into a bin. "Please. Didn't college ever teach you anything? I'd never leave you hanging."

You would have figured all the free drinks would have been taken by now, even if you did find a bottle in a bush. But still, an untouched one? Maybe this one is just too far from the rest of the party.

You open the bottle easily, with maybe too much practice. Marlowe claps, your cheeks burn, you drink from the fizzing top, she cackles.

"Numbers?" She challenges, taking it from you.

"I'll go odds. Range?"

"Fifty."

"You little bitch. Go ahead." You laugh.

You developed Numbers back in college with her, when you'd both gotten bored of every other drinking game. This game has nearly killed you about a thousand times.

You go a few rounds and then you have to stop to laugh and swipe the fizz from your face. "Sorry. I gotta slow down. I'm gettin' old."

She suddenly drops to a half crouch and swats your hand, *hard.* You flinch back, "Ow, dude, *what?*"

"Gotcha." Her eyes glitter. "Tag, you're it." Marlowe takes off running. Over her shoulder: "You're not fucking *old,* dude!"

A moment to make a heart weigh nothing on a scale, like a body.

To be fair, it would be a bad job hosting to leave her.

You limp after her, drinking the new champagne. You try not to run. You're not limber like her.

Long stretches of her legs flash out from under her dress. She looks like Artemis, chasing down the moon.

You, on the other hand, would look silly, in your sensible thick heels, sprinting across his grass, pulling your dress down to cover your ass. You half trot, keep your head an owl to be sure nobody is seeing you.

You call after her, hushed at first, then annoyed as the space between the two of you widens. You are not kids. This isn't how adults behave. This isn't appropriate.

Also, why is she dodging your questions fucking *again?*

A quiet anger comes around, an old wound, the kind of thing that never feels good to touch but also never finishes rotting. She slips inside ahead of you, and you yank the door to follow. She didn't even hold it open.

Now you turn a corner and she's just *there,* crouched in a corner of his oversized and ostentatious Tuscan-themed kitchen, angling herself so the huge marble island is placed between your bodies. When you take a step forward, she takes a step to the side.

"I'm gonna fucking kill you," you say, but it has exactly no malice in it. You can't help the horrible Friday giggle in your chest, and you can't stop smiling, wild and uncaring while she bares her teeth at you, snapping back in the air.

And then she turns, and you are both running, opening closets and offices and drawing rooms and walking in on couples having sex. Your thighs hurt.

You catch up to her in a guest bedroom. She squeals and jumps when she sees you, trapped in a dead-end. "This house is fucking huge!"

"Okay, stop, seriously. This isn't funny." Even *you* don't sound convinced. You whiny, nagging bitch. You hide the fact you have to heave in a huge breath. She doesn't even seem winded, and meanwhile you're like, dripping in sweat.

She groans and throws herself on the bed. "*It isn't funny.*" She does a good imitation of your voice. "Keep drinking and tell me that again."

You put the bottle down. "I shouldn't."

"Too old?"

"I have stuff to do in the morning."

"You used to be fun. You used to be *funny*." Her eye roll kind of hurts your feelings. "It's still super early."

"It's like, two in the morning."

She checks her phone, snort-laughs. "Oh. Whoops. We should get back and take down the tent. My boss is going to kill me."

You sit down next to her, careful to be sure you only place a small piece of your hip on the bed. Now it's not obvious how much weight you gained—she won't be able to feel the dip in the mattress.

You pick up the bottle again. Pretend to be sober enough to read the label carefully, in the original French. You still "speak" French casually. As a party trick. As something you learned so you could follow her to France. As something you learned so you could ask her, just the once, the thing you will never fucking be brave enough for again.

She groans. "Ugh, now I thought about it. I for real should be going. I have to wrap up the decorations and everything."

You should let her leave. She needs to go. Every time you look at her, you feel like you got slapped. Your skin prickles. Your stomach flips.

"Can I say? I do super like the whole psychic outfit." You reach up to push her hair back behind her ear. "Is there a place where psychics go to get their costumes? Or is it, like, some kind of, like, warehouse situation."

"Thanks, I ordered it online. I think it's technically a prom dress." She straightens to examine her outfit, lets out a giggle. "Oh no, I'm drunk. Fuck. I can't hold my liquor anymore. *That's* getting old."

"Oh, babe, oh no. I'll order you an Uber if you need to get home."

Head shake. "Can't leave the company van, though."

"Psychics have a company van?" At her nod, you bite your lip. "I mean, like it's okay if you stay. And like obviously we have enough beds. No problem. As long as you're out by the morning. There is a planned hangover brunch though."

You don't even think Adam will notice. Once while you were out dancing with him, you disappeared for five hours to throw up under a fire escape rather than in the tiny club bathroom. When you'd shown up again, he'd just said—" ██████████ ."

"I don't know, dude." She takes a deep breath. "I feel like I should check in with my boss too."

"Adam has like, makeup wipes and the basics in every bathroom. And you can obviously borrow anything else you need from me."

She blows out a breath. "Drinking on the job, huh?" She pushes her hair back, grimacing. "Not a good look for me."

"I've worked retail *and* as a waitress. You're fine. I've seen worse."

She picks up her phone. "Honestly, if you're *sure* I can stay . . ." she flicks her eyes to you, you nod emphatically, wave at the phone. She slumps with relief at the gesture. "Okay, let me just text my boss. She mentioned it might run, like, super late. I'll tell her, like, I'm too tired to drive and you were kind enough to offer this to me."

"Are you kidding? Feel free to tell her we're keeping you for a fucking second morning party. Bill the son of a bitch."

Her thumbs hover over the screen, mid-typing. "Are you. Serious?'

"Have you seen this place?" You snort. "He won't notice the price difference." So what if he'd be pouty about it. He was already gonna throw a fit about the brisket.

You'd seen his budget and all the air had blown out of you (*more than your student loans*) but when you'd brought it up to Lacey, she'd winked and said *think about what he'd pay for a wedding. We hate them, but we would love to marry a capitalist.*

"I have so much to tell you." Marlowe finishes her text and then yawns into her hands.

"Literally please do." You take your shoes off. They're wet with grass. You finish off the champagne.

"Don't you like—I feel worried your boyfriend is gonna be mad I'm stealing you. It's his birthday. Wait, is it like his actual birthday, or has that passed?"

"He's fine." You yawn too. You are suddenly drunk-tired, the kind that is immediate and painful, angry and necessary. You lay half-upright on the stacked pillows, careful to be far away from her. Hands crossed over the now-empty bottle. "Come snuggle and tell me your entire life story."

For a second, she doesn't move, and your spinning brain shrieks *stupid!*

But then the mattress shifts, and her body presses into you. "Hi," she whispers.

You turn over and look at her, almost nose-to-nose. "Hi."

"Hi," she repeats.

"So how was France?"

"Colder than I thought. How was the writing job?"

You struggle to remember what she's talking about. Oh right, one of the many ways you have failed to have a life! You snort. "My boss had to close the company three weeks after I was hired."

"Wait, what?"

You wave your hand vaguely, and then laugh when it makes the bottle rock between the two of you. You pull it up tighter to your chest. "It was a whole thing. Like, *fraud.*"

"Okay, I just, like . . . got fired." That weird, high laugh.

You don't like that laugh from her, so instead you playact trying to recork the bottle with your teeth, one eye closed to stabilize your vision. She giggles while you growl. You give up and toss the bottle over her head (she laugh-yelps). You figure—*I'll handle that when I'm sober.*

"Watch this." You clap your hands and the lights go off and the running lights come on instead. The stately-clean *modern feel* gains a low orange tint, turning the room into something private, masculine, dark.

You might not love everything about Adam. But the man *does* know his shit when it comes to houses.

"Oh, I'm gonna fall asleep, though," Marlowe whispers.

"Then go to sleep." You whisper too. It's wrong to talk loudly now, not the right atmosphere. You wiggle your way closer to her. "For real, how's your mom?"

"Doing better." Her voice is blurring at the edges. "Thank you for asking. How's yours?"

"She's good."

"We love your mom."

We. "Yeah." You have a million other questions, but your body is too heavy. Pulled through the floor. Tired to the back of your nails. "Thank you for coming tonight."

"Best night of my life," Marlowe says, slurring.

Mouse wakes up first. Her hair is a mess and she smells like sweat.

She cringes at the phone screen light before reading the time— *4:53 a.m.*—puts it back down, staggers to the closest bathroom. She's disturbed to find she's still a little drunk. She splashes water on her face and makes herself pretty-ish, swiping at her smeared mascara and putting on concealer over the remains from last night. Her bra is giving her a bruise over her ribs, but whatever.

You are a good girl. You are being a good girl. You are in love with the perfect man in his perfect mansion.

You tiptoe back, hovering for a moment over Marlowe's frame, just watching her sleep. Knowing that if you get back in bed, it will be intentional, now, to have slept next to her. Knowing you should go find Adam next.

Marlowe cracks open one eye. Pulls you down next to her. Throws the covers over both of your bodies. Pulls your arms and your legs so you spoon her, her slim body a crescent moon against you. Effortlessly, perfectly comfortable.

"I fucking missed you," she breathes, and then she falls right back to sleep.

there is probably a better word for it, right? the silence that is growing a keen edge inside of you. there is probably a name for it. tuck your rabbit heart back into the burrow.

you can shake while shoving your hands through the bargain bin. you can tremble on your way down the aisle. it doesn't have to be pretty. an echo is also a noise. so what if joy has become diluted through refraction. just get what you were coming for and go.

life is not a miracle; it is a salvo.

You miss writing poetry with her.

It had started as kind of a joke back in the first year of living together. You had been burned out on writing; she was full of ideas. You were showing off, in a sense, almost flirting. Sometimes she was a better writer than you were because she wasn't trying as hard. Her natural abilities both made you love her more and also made you hate her a little. You don't have *inborn talent*—you have skill. You have been writing since you were in the second grade, obsessively. All that practice eventually adds up to something.

You haven't been able to write anything in months. You used to write about being in love with the sky and sea and air. Most days now: love feels like a cracked window. When you try to language it, you find that you keep writing about dead leaves and furnaces.

The summer has released itself into a temperate fall. You sit outside of Adam's house on his beautiful lawn in his beautiful chairs. Writing in a journal you spent too much money on, head titled to the side as the world sighs into gloaming. You hope you look beautiful, enchanting, absorbed. A bug lands on your arm and it makes you jump. It flies off, which is sad—it just wanted to greet you. It would have been nice to make a friend.

In your neatest handwriting, you write: *Adam is a kind man*, and then stop. It's factually incorrect. You usually tell your parents he's *nice*. Both are four letters, but you like that *kind* and *nice* share only half of their identities: *i* and *n*.

You let your handwriting shift. You've been with this man for *so long* now, you should be able to write a poem about it. You let the letters curl into a less-legible, more-honest script.

adam holds me at night. Factually incorrect. Instead, he gets annoyed if you ask for too much cuddling. Everyone sleeps differently, after all.

adam likes to ▮▮▮▮ *e me.* Factual, finally, but hard to look at. You scratch out the offending letters before they can sink too deep into your skin and leave a brand. Already your cheeks burn.

You try talking around it instead.

adam likes me on my knees. Accurate.

adam likes to be worshipped as if i am not a human being. More accurate.

adam likes me. Very possibly untrue. Needs more research.

Marlowe once wrote a poem about fucking you. How you'd pant her name until it made a constellation. A ratification of desire above you both, glittering in a canopy between bedposts. She knew you wanted her so badly that you melted the sheets under you.

And fuck it. She can't have that back, ever.

So okay. You're going to write a poem without her in it. You're going to write a poem that doesn't walk around her either. You're going to write a poem about Adam, whom you love.

Are you more mad that she left, or are you more mad that you wanted her to stay?

You write: *adam* and wait for the rest of the poem.

You used to write so much. You used to have hundreds of poems. You used to have to get out of bed to write. Sometimes you'd even dropped out of conversation, mumbling a line to yourself, typing it out on your phone in the bathroom. You used to have to edit yourself down, to beg yourself to shut up. You used to always be in the constant state of writing a book.

You used to write about *everything*. It was hard to get you to *stop* writing. You used to write about puddles and stand mixers and apple juice.

You think of air vents and car exhaust and the vet bill. You think of Richard Siken and of hot glue guns and a ceiling fan.

You google the names of your favorite poets, but their words are opaque to you. Even your heroes cannot penetrate whatever plastic is wrapping around your brain. Words used to be special to you, right? You used to hold words against yourself so tightly they would gnaw within your thigh bone.

This is your skill. *This* is your talent. You used to be fucking *gifted*.

You just sit there, staring at the four letters of his name, and you write nothing.

Whatever you are feeling is in the fourth dimension and you only have access to three of them. You are experiencing this feeling only because it passes through you in a plane. You have no idea the true shape of it.

You wait until long after more bugs come out and are crawling across your wrists. You wait until the crickets are all harmonizing. You wait until your jaw cracks. There is no sound of an owl. There is only the far-off highway.

From this distance, the cars passing almost sound like sighing.

under his hands, your mind; to mush and shadow puppets.

there's no ghost. oh fuck! only your own face in the windowpane. the house wasn't haunted, it was *waiting*.

i keep thinking about being seven in a restaurant, having my first panic attack, suddenly convinced the world was going to end at any moment. i keep thinking about how i sat there, staring in mute terror at the ceiling. even if i'd had the words for what was happening: i still wouldn't have told anyone. maybe i was just born wrong, and i never grew the right kind of self-advocacy.

i don't like to scream, even in an emergency. it just feels wrong. shameful. embarrassing. i am missing one of the most basic forms of human self-defense. one time i accidentally caught my sleeve on fire and it wasn't until after when i was dressing the burns that my friend said—*it's kind of weird you did that while staying completely silent.*

i keep having nightmares about the dead cat. i sob to him about needing to get out. i think they closed the last road for me a few miles back, but i don't know what else to do, so i just keep walking. i don't know what i think the cat will help me with. sometimes i can touch him, but mostly his body just scrambles near the fringe of my dreams.

he asked me in the last one—*will you please just let me sleep?*

◇

You come home early. Adam had not *technically* kicked you out—but he wanted to have *the boys* over, so he'd kind of implied you were annoying to be around.

Kaisa is drunk on the floor, sobbing in a heap.

You stare at her, your hands fisted around your keys. Holy fuck, you should say something. Say *anything*. Instead, you weirdly look at your phone, as if you're expecting a text message. The same text message you've been hoping to get for, like, ever. It still hasn't come.

Her friend is petting her head, holding her gently. Other people you don't recognize kind of stand around awkwardly. One of them takes you gently outside.

They tell you that, sorry, Kaisa's just gotten out of a bad relationship, and needs some space, can you please go *anywhere else*?

You say *oh my god I'm so sorry, of course, let me just grab my things.* They make a face like you're saying the wrong thing, like even that small intrusion is too terrible, too big.

You have to awkwardly step over her to get into your room, which is terrible. You put your hand on her head and murmur something quietly, but it's uncomfortable and weird.

You don't really have that many things to grab. Most of your clothes are at his place. This isn't even your home. Why are you back here? You're *his* to take and hold. And now what?

How fucking funny. In trying to have two worlds, you belong to neither.

You don't *have* a home. Just two places you are unwanted, and no place to go.

there is a garden at the start of God and a garden at the end of God's son. humanity begins at the base of a tree. judas will hang off the branch. Jesus spends his last night below an olive tree.

humanity destroys itself twice, in a sense.

one: eve says yes. we will punish all women for it. to serve, in order to make up for the weight of our extra rib.

two: it is a man that sentences Jesus to death. in Jesus's death, we are all saved, amen.

we get the phrase *washing your hands of it* from the passage where Pontius Pilate dips his uncalloused fingers into a basin and says—*fine, but I don't like it*. men are generally forgiven for this moment, maybe because it was a *woman* that gave Pilate life in the first place, so it's actually probably *her* fault.

it was men that put Jesus on a cross and it was men that hammered the nails in.

men are allowed to be priests and popes and bishops. not women. we aren't allowed to read the words aloud without somehow casting a stain upon them.

what do we do in the world we have left, after we have been cast out? who carries the weight of the sin? who walks in the shadows, once all the clouds have come in?

we got dave when he was a kitten. the shelter said he was old enough, but honestly, he might have been a week or two shy of it.

he was *my* cat, although he technically belonged to the family. i have to admit i arranged this. it is still one of the most selfish things i've ever done. we got him in the summer, and the rest of my family sleeps with an air conditioner on. i spent the first three months waiting until they'd all gone to bed, then I'd sneak past their closed doors just to hang out in the living room with him. he and i would curl up on the couch, feeling small and lost together.

he didn't have the name *dave* until about a year into his life. my dad called him █████████, after a wine god. for a while, we tried a few nicknames, but more often he was just *the cat*. no one called him ██████. it just wasn't *right*, but why get upset about that. it's pointless to care about the name of a cat. it's a *cat*, not a dog.

the name just arrived in my head one day. it fit him so *well*, is the thing. by that point he was *my* cat, and everyone knew he was *my* cat, sure. but dave suited him so perfectly, if you called *dave?* out into the house, you'd reliably get an answering meow. it always made me laugh, like he was saying, *yeah?*

he liked to crawl to the top of ladders and then reach under the rung to play with his tail. i am terrified of heights, and would spend hours posed nervously underneath him, worried he would fall. to my knowledge, he never did.

he was an unbelievably gentle cat. he never bit nor scratched us, no matter how rough us three kids got. it was rare to even hear him hiss. the few times i picked him up wrong and a stray claw would catch me, he would spend the day by my side, appearing to apologize for it. in my teen years, i once put him in a petsmart dress for all of fifteen minutes. he didn't even bite me during *that* entire experience. i would have honestly deserved it.

every time he purred, he would drool. he purred a *lot*. i googled it pretty much every month, worried that it was something bad. it turns out certain cats just drool when they're happy.

he was weirdly well-trained, considering we never trained him. he would most reliably come if i was the one calling him, but pretty much anyone could say *dave* and he'd trot his little legs along. it was a good party trick in the rare event my friends came over: i'd say *oh want to meet the cat?* and then i'd just *call the cat*.

legally, the cat was under the name my father first chose. my father was the only one to refer to the cat that way. every other person i know called the cat *dave*—even the *cat himself.*

when my cat died, the vet said goodbye using the wrong name.

Mouse's phone is on the bedroom floor while she does her morning Pilates Intense Burn Challenge. She hates cardio, but Adam likes her flexible and has recently implied she's chubby. She pauses *Workout Playlist #12* on her Spotify.

Oh shit. Lots of missed text messages. She scrolls, chewing her lip. She has to read each one about three times: none of the information actually sinks in. She wraps her fingers around her wrist. She wants a Boston cream donut. She goes into the bathroom and ███████████ until her head spins. She brushes her teeth and stares blankly into the mirror.

You are an adult, Mouse. You are going to handle this like an adult, Mouse. You are going to figure out what to do, Mouse. One thing at a time.

First, call in sick to work. You're not going to be able to do anything today. At all.

Now what.

You go find Adam, but he's not in bed. Fuck, did he even *come* to bed last night? You'd gone to sleep early, unwilling to put up with a fight.

You take off your shirt but keep the bra and yoga pants because it's too much effort to change right now. And who knows, maybe TMZ will look through one of the windows and see you being a slob. You only take a few steps before shame makes you backtrack and put the shirt back on.

You find him passed out on a couch in the basement.

"Adam. Wake up, baby. It's almost ten in the morning."

"████████?" He looks distinctly hungover.

You open your mouth, but no sound comes out. Just kind of a hollow choke.

This isn't for him. You can't tell him about this. Not quite a space like Elijah. Just one where you know he *couldn't* exist.

Besides, you're old enough for a mortgage (not that you have one). You are supposed to be calm, and cool, and unaffected.

"Nothing's wrong, baby. How are you feeling?"

"█████?" He still hasn't fully opened his eyes. "████████?
████████████."

"Did you drink any water last night?"

He spits on the floor.

You dance to the side. "Do you need anything?"

"████████. ████████████?"

"You left it in the bathroom. I set it up to charge while I got ready this morning. Want me to go get it?" You are suddenly exhausted. You need an Advil.

"████████████."

You tut and push his stringy hair back. "I'm sorry, baby. Want me to make you some eggs or something? I can get you some soup?"

He barely sits up, opening one arm toward you. An invite. "████,
little Mouse.████████████████████████"

You fit yourself against his body, even though the two of you do not fit on the couch. Most of your body is hanging off of it, held on by your balance and a leg firmly on the ground. He smells like vomit and sweat and Tanqueray. *You love him, and you are in love with him.* He wraps his arms around you.

Your skin is shivering. You hate touching him. Ants are moving in calligraphy everywhere he makes contact. God, aren't *you* the sensitive one.

His breathing has already slowed down. He is probably still drunk. That is fine and understandable. This is something that can happen, like how the thing with Marlowe is something that can happen.

And hey! Maybe you misread those texts. Your brain has been kind of foggy and weird lately; maybe you misunderstood. And even if you *didn't* misunderstand . . . well, it's better than spending the time thinking about food.

You lie there for an hour, your hand on his chest, your body uncomfortably perched, and then you give up pretending.

When you slip away, he doesn't stir. You'll bring him a glass of water. That is doable. That is control. You walk toward the kitchen.

You hold your phone awkwardly, your thumbs ghosting over your mother's number, thinking. It is the adult thing, sometimes, to call your mother when you are kind of nauseous.

You settle for texting her. *Heard there was a storm last night by you . . . How are you?*

You get Adam his water, sneak back out of the room. Scroll Instagram mindlessly for a bit, just standing completely still in the hallway. You only notice you haven't been moving when your knee starts twitching.

Oh. You know what to do. You dial Lacey.

She picks up immediately. "Holy shit, ███, I saw. I'm legit already on my way over."

"Okay. I am gonna hop in the shower."

"I love you. I told Tanner not to expect me home. I'm comin' straight to you, baby girl."

"I love you so much, dude." You aren't going to cry. You are *not* going to cry.

You should actually call your mom. You should congratulate Lacey on how the new boyfriend seems to be a good one. You should do something. You need to do *something*.

You go take a shower.

You strip down, examine your back, trying to see your ribs through the skin. Hold your stomach in your hands, so that the pooch you've developed is separated from your abs and becomes a formed mountain. You turn around slowly, finding scrapes and acne. Maybe if you are good and finally eat less, you can become a skeleton and finally match the monster inside of you. A skeleton would look good at a wedding. A skeleton would be glamorous.

You take a long time in the shower. It feels good to take a long time. It feels very bad to take a long time.

Growing up, your family lived on the edge of a streambed. It had flooded almost every single year, and the power would go out for long periods of time.

Your father used to collect rainwater in big tubs, and you inherited the habit to keep your plants watered. It felt mature and eco-friendly, carting in big blue bins to sprinkle over your forty-eight leafy friends.

You should have pressured Adam harder into those zero-waste toilets and showers that run on next to nothing, but the truth is that you are a bad feminist and a bad environmentalist and you like the fancy shit just as much as he does.

It is bad to waste water. You turn your hands over each other, examining the way the water runs up and down your wrists.

Marlowe is getting married.

Eventually you step out of the shower and into a towel. It is still happening. Instagram is still full of congratulations to her.

Your mother hasn't texted you back. It's time to call her. Your cooling skin starts dancing again. What if she doesn't pick up. What if your mom has fallen in the darkness while your forty-year-old boyfriend was getting drunk last night. Maybe your mother knows about Marlowe and is already celebrating. Maybe your mother is dead like you will be soon. Maybe—

Mouse's heart gets too high and fast and she has to sit down or she will faint. She folds her fingers into her palms and hears her stomach gurgle with last night's fried dinner and the whole world starts spinning. The world is ending, the world is ending and we're all going to die. Is that an explosion? It was an explosion, it was right there and now the world is *ending*, fuck, you don't even *love him* and now your life is fucking *over*. Holy shit the nuclear war is here, they've open fired, there's nowhere to run, you're gonna *die here*, right now, in this fucking *horrible* bathroom, wet and naked and terrified.

Bitch! Stop drinking and you won't have anxiety attacks!

She puts her head between her knees like her mother taught her. She waits until the gurgling dies down and then finds *Mama* in her contacts and hits *Send*.

Her mother picks up.

You cough. "Hi! No, I'm okay. Just checking in, do you have a sec? Okay. Oh, before I forget—I just sprouted some lavender from that plant you gave me, and—yeah! It's doing excellent. Hey, you remember Marlowe?"

A pause.

You realize suddenly: you have never *officially* told your mother about Marlowe. She has never officially brought it up either. Your parents *did* seem happy that you got a boyfriend after, though. That might not have been about the *gay* thing, though—maybe more that Adam actually calls you his girlfriend.

"I do, yes?" She makes a sound you can't place the meaning of. ". . . How is she?"

The words *Marlowe is getting married* can be rearranged into *ad aegis egret, lim worn trim*. Is *lim* a word? *Egret*, meanwhile, is a *great* word and a very lovely bird, although you struggle to tell them apart from herons and other members of the Ardeidae family.

You do that annoying cough again. "I told you she's back from France?"

"You told me she's back from France, yes. Listen, honey, I was in the middle of—"

"Marlowe's—like, she's engaged."

"Oh." She shifts and you can practically *hear* her expression over the phone. "How are you . . . doing?"

Extremely bad! "How's the dog?"

She obviously notices your entirely unsubtle dodge. ". . . He's . . . great." The trepidation in her voice slinks its way into your heart. You hear her switch the phone to the other shoulder. "Your father tried to take him to the dog park yesterday, and he spent the whole time being annoying. Like, *screaming*. It made the other dogs howl too. They literally got kicked out. Did you know you can get kicked out of a dog park?"

"Dog park anarchy choir." You huff a breath out. "How's the job?" Then—"Wait, were there, like, dog park bouncers?"

"No dog park bouncers. But the job is good. Todd in HR just announced he's gonna be having a baby with his wife, so we threw him a little party."

"Oh, *cute*."

"Did you look into that job listing I sent you?"

You didn't. "Yeah, I'm cleaning up my résumé before I apply to it though." You're neither cleaning up your résumé nor are you going to apply to it.

"Okay, good."

"I—like I wish I could hang out with you guys more. I'm sorry I haven't been home a lot. I wish I could be there more often. Things have just been . . . really insane." They haven't been, you're just a bad daughter. Also, you really shouldn't use *insane* as a descriptor, that's casually ableist of you.

"I wish you could be here too, honey." She sounds surprised. "Don't be sorry."

"You know, I saw her, like. A few months ago."

"Her? Oh, Marlowe. Right, I remember you saying. At Adam's party."

You sniff. "I think it's the same guy she had to send text messages for."

"I can only hope his text message skills have improved in the interim."

"She could have, like—we have a group chat. The thing that literally is *for*, you know. Communicating. Like it's so fucking annoying. I don't even know why I'm surprised by it. But she could have said something. I fucking—I found out from an Instagram post."

"Oh my God, ▆▆. I'm. I'm so sorry. How are you . . . feeling?"

Egret is a word we get directly from Middle English, not from *regret*. Actually, *regret* has its origins somewhere in Middle English too, but mixed in with the old French *regreter*, which can be loosely translated to "bewail"—used mostly in terms of loudly mourning the already-dead.

You pick your thumbnail off. "Do you think they have to list the cat in the prenup? Toothpaste, I mean. If he's still alive, I guess."

"Pets are listed in prenups, yes," your mother says. "Why do you think they'll need one? Isn't she Christian?"

"It's *fast*, right? She can't have been dating this dude for more than a year or so."

She makes another noise you can't place. "Well, you know how it goes." She sighs. "Some people rush into things."

It's probably cheating to use Latin *ad aegis* in one of your anagrams. You don't like that you could make the word *eel* in there, but you don't know why. You want to keep *egret*, it sounds nice. It bounces around your head in a spiked dust bunny.

You check the time. "Oh fuck. Mama, I gotta go. I have to go get dressed, Lacey's coming over."

"Oh, that's fun."

"We're going to get *rip* drunk," you report cheerily.

"Oh honey," she sighs. "Please be careful. You only have one liver."

You both say goodbye-I-love-you. You stare at your phone for an extra few minutes, completely forgetting what you had wanted to start doing. You don't really want to clean, but you should make sure your underwear isn't, like, everywhere. *Oh.* You need to put clothes on first. Okay, so.

You choose something baggy at first, but then hate how it makes you look, so you switch to a tan turtleneck and black A-line skirt. You don't want to look nice; you want to cry. You *need* to look nice, or you *will* cry.

Once you've slapped on makeup and clothes, you start your examination of the mess from the night before. Thanks to Adam, the house is trashed. You're glad you locked the liquor cabinet around midnight. It didn't matter, he just went through the other off-limits-to-you wine cellar. (In Adam's defense, you'd have emptied it easily). You feel bad for the housekeeping staff. None of them actually deserve this. You know a good deal of them now, and they're all pleasant to you, if awkward. You are terrified they will think Adam's mess is *your* mess, so you tend to keep your things extremely tidy. You would rather die than be associated with the way he treats them.

You water your plants, at least. Staring long at their leaves when really you are staring-hard-at-nothing. You run a soft cloth over the palm fronds. To your knowledge, none of your plants have become carnivores yet.

When there's nothing else to do, you go wait for Lacey in the kitchen. You google it. The difference between herons and egrets is mostly their size and the color of their legs—egrets tend to have black legs, while herons will have lighter ones.

"There you are." Lacey is twirling her keys when you rescue her from wandering the driveway, looking for the front door. "I get lost finding this place every time."

You hug her too long to be casual. "Are you hungry? I think there's leftovers."

She declines, but you arrange a plate for Adam, just in case he's ever awake and living again. You stare at the Tupperware container and think about taking some breakfast for yourself, but hate the notion of eating alone.

Lacey looks at you with a frown. "Wait. Are *you* hungry? Did you eat yet?" It isn't clear to you what this means—if you've been eating too much or too little. Either suggestion makes you uncomfortable.

"Adam, like, actually tried to party on a Wednesday. I was, like, doing paperwork in bed. They drank *wine mixed with gin,* Lace'. Hello?"

"Is he like, okay?

"I don't know. Last I saw him he was asleep downstairs. I think he started drinking at ten in the morning yesterday. And I saw him take a shot at fucking *three-thirty a-fucking-m.*"

"Like? After drinking *wine?*" She gags. "The very notion of a shot just, like, lays waste to my entire gut bacteria. I literally hear them screaming."

"Me too. Can you believe he's *forty?*"

"We're about to take a shot, right?"

"Yes, obviously." You pour her one immediately, shoot it with her, gag, and then lead her through the rooms and all the wasted spaces. You sit her down in your greenhouse. "Do you care if I, like, go bring him his food? I don't want him to, like, die."

"No, let him starve. You and I will stay here and build a fort and take over the house and build an anti-man society."

"Don't tempt me Lace'. Because honestly . . . ?" You leave the rest unsaid because it is obvious, and then go take the plate to your boyfriend. Back up one flight of stairs and down two more. It kind of smells like mildew down here, but in a weirdly crisp way. You put the food on the floor next to him.

You push back his hair again, humming. "Hi, baby. You need to eat. It'll help."

He peeks one eye up at you, snarls, turns over and goes back to sleep.

Well, okay. Problem solved.

When you find her again, Lacey has wandered into the backyard. She shades her eyes against the sun and smiles at you. "Do you have a sweater that I could borrow? It's colder than I expected."

"I have something but it's dirty? I don't have, like, a lot of clothes here anymore."

She raises an eyebrow. "Haven't y'all been dating for, like, ever?

"He's got, like, a super-fast washer and dryer so I just . . . clean what I need? I don't know." You sit down on his marble steps. She sits next to you.

"Fuck. I thought she'd, like, be the last of us to stay single." She sighs into her hands, rubbing her arms to keep warm.

"I legitimately cannot understand how neither of us won *that* race."

"It's God's punishment for having a body that simply will not quit." She looks up to the house. "And *don't* think that I don't know it's fucking ironic that the queen of noncommitment is the first one wed."

"It's like. A dramatic irony though, to be honest."

"I can't believe she didn't tell either of us. I want to be like. She's dead to me. But I'm tryna, like, get my karma right. I'm not supposed to wish death on anybody." She frowns. "I'm telling everyone I know that we don't talk anymore because she thinks aliens abducted her."

Spooked, you check to be sure your antennae are tucked away.

"Okay, say more."

"Like about aliens?"

"Like, tentacle aliens, or, like, friendly meep-meep aliens?"

She snorts down her nose. "Hang on, wait. Do you think aliens say *meep-meep?* Like the fuckin'—*Looney Tunes* bird?"

"Oh, I meant the Martian from the *Looney Tunes*, huh?"

"Road Runner."

You pick a piece of glass out of the rosebushes. "See that is a good point though, because she, like, *absolutely* has get-kidnapped-by-an-alien vibes. Like *that* makes sense for her."

"She *does* though. Like, I'm glad *you* said it, because, like, she *does*."

You chuck the glass further into the bushes. It would be nice to be reborn as a bird, but if you ever came back, it wouldn't be something so graceful as a heron. You'd come back wrong, and they'd have to stake you through your heart.

Lacey shivers and then shakes her head, splaying her fingers. "Okay. Let's just rewind for a second. Like, just for a second. So, first: she breaks your heart."

"Uh, ouch?"

She barrels on. "*Then* she comes back from France without saying anything."

"Well, she says *something*, but it's to the rest of the internet first."

Lacey points to you. "Exactly."

"We love a considerate queen."

"So after very casually ignoring you, she meets *us* in a mall. Where, *let* it be known: she proceeds to *ditch us* in order to *text for her boyfriend*."

You laugh and raise a finger. "Slight correction: to *assist* in her boyfriend's texting."

She nods solemnly and rests her hands on your bicep. "Objection noted and accepted. It was a matter of *assistance*."

"Do we think she went home to take it up the ass?"

Lacey gives you a dark look. "Don't be stupid. Of fuckin' course she did. Have you ever met her. She took it up the ass *hard.*"

"Ah. You know? You're right. Continue."

"Where am I?" She splays her fingers, tilting her head.

You squint at the horizon, walking the conversation backward in your head. "Oh. She leaves the mall."

Lacey nods sharply. "*The mall.* Yes. Okay. So. You don't get a single fucking apology. No mention about how shitty she's been. And then— literally by sheer fucking *happenstance*—you see her at Adam's birthday party, where she is pretending to be a *literal psychic.*"

"She did also send that one weird text saying she had something important to tell me and then never fucking told m—wait fuck, *Lacey.* What if *this* is what she wanted to say?"

"It better fucking *not* be, because she had *plenty* of opportunities!"

"This is so fucking like her."

"Mind you, at the party—all of a sudden, she loves you again! She sends this fucking cryptic-ass text so that you're roped back in again to her *bullshit.* And doesn't. In that whole time. Fucking tell *either* of us. That she's thinking about marrying this dude."

"Right. Literally at the party—all of a sudden, we're *best friends* again." You snort. "All that shit about *you're my favorite person.*"

Lacey lets out a groan. "Oh, my god. I am *still* not over the fucking *favorite person* speech, don't even fucking talk to me about it, I will fucking *kill her.*"

You and Lacey have rehashed the birthday party experience enough that Lacey actually might remember it more reliably than you do. You both quote *something let go inside me* at each other in inappropriate settings.

You huff a breath into your hands. "She's playing with me, right? Like we can both agree she's playing with me?"

Lacey looks ready to fight, her scowl deep. "Okay, at this point? I hate this girl. I'm just gonna say it. I hate this girl."

You shouldn't have chucked the glass. The roses don't deserve that. You sigh, deflate pretty much immediately. "Like, I'm fine." At her look, you sigh again. "I'm just confused. I mean—where has she fucking *been* this whole time? What could she *possibly* be doing?"

"Being an absolute whore, evidently."

You scoff a laugh. Your cheeks warm in the bad way—you're close to crying. Or you're tipsy. Oops. "Did you know—like, recently, I learned seahorses are mostly bones? How fucked up is that?"

"You love a fucked-up little animal fact."

"Can I be an asshole? Like can I be rude?"

She barks a laugh. "God, *please* do."

"I was a fucking *prize* of a partner, dude. There is *no world* in which she's doing better than me. Like this dude *cannot* be all that."

"Do you want another drink? Like, are we getting drunk? Am I driving you back to your apartment to get drunk *there?* What's, like, the situation." At your look, she points to you again, scolding. "I am *going* to take care of you, and if you try to get out of it, I will literally kill you. Karma be damned."

You shrug. "Do you wanna order brunch or something at least?" Wait, fuck. Why are you offering to eat?

"Yes? Absolutely? You're close to that little waffle place around here, right?" She stands up and brushes her legs off. "Is there anything on my ass? Can you check?"

"Yeah, hang on, you got a leaf." You tug it off, pinching it between your fingers. "I think the waffle place got, like, health coded. But we can check."

"Okay, did you hear the seahorse thing on *Radiolab?* Because now that you say it, I remember hearing something like that."

"Maybe? I've been listening to like, a lot of podcasts lately." No, actually. You learned it on Twitter.

Lacey's wearing a satin, pink blouse. It's nice. She didn't used to wear a lot of pink. You think of who she was at fourteen and then think of who *you* were at fourteen and cringe. At least when you got out, you took her with you. "Hey, how're your parents? Did they get the house?"

She rolls her eyes and takes your offered hand. You both pick across the perfect marble steps, wading through booze cans. "You know they could have? But my father said there was too much light pollution."

"The man is rabid about his telescopes." You hold the French doors for her.

"How's your mom?"

"Same, basically. She's been watching reruns of *Murder, She Wrote,* and now thinks I can write the next great American murder mystery. It's like, cute?"

"I mean it's absolutely cute but—correct me if I'm wrong—you write fantasy."

You pick up the bottle. There was a time where you didn't have an opinion on fancy alcohol. In private, it all just tastes like a bathroom. Not that you'd ever admit it, even to Lacey. Now you say things like *smooth.* Thanks, Adam. "To be fair? It could be a mystery and have, like, lasers in it."

You grab two water glasses from the kitchen and then pour two silver margaritas, heavy on the tequila.

She holds it with a strange look on her face. "Okay, we can drink, but, like . . . should we wake up Adam or something?" Her eyes briefly narrow. "How . . . are you guys? Um, sorry if this is weird but . . . Why isn't he here for this?"

You freeze. Bottle in your hand, you feel duplicitous. You wonder, wildly—*is that a hint?* But what would she even be hinting? You've told nobody what's happening.

She shrugs. Knocks back a quick gulp. "Nevermind, fuck men."
Her smile is stunning. "And fuck Marlowe too."

Your hands shake putting the cap back on the tequila. You
shouldn't really drink on an empty stomach, but who's watching.

She comes over and rests her head on your shoulder, humming. "I
miss you."

"I miss *you*." You think about pouring grenadine into your drink,
but it's not worth the extra calories. You lead her to the hidden bench,
tucked between peace lilies. "Sorry work has been crazy lately." Mostly
you spend your weekdays with Adam, and then you're too tired to
drive all the way back home, much less out to where she is.

"Literally not a problem. Tanner is, like, working on this big
promotion, so I'm usually running around making dinner and things."

"Wait, that's super exciting. I know he was working for that; I'm
really glad it's going well." You pick up a piece of champagne wrapper
from the velvet couch cushion and push a glass table over so you both
have somewhere to put your glasses and sit. You drag a bowl of fruit
in front of her, only to immediately realize you have no idea how long
they've been sitting out here. They might be rotted.

"I mean, at least you can go to the wedding with Adam, though,
right?" She settles herself on the floor, so you follow by her side, bottle
of silver between you.

You flinch at the idea there's going to be a *wedding*. And you don't
even want to *think* about asking him to come with you. You couldn't
handle the dual rejections. Or worse, he'd say yes and forget. "Yeah,
right? Like, at least I'm seeing someone."

"And that someone is *rich*."

"And he's rich." You splash more tequila into your drink.

She reaches over and picks up a piece of your hair. "You like
him, right?"

"I super like him." The words hang flat in the air.

She looks over her shoulder. "Does he have work today?"

"Nah." He only works when he wants to, which is rarely. "He's just downstairs, recovering. He don't feel good."

"Oh." She pulls out her phone.

"What, *oh?*"

Lacey doesn't look up. "No, I just. Like. This is a big deal to you, right?"

"Okay, to be fair, it shouldn't be."

Lacey texts something to Tanner. "I guess, I mean—it's like cool he's letting us have girl time, I mean." She finally squints up at you. "So just us for waffles?"

Mouse closes her eyes.

there is a restless buzzing that has come up over everything. no matter where you rest, you cannot find comfort. humming blood termites. like a sleeping limb, but somewhere too internal. static, or electric cotton.

you try working out more. you try more protein. maybe your soul needs some kind of professional rug cleaning.

everything feels fake. the days melting like glass, a gray slurry. in and out and in and out. so often you wake up with an annoying chime in your brain—*every day, the same day.*

ocd is a bad friend, but it's trying to protect you, at least. listen closer. it was a bad day today, so you must establish a new rule about what you have discovered—no more oat milk in your coffee, you drink it black now. you put too much salsa on your plate and that's why your cat died. you wore the wrong socks today and that's why it always hurts during sex.

if you want to keep drinking, you need to stop eating, and you *need* to keep drinking. if you want to keep any of the friends you have left, you're not allowed to wear yellow anymore, ever, even if Adam approves. if you want your family to live, you need to shut up and turn over and let him you.

even Mouse starts getting frantic, her rabid claws scratching away inside your ribs.

you read once that rats will chew their way out of a body. lucky enough for you, she's an alien, not a rat.

but even she can't work under these conditions. life without desire is a synonym for grieving.

◇

you have been convinced for a long time that anything born of this Body would not be worth saving. apologetic, you skirt your own cartilage, betray the night to seduce the day.

you've convinced yourself humanity is circumstantial.

fool's gold, you stand perfectly still in the headlights. they'll think you are a deer here, a rabbit; mistake the smell of the woods for panic. if you remove your canine teeth, the howl will fade; the mist that yearns over your life finally will dissipate. talk about *manifesting*. stretch out your roadkill frame, adjust the dress of your ghost. if you paint over the debris with riot colors and a laugh—they will mistake the shattered glass for snow. if you are rapturously perfect and pray the right way and kneel with a bruised body and lay your lamb neck down: you can finally glint into God's eyes, captivating. all the elegy of your life would rewrite into an aria. they will miss the fact you are a horror movie. when a monster suffers, that is heroic. now your gore is actually an altar.

if you would only be careful, and perfect, and pretty: you could be delightful. even better: you could be capable of *feeling* delight.

high cost, but whatever. that's what you want, right.
your body is a strange animal in the angel-hair light.
look at your hand. look at the sun. look at yourself.
is this it? is this it?
we sat down, and sorrow won?

◇

you mull over your shitty phone while curled up in his fancy bed. the
idea just arrives, as if it had been sitting in the cabinet of your mind
for a very long time.

"i think," you say to him. "i'm gonna stop drinking."

when you look up, he's watching you. standing awkwardly in the
doorway with two glasses in his hand. he had poured you a whiskey on
the rocks—a gesture that's oddly endearing, to have done it without
your asking.

the look on his face has a twisted, strange cast to it. almost grief,
almost confusion. he carries the glasses out of the room and comes
back, hands empty. drapes his arm around you. he smells like sweat
and pine needles.

oh. he's a complete stranger to you.

"He's upset I'm gonna watch the cat while they're on vacation."

Lacey rolls her eyes. You're helping her push a rusty cart though
IKEA. You're only excited for the plant section and have been causing
chaos in the meantime. She is gently preventing you from injury while
she works through the first half of her list. You're folded over the top
half of the cart, seeing how much of your weight you can put on it
before it tips toward you.

She spins a desk chair, consulting her notes. "He's upset . . . *Still?*"

"Well, he's allergic."

"You're allergic too."

"I wasn't like, always allergic." The cart tips and you flinch when it slams back down onto the concrete. You leave it to go spin chairs with her, throwing yourself into a high-backed black leather one that has less torque than you'd hoped. "But yeah. He's like—*you can't bring the cat.*"

"To your own apartment?"

"He's like—*oh, you're gonna keep the cat once you have it, and then it won't live at yours, you'll bring it to mine*, blah blah blah."

"Is he, like, does he think he can, like, stop you? Oh, this one is nice."

"Let me see." You swivel. "For the living room?"

"Office."

"*Oh, look at me, I'm Lacey, I have an office, I'm rich now.*" You grin through your bad impression; she snorts and rolls her eyes again.

"I'm not rich. I just hate doing my work at the tabl—"

You wave at her. "Oh, no, I get it. But how about this here puce one?"

She wrinkles her nose. "Oh God no."

"It's heinous, I hate it, please buy it."

"At some point I'm gonna put tranquilizer in a little dart and just take you out in one swift move." She mimes the action, which looks more like strangling you.

"Anyway, so I'm like, my parents are going out of town. Nobody else can take care of the cat. And this is *my* cat, I've—"

"Haven't you had him since you were, like, in the eighth grade?"

"*Exactly.* I grew up with this little dude, who is the most perfect little Siamese joy of my life, like *never* scratches, *always* purring—"

She's nodding, sorting through office décor. "Right, he's literally the perfect cat, so—"

"And then this little bitch says—get this—it—and I'm *quoting Adam directly*, Lacey—it, quote, *'creeps him out'* that we named the cat Dave."

"Shut up." She puts down a painting. "No, he did not. *Why?*"

You nod violently and push yourself around in a circle again. "I shit you not."

"Is he fucking—like does he think he *owns* you?"

"He thinks he owns me." Somewhat literally.

"Dude, he can fuck off. You fucking love Dave. *I* love Dave, and I don't even like cats. What the fuck."

"So I tell him, like, it's *my* cat, I'm gonna just keep him in my apartment for the month, it's not a big deal. I, like, did all the planning for it; Kaisa's on board and super excited, I'll be on allergy meds the whole time, it'll be fine. I mean, Lace', I moved my *plants* in preparation for this. Do you know how long that took?"

"Right. Yikes."

"I will say? The plants do *not* fit in the apartment."

"Does Kaisa like them?"

"Oh, they're delighted. They think it's, like, homey now." You actually secretly love it too. "But it's *dangerously* close to a Rainforest Cafe."

"Your first panic attack was in a Rainforest Cafe."

"This is true." Your horror had been witnessed by a faux silverback gorilla, his button eyes unblinking. "Anyway, so *then* Adam goes on about how I'm *obviously* like—again, *direct quote*—'manipulating' him, because I *clearly* hope that *he'll* offer to take Dave, just so I have more room for the cat to be in. And that *he'll* end up taking care of the cat, etcetera, etcetera."

She rolls her eyes. "Where the fuck is this even *coming from?*" She takes a picture of a tag with her phone, and you have to scurry to keep up as she moves into the dining section.

"Where *is* this coming from! I legit handle every—anyway. So I'm like—literally, this cat is so old, he's staying with me. I don't feel comfortable taking him to a boarder or a different house or anything. My place at least smells like me. He's gonna be super upset about being moved. I do not know how to say this more clearly. The cat. Is staying. With *me*."

"What am I not understanding about this? What is his fucking problem?"

"Your guess is as good as mine." You drum your knuckles against the table she's reading the tag of. "How big is your new space?"

"Well, Tanner picked it out, but it's honestly too big for me. It's got, like, three extra rooms."

"In the city?"

She flutters her eyelashes at you. "You think you're the only person alive to date someone who makes money?" She winks, but you drop her gaze, weirdly embarrassed. She runs her hands over the tabletop. "We can afford it, but I'm like—what do I need this for? It's honestly kind of, like, pointless."

"Right, but you'll, like, use the space. Like, that kind of thing always ends up being kind of helpful."

She hums neutrally and takes a picture of the tag, following your action and drumming the table too. "Is this ugly?"

"I kinda think all tables are ugly?"

"Remember my grandma's table?"

"Okay, not that table."

"Well, my grandfather made it for her," she says, which she probably knows that *you* know, like how *she* knows about the Rainforest Cafe. You like the table story, actually, but she doesn't tell it. She twists her lips and glances at you. "So . . . What are you gonna do?"

"I mean, I'm taking my fucking cat home."

She nods once, sharply. "Exactly. Fucking *good* for you."

"Thank you." You put your hand to your chest and bow your head like you're an opera singer accepting flowers. "Okay, so. But get this. Like. We've had this *huge* argument. And, like, the plans are all made. Some of them can be considered spite-plans, but that's beside the point. I have the meds, the space—my roommate can watch Dave if I need her to."

"Literally perfect. So, like. *Good* for you. Actually, like, how *is* Kaisa?" Lacey's voice is high. From experience you know it is her best impression of asking casually.

You grin. "Kaisa is good. She's been single for a little bit, you know."

"Oh?" Her squeak makes her laugh at herself. "She's just, like, so cool—I don't know, it's just surprising."

You should be a better friend to Kaisa. You pretty much know nothing about them. "I think she just got out of something rough, to be honest. She's, like, taking time off from dating for a little bit."

"Yeah, honestly, that's pretty smart of her."

Kaisa is always doing something smart. And cool. And interesting. Wait, are you jealous of her?

"Is she, like, okay?" Laccy doesn't usually ask this many follow-up questions. She flips you off at your shit-eating expression. "What? Don't look at me like that. I'm just like, like, I'm just like—it's hard! Like, to get out of something—hard. Like, I'm just concerned for her. I know I'd want my friend to be out of—oh my God, stop smiling like that. I'll kill you."

"Remember how, like, five times in a *row* you made out with her in a closet when you came to visit me at college?"

"Oh my God. Listen, she's *pretty*. Also, it wasn't always a *closet*."

"But yeah, she's fine. Or, like, she's getting better."

"That's really good to hear." Lacey genuinely looks relieved, because she's a better person than you are, and cares about things like that. She cuts her eyes up to you, and then down to her hand. She takes a deep breath. "It always makes me so scared to hear about stuff like that, like—I never know how to help, and I'm obviously the type to try but . . . You know, when your friend is stuck in a bad thing, you just kind of have to just, like, be there for her as much as you can, and hope she gets through it."

The shift in tone has unseated you. You don't know how to answer that. Fuck. You *should* have helped. You stare at the lighting department's spinning globe arrangements. "God, I love that freaky little one with the orange."

She takes your hand for a second and you both watch the thing twisting. "I am really sorry to hear that about Kaisa."

"You would be," you joke, but it comes off annoying and cruel. You regret it immediately. You are coated in shame. Why *didn't* you help her? Why didn't you notice? Why didn't you say anything?

"Stuff like that always makes me . . . think." She takes a deep breath. "Like, what kind of relationship am *I* in, am I safe to leave, what do I think I could take with me? What am I getting out of, like, staying. Like, it's good to—ask myself these things. Like. I know—like, if anything happens, you'd be there for me."

"I'd kill Tanner in his sleep."

She doesn't laugh. She squeezes your arm. "I wish I could . . . that I could have helped her. Just let her know—like—it's okay. Lots of people love her. She didn't have to, like . . . stay with someone who was hurting her."

Her voice trails off into a murmur. She has barely looked up at you, but she's completely right, even if she hasn't been accusing you. You should really, really be a better friend to Kaisa. You are *so* fucking selfish. You had been too focused on Adam. Are you a narcissist?

You aren't sure you really understand where this seriousness is coming from. It makes your skin crawl. "Yeah, it's nice to see her doing better. And, like, I think. She's really . . . strong. Or, like, she takes things . . . in her own way."

Lacey doesn't even seem to notice she's changed the tone of the conversation. She squeezes your arm again and then picks back up her list. You cross your eyes at the lighting department, trying to get the bulbs to switch over each other and trade places.

Lacey clears her throat. "Yeah, I remember her being, like, pretty, like—"

You need to clear the tension, aim a cheap joke. "Yes, we know they're pretty, Lace'." You wink, she laughs awkwardly. You lean into the joke, pretend to make out with a plate. "Oh Kaisa, you're so pretty."

"Oh my God." She laughs for real now, picks up a plastic lemon and mimes lobbing it at you. You flinch, which both of you pretend not to see. "I meant, like, she's pretty—no, stop—*intentional*," she says to the lemon. She puts it back down among the dusty grapes and limes.

"Ooh, *intentional*." You waggle your eyebrows.

"Do you want to die? Is this, like, where you want to die? In an IKEA?"

"I mean, my body has no resale value, but I do find comfort in the idea that someone will try to rehome me as a set piece of their smorgen-dorfen-klienin."

"You do know, like, Swedish is a real language, right?"

You shrug. "Anyway, but, so—" You clear your throat. "Back to Dave, right?"

"Oh my God, there's more?" She starts walking again, and you follow her.

"There's more," you nod.

She stops in her tracks and pins you with a look. "There better not be, I'm *already* homicidal." She looks back down at her phone. "And, like, what else *could* there be? You said you were taking your cat, it's not his fucking problem."

"One would *think!*"

Lacey groans in response, gritting her teeth at you. She takes a seat at a kitchen island, and you lean across it to talk to her.

"Hold on because it gets *worse.*"

She points at you. "I'm holdin' on, but I need you to understand that if you continue, you *will* be an accessory to murder."

"You know? It's an interesting Marxist approach to share the blame of a murder." You tilt your head to the side. "Can I redo that joke and say Agatha Christie instead?"

"Everyone knows Agatha Christie and Karl Marx are the same person."

"I mean. *Have* you seen them in the same room?"

Lacey darts her eyes around suspiciously and holds up her hands. "To the NSA in my phone: I just want to say, for the record, I am not sure that crowdsourced murder is the correct usage of the term *Marxism.* And! I do *not* believe Agatha Christie is Karl Marx. For the record." Then she mouths at you: *they're the same person.*

You laugh, messing with the fake faucet. You wonder what mirror Marx and Christie would have to switch through. "Anyway, *so.* To recap."

She cartwheels her hand to say *go ahead.*

"When we last spoke with our subjects: my parents are going on a trip they've planned to do since forever. Even though I have allergies, I have decided I will take my cat for the time they are gone. I have told my—" You stutter over *boyfriend,* choose a different word, "I've told Adam that while it might shift things for a little bit, I should spend more time at my apartment while babysitting Dave."

Lacey nods. She is reading the tag on the granite countertop. "Which is completely fucking normal."

"He tells *me*—"

"Right, this is all a ruse to import Dave into *his* house, somehow."

"Exactly. *So.*" Now it's your turn to pin her with the Look. "I'm, like, maybe he, like, just feels weird about how it's gonna be, like, a month. And to be fair to him, it's kind of different from how we've ever been in the relationship. Maybe he's just lashing out."

Laccy gives a side-to-side head tilt *maybe*. She gets up and starts messing around in drawers, pulling them open and closed. "I mean . . . okay?"

"But then, get this." You hold up a finger. "Adam *calls my parents.* Like to talk to them about not giving me the cat. And he tells them, like, how this is probably just another thing for him to worry about, how I'm always fucking depressed and suicidal, blah, blah, blah. He says, '*She has no self-control.*'"

"Sorry—*what?* And . . . *what?*" At your *uh-huh, right?!* nod, she grits her teeth again. "I will kill him." The way she says this is not the way she has said it before. She says it like a promise.

"Okay to be fair it is, like, *objectively true* that I'm depressed and suicidal. But I mean, I'm fuckin' *trying,* I've actively been looking for a therapist." You won't make eye contact with her, wandering in her wake while you both navigate to the next showroom. "But yeah, I'm just, like reeling. First of all, don't fucking talk to my parents behind my back. Secondly. Like. With my fucking *laundry list* of mental illnesses, he just goes and adds like—oh, also? No self-control."

"This is fucked up, dude. It's not even fucking—like it's not *true,* you have, like, an actually *insane* amount of self-control."

not to call semantics, but it *is* true. you're not even really yourself, so it's hard to have self-control, since i'm not there to do the controlling. thanks, mouse.

You clear your throat. "Anyway, so it just got too wild after that. So I went home, you know, ate ice cream, stomped around. And a few days later I called my mom." You lean closer to her, unable to stop the grin on your face. "And get this—before he had even called, they had canceled the vacation."

She frowns, turns to you slowly. "Wait. *The* vacation? Their two-years-in-the-works trip-around Europe? They . . . canceled?"

"They. Canceled."

"Wait. Hang on. So you don't even have to watch Dave. Like . . . no cat?"

"No cat."

"Okay actually?" She pauses, her nose scrunched. "I'm sorry but that's kind of funny."

"Okay *thank you.* I told Kaisa about it and she was like—*oh I'm so sorry.*"

"Well, they're nice, I'm evil." Lacey winks at you. You wink back. She winks back twice. You wink back three times, she winks four. You fuck up the fifth and just blink, you both laugh.

She sighs. "It kinda sucks about your parents, though."

"My mom was so excited, dude."

"Oh, don't, I'll actually cry, I love your mom."

You love your mom too. You help Lacey put a lamp into the cart and she takes a picture of two more tags. Her list is still so long, and she always seems to just pick up what she wants, not what she can afford. You're saving up to buy another monstera plant. You play with the taps on an empty sink, playacting doing the dishes.

She sends you a quick look. "Okay. I have a bad idea. But you know what you should do?" She angles her phone at another table. "Hang out with Marlowe."

You drop your imaginary plates. Lacey doesn't look up. She had better be pretending to be that interested in the grain pattern, because you want to bite her. "I don't even—I couldn't—like I—where could I even, like—"

"I could come if you're nervous," she offers.

"I'm not nervous."

"You sound nervous."

"I haven't actually spoken to her in, like, years. Like, the party was the closest we got."

Lacey shrugs. "I saw her comment a few times on your posts."

"I'm not gonna *block* her, I just don't *talk* to her."

"Hear me out." She turns a large glass jar around in her hands. "We go to yours—or mine, or whatever—we hang out." She shrugs again and pitches her voice upward. "It's, like, I *kinda* maybe . . . wanna know how bad her life is. Maybe. A little."

"You just want to see Kaisa."

"She—I—no, okay, don't look at me like that. I am suggesting— *stop oh my God*—seeing Marlowe because I just . . . *maybe* want to see if karma actually caught *up* with her. And I think, like, if Kaisa is just getting out of something scary, actually it *would* be good to invite them, just to, like, give them something to do. I—*stop!* Okay. But— no, for real, Marlowe owes you. Like, if she's even, like, a *little* sorry for eating your heart and being like *oh no! Commitment! I'm allergic! I'm dying!* Only to immediately get married. She needs to see you're fucking *powerful.* Unbothered. Happy."

You open your phone again. No messages from Adam.

There is a very quiet puppet show happening inside of you, and the mallet keeps coming down, and the audience keeps laughing. Are you behind glass? Can you feel this?

"Okay." You mumble it into your collar.

"Wait, actually?"

"Okay, listen, try not to be so fucking victorious about it, I mean—"

"You just, like, agreed to that so *fast?* I thought I'd be arguing with you for, like, at least a minute."

"You have to come, though."

"I'm busy."

"You promised and I'll fucking kill you. Please come. Lacey—"

She laughs. "Oh my God, do you know me? I'm *going* to be there."

At the still-blanched look on your face, she counts out on her fingers:

"I'm there to *drink*. I'm there to *support you*. I'm there for the *drama*."

Your shoulders relax. "You just want to kiss Kaisa again."

"Oh, you and *I* are going to make out, I want to make Marlowe jealous."

You laugh, blow her a kiss, and then try juggling some plastic limes only to drop them. You chew your lip. Chew your collar. Chew your nails. "Okay. Before I do this. Will you actually come?"

"I'll actually come."

"Okay, pinky promise."

She knows the drill. You both loop pinky fingers and kiss your fists at the same time. "If you're lying, I'll cut off your pinky finger," you warn her.

"It's not even my favorite finger. You should use my middle one next time."

"Alright, Hot Topic." You pull out your phone. "You know what? Fuck it. I'll text her."

"Oh my God. You're actually doing it?"

Your fingers pause over the text. "Okay, so I've said—*Hi, Marlowe! It was nice seeing you the other day. I was thinking of having a little get-together to celebrate*—fuck, I don't have anything to celebrate."

"*You* don't." She politely doesn't say the rest: *but* she's *getting married*. "Did you use an exclamation mark after the *Hi, Marlowe*?"

"Yeah, is that too much?"

"It's fine as long as you use two or more. It's more, like, personal."

"Okay hang on." You click back up. "Exclamation, exclamation,

exclamation . . . flower emoji, rainbow emoji. I could slap like a tiger or a crown in there to make it really incomprehensible."

"Perfect, continue."

You hover your thumbs for a moment, chewing your lips. "Okay. *It was nice seeing you the other day. I was thinking of having a little get-together at my place while the weather is still good. Would you want to swing through?*"

"Nice. Casual but friendly."

"The weather makes no sense as being a factor, but whatever."

"I mean, it's fine."

"Okay, send it?"

"Send it."

You send it, squeak, drop your phone into the cart. "Oh my God." Your heart is strangely fast. "Okay. That was bad, right? Maybe I can unsend it?" You reach for the phone, but Lacey slaps your hands.

"Help me find cutlery."

"That's on the bottom floor."

"Really? Huh." She makes a mark on her list.

Your phone buzzes. You both look at each other.

From Marlowe: *ABSOLUTELY.*

From Marlowe: *It was so, so good to see you too, Depot. Missing you badly.*

A horror story: you wait with your body shaking outside the car door. In this movie, you are a ghost. You are never given a speaking role.

He rolls his window down and asks you which way you're going. Stick your hand into his throat and pull out the vocal cords and shove them into your body.

There is something so beautiful about finally giving in and letting yourself be ugly.

◇

You stand in your tiny bathroom with seven candles burning because you don't like the numbers six or eight. It is supposed to smell like fall in here, but you can only afford candles from the clearance aisle, so it's more like a muddy apple crisp. Your music plays over a shitty USB speaker.

You rearrange the decorations on the wall again, and then start on rearranging your tiny guest basket where you keep extra tampons and hand lotion and soap. Fancy-looking shit. "This was a mistake, huh? I'm an adult, I can say this is a mistake. It's a mistake."

"Oh, absolutely. When I suggested this, I legitimately was joking." Lacey is a little tipsy already. She has a small smudge on her chin, and she tilts her head toward the light while you fix it for her. "This is going to be a shit show. We heard she was getting married, and we thought—*golly! We should text her so we can hang literally only a month later.*" She holds up a finger. "*Which* . . . is why you should start drinking more. I want neither of us able to stand." She dips a tissue in micellar water and goes after the smudge too. "When is she coming?"

You kiss her with a *smack!* sound, pronounce her free of smudge, and then look at your phone. Missed messages from Adam: zero. Who the fuck cares. Fuck this dude.

Messages from Kaisa: three. They are all sweet, which makes you not want to answer them, because you are not sweet. She's working until later in the evening, but she was so surprised and happy when you asked her to join—*Oh! That sounds really cute and lovely.*

From Marlowe: *Hi bb. Leaving now <3*

Just stopped to get mixer/vods/tequila etc. Want anything?

"She says she's at the liquor store." You scroll up. "Like probably between fifteen minutes and half an hour?"

"She's only picking up liquor *now?*" Lacey rolls her eyes. "This is why we didn't invite her to dinner."

You text back: *Omg. ty ily. We have spite & vodka here if u want that.* Then immediately: *Fuck lol *sprite and vodka.*

From her, immediately: *No, we got spite too fuck capitalism let's goooo*

Her: *lol*

Her: *okay im gonna get some stuff for sunrises.*

Her: *whosssss else is be there so I get enough*

You: *Just Lacey & maybe my roommate Kaisa later lol not much of a parrttyyyyy but we old out here*

Her: *I LOVE LACEY!!!!! OMFFGGGGGGGGGGGG. And omg I totally forgot about Kaisa!!!!! Wow!!!! Can't believe y'all are still roommates.*

Her: *Oh we getting LITTTTTYYYYYY 2NITE!!!*

Her: *Okay checking out now I'm so excited y'all.*

You pose in the bathroom mirror, which is nicely and purposefully warped to make you look tall and thin. It takes you seven embarrassing minutes of sucking in before you give up and change poses to be less in-frame. You hesitate before you send Adam the result. Bra courtesy of bargain bin at Victoria's Secret, body courtesy of expert photo manipulation, panties from, what . . . Walmart?

"I've been thinking a lot about gargoyles," you say, apropos of nothing.

"Ah. Is that this week's current monster lore obsession?" Lacey peeks in at you, wrapping herself around the doorframe. "Come do my makeup?"

At your gleeful nod, she pads into the room with you, helping you into your tight little dress. You hate how you look in this one. It's so obvious that your weight distributes in weird ways. You're gonna have to change. The problem is that you can change only a certain number of times, or Lacey will get worried. The *other* problem is that no matter what you wear, it's gonna be you, in a dress, trying to look nice. Stupidhead.

You kiss her hand for the effort and then follow her back into your room. "But yeah. Something about stone angels and gargoyles. Like, these things we make to watch over us, carved *into* buildings. It just *gets* to me." You pinch your free hand together in a mock chef's kiss motion for emphasis and then take a swig of your drink. "What kind of a look were you feeling?" You gesture to your face to signal *for the makeup.*

Surely *something* you own isn't fucking heinous on your frame. Someone would have told you if you dressed badly *every* day, right?

"Stone angels and stuff like that always remind me of that *Doctor Who* episode." She pulls out her phone. "Hang on, I had reference pictures for the makeup. Lemme look."

You're so fucking sick of your closet. Half of these clothes should be donated anyway; the other half are just work-related. Did you ever actually have a personality? All your "nightlife" clothes are from when you were, like, nineteen. It's embarrassing. But how are you gonna come up with a new wardrobe? You don't have the money.

You wish you'd thought to get a new outfit for this, but that would have been actually trying. You are not supposed to be actually trying.

"I really hate what they did with that whole weeping angel plotline," you tell her over your shoulder. You push your stupid clothes around listlessly and then go to make the music louder, putting on a playlist you specifically made to get drunk to.

She takes a huge pull from her drink. "*Don't* even talk to me about it. Do not. You *know* I will get upset."

You aren't done with your makeup yet, but you pat your bed to get her to sit down on it, gathering your supplies around you in a glittery palette nest.

She shows you the phone. "I was thinking, like, kind of a sunset?" She lies back, her hair fanning out behind her.

You study the pictures. You are probably moderately capable of doing a good job. You run your eyes over your colors, thinking, your hands hovering. You pick up one of the fluffier brushes and hum, running it in idle circles on the inside of your wrist.

She takes a sip of her drink while she waits. You drink too. She lies back down and you straddle her in order to get close enough to do your work. This moment—this is one of your favorite things. It is familiar, intimate. You have done this about a million times with her over the years. In different dresses, in different beds. But it is always her and you, and the massive amount of love you have for her. The kind of thing that outlives a planet.

She scoots to make you both more comfortable. Clears her throat. "So. Okay. I am gonna ask you something, but I don't mean, like. Anything *bad* about it."

Oh, shit. Does she know? Has she noticed? You force a laugh. "I'm scared now."

"Okay. So." She takes a deep breath. "How did you know you're, like, gay?"

Ah. *That* question. You blink, realizing that in your many years of friendship, this is the first time she's asked about it. She knew when you were fifteen. Talk about patience. You tilt your head to the side, considering. "You know? I don't know that it was, like, a specific moment. It just. Like. It just made *sense?*"

She sighs. "You know how I'm always, like, drunk when I talk to you about how I might be bisexual?"

You hum an acknowledgment, moving slowly, applying primer to her lids. It feels like this is a very important conversation, and if you strike too quickly, it will vanish. "Yeah?"

"It's like . . . I feel bad, because I genuinely *love* Tanner. And it feels stupid to like . . . tell my family *now*."

You set the primer and pick up a thinner brush, running it through the purple you're going to use at the corners of her crease. "Yeah. But, like, it's hard to come out. You should take the time you need."

Lacey adjusts her nose ring. "I just wish I'd, like, figured it out, like—before I started dating him."

You dip the brush into a lighter color. "Yeah, no. I definitely hear that a lot. Like. When people find their life partner or whatever, they start figuring out, like, who they are."

"And like. Tanner's so fucking cool with it. And I'm still like—let's not tell my family. Like they're *technically* cool or whatever, they don't vote like dicks . . . but like. If I tell them, they'd *know*, and it would *change* things."

"Right."

"It's just that sometimes they say stuff and my skin crawls and . . . I'm like . . . it's probably better to just keep it inside?"

Your heart breaks a little at that. You want to cry, and have to pause to keep your hand from shaking. "Oh, Lace'."

"I just know like . . . if I bring it up, it's either going to get ignored, or it's going to be, like, a whole *thing*, and I don't know that I *want* that? And I *know* my mom is gonna be like—*what about Tanner*, because she thinks *bisexual* is just *gay but shy*."

You can't help it, you fold yourself down against her, wrapping her in a hug. "Oh, my love. That's fucking awful."

She sighs into your shoulder. "I don't know. Like, what's the *point?* Like, it won't change anything. And it *shouldn't* change anything. So then I'm like why would I tell them, even? Like, if it's just going to upset everyone?"

"Lacey . . ." You don't know what else to say, so you sit back up and go back to the makeup. "This is so hard. I'm *so* fucking sorry."

She gives a harsh laugh. "And I know, like, that I tell them about my day and stuff, so why would *this* be any different? Like, if it's *really* not going to change anything."

You hold your hand against her cheek, trying to send all of your love down through your palm and into her skin. "Lacey. You'll kill me for saying this but, like, it needs to be from *you*. You need to do what feels right *to you*. Like, I can't . . . decide for you."

She groans and then grabs your wrist, opening her eyes. "Oh my God. Sorry. This is supposed to be, like, *your* night. I'm sorry that I'm even bringing this stuff up."

"Lace', are you okay?" God, you fucking suck. How come you haven't noticed she's in pain? She's, like, the only person on Earth who cares about you who is not biologically related to you. Do better.

She closes her eyes again. "I have dreams I'm single and you're married but we live in a house together. And we invite people to, like, our goblin gathering. We live in, like, an ochre house or whatever. Discussing Audre Lorde and listening to "Ode to Joy" every morning. Oh, and there's, like, a little garden for you out back. And I keep goats."

"Oh, I love that. I have dreams where everyone dies. Give me some of *that* dream juice."

"*Dream Juice* is, like, the name of my new essential oils brand." She laces her fingers into yours for a moment. "But the brand is absolutely a multilevel marketing scheme."

"I think you should tell your family only if it's safe to do so." You click your tongue at the tiny mistake you make while switching between eyes. You lick your thumb and rub the mark off of her. "Sorry. Fixing the error in post."

She groans and pushes your wet hand away.

You get the feeling—whatever moment was happening, it just passed without you knowing how to handle it.

She tickles you. "I can't believe you didn't laugh at that joke. Also, I hate it when you give me real advice. I have to, like, hear stuff I already know and don't want to *admit* I know."

"I love you," you say, because there's no other real thing *to* say. "I'm here forever if you want to talk. Also, your makeup's done."

"Bitch, you fucking *better* be here forever. Are you kidding me? Do you think I could do this alone? If you ever fucking die, I'm just going to learn necromancy." She wiggles out from under you and examines the makeup. It actually looks really good.

Was that a friendship test? And why does it seem like you failed it? You should be better about this. You need to figure out what you *should* have said, and never make this mistake again.

You subtly change three more times before settling on the first dress, even though you now fully hate looking at it. At least it makes you look curvy. You are comfortably tipsy. Thank God almighty.

You don't hear the knock over your music. A curated playlist you named *Coke Is Extra*.

Marlowe is in all black, and way more casual than you are. Fuck, you shouldn't have dressed up, it is so immature. She's holding a bottle of Don Julio in one hand, brandished like a mallet. Threatening in an extremely cute way.

She drops into a gremlin crouch. "Hello, my pretties." She wraps Lacey up into a hug so all-encompassing that Lacey squeals. From her place under your best friend, she says, "Oh, *fuck* yeah. Baby the band is *back*. I *love* your makeup, Lace'."

Lacey wiggles back down to the floor and says something you don't catch. You are staring at Marlowe as calmly as you can. She looks happy. Concrete. Whole. She's already laughing. Her mouth so perfect. She flicks her eyes over at you, winks. Says she likes all the plants. Says she likes the way you (Kaisa) decorated the apartment. Walks into your kitchen to put the tequila down.

Marlowe goes through the cabinets casually, as if she's lived here before and you just never realized. Maybe your organizational habits are just predictable based on your previous shared arrangement. She gets down three of your mugs (cat cup, *rescue a greyhound!* cup, IKEA cup), nods while pouring two shots into each.

You forgot how practiced she makes everything look.

She winks at you again, splashing only a little bit of orange juice into the tequila. Lacey sends you a look. Marlowe hands out the shots.

You all link arms around your drinks without agreeing to do so—old habits. A knot between wrists.

"Okay, okay, okay, okay, okay." Marlowe shakes her hair back from her face. "I am *so* fucking glad y'all wanted to do this."

"It has literally been seven thousand years." Lacey inhales sharply through her teeth. She looks fucking stunning. "I'm gonna, like, fucking die. I'm letting you all know I'm gonna die. I'm, like, already kinda drunk. We are *twenty-eight*, bitches."

"Oh, we are gonna *die*, absolutely," Marlowe nods solemnly, even though you know she's still twenty-seven, a full year behind you both. "That's, like, the endgame."

"Let's get drunk," you say.

Lacey locks eyes with you before looking into her glass. "Uh. . . . Can we, like, cheers to being friends. Like, even now?"

Marlowe straightens her shoulders. "No, yeah. Cheers to being friends. And to making up for lost time. And to being with people I love, even though it's been a while." Marlowe's sudden seriousness makes all of you pause.

The music is suddenly stupid; you're too old for it and trying too hard to keep up with *the kids*. You somehow forgot she could do this—make something feel incredibly important, just with an attitude shift. You all stare at each other.

"Also cheers," you say. "To your, like, engagement?"

Marlowe laughs. "Okay! This is *not* about me. I will *get* my party. This is about *friendship*. I mean, like, *fuck* a man, dude. Fuck—you know what? Fuck *all* men!"

"*Fuck all men*," you all shout, and then the octopus of your linked bodies moves in a wave, sloshing liquor as you throw it back. You all hiss or howl or shriek.

Marlowe immediately refills the glasses, and then puts them down. She catches Lacey's hand before grabbing yours too. She holds the two of you in her little circle.

"Okay—okay. I need to say something, and it's kind of heavy, and I need to say it immediately."

You and Lacey freeze. Marlowe stares at the floor. "I've been . . . a really bad friend." She scoffs at herself. "A *really* bad friend. I know it. I've . . . like, I'm . . . I had a really hard time. But I've . . . like. I've started taking meds, and I think they're helping. I'm trying to find a therapist and I'm in, like, a thirty-day trial for CBT. I want to actually try and be good to everybody again."

You shouldn't be playing this dumb music. You stare at Marlowe, squeezing her hand. You repeat something you heard Kaisa say once: "Marlowe, that's really brave of you to share with us."

She looks at you, directly into your eyes. "I'm sorry," she says. "I'm really fucking sorry. And I am gonna try really hard not to let it happen again." Tears well up in her eyes, and you reach up to her cheek without thinking, stroking your thumb over it. She catches your hand and leans into the touch. "I'm gonna be better, I promise," she chokes.

"Oh, my God," Lacey is now also crying, "Stop this. Fuck. It's so okay, come here," and then you are in an octopus again, this time the three of you pressed against each other in a too-tight, limb-smash hug, squeezing and sniffling and giggling and tangled. Each of you saying *I love you, I love you, I love you it's okay, I love you, oh my God.*

Marlowe steps back and wipes her eyes and says, "*Whew.* Okay. One more thing. I'm just gonna say *one* thing about the wedding, and then the wedding is off-limits for the whole night." Her eyes glint. "I'm saying it now so you know I wasn't asking just because I'm drunk."

She picks up the shots she had prepared and doles them out. You know suddenly what's about to happen, but there's no place to take the car off the road, so you just hit the side of the truck.

"I want you both as my bridesmaids," she says.

Lacey squeals and wraps her in a hug. Liquor sloshes. You force a wide smile and nod as if you are trying to swallow a centipede. In the dancing you all align the glasses again with an aggressive clink, and then the deal is struck and slathering down your throat.

You almost throw up the whole shot into the sink but instead carry half in your mouth while you force the rest down. You like this casual metaphor: the poison takes effort. Pretentious bitch.

Later, in between the chatter and the dancing, you sit on the toilet and close one drunken eye. You type into Google one of your favorite phrases: *weight loss before and after pics*.

You stare at the words and then delete them. You take your time replacing them, your fingers almost numb while you slowly type out: *where can I find a therapist.*

my childhood cat is dying in my childhood home. this is obscene to consider on the international scale; dave is sixteen and very old and, by all accounts, very happy. i got the update at 8 a.m. through facebook messenger. my mother's carefully worded consideration evolved into the robotic planning of my grief.

i canceled a few plans. i wavered on driving the two hours to say goodbye to him, suddenly struck by how many small and stupid things in my life have to get done. i have to get my oil changed before i leave. i bring along my notebook just in case i can manage to get through some of my work.

and then i get in my stupid beat-up car and drive the stupidly familiar route 2 and weep stupidly all ninety miles. four hours later, dave dies on a table, flat like a pancake. i went home to ensure his murder.

while he dies, i want to say *i love you, be good* and *you were a very good cat*, but the vet is in the room, and i feel weird about it. i know i am missing my chance.

he will be the last cat i ever own. i've since developed an allergy.

we put him down while he was still crying, calling out for something gentle in the dark.

i hope he wasn't scared. he died like a memory; singing and soft.

sometimes, to love a thing is to touch it just softly, and say goodbye before you're ready.

You meet the angel on a backroad past a broken farmstand, sitting on a stoop of the abandoned gas station. A tickling of grass itches the air along the cracks of white concrete. Your allergies are killing you. The sun is setting, but today is a day that has been yellow no matter what time it is.

The angel is chewing a peach, which you're pretty sure is out of season. Juice is dripping down long tendons. The angel's limbs don't stop in the right places, but the wings are smaller than you'd anticipated.

You hadn't seen that it was an angel until you turned in, had just assumed it was a person. But it is an angel, although the halo is surprising—it is not yellow or gold, like the paintings. A carousel of silent, rotating flame. It reminds you of your chemistry class in high school.

You had googled how to get here because you needed gas, but now there isn't gas here or in your tank. There isn't service either. Maybe you could walk back to the broken farmstand and ask for a gallon— but do they even take Visa. You don't have cash.

You could maybe get another three miles on fumes. Your car has started to shudder.

You get out of the car and hold your hair in fistfuls like the tall grass. You want to scream, but don't want to bother the angel or look insane. You sit on the hood of your car for a second, debating the next steps, taking deep breaths. You stare at the grey horizon and wish you were in Nebraska. You wish you were in Tallahassee. You wish you hadn't ever come to this planet, where the people smell like overripe dessert and talk too much about the exorbitant price on dreams.

The angel licks the juice off a wristbone. On your arm, that joint would have been your elbow.

You look at the angel, try for camaraderie. *Is it better up there?*

The angel squints most of its eyes up toward the clouded sky, leaving a few pairs trained on you. *It's quieter.* The angel has sharp teeth, where it has a mouth.

Against your better judgment, you ask: *Whatcha doin' down here?*

The angel takes another bite. The peach doesn't seem to be getting smaller. It turns the peach while it eats, a familiar gesture. The twisting seems to reveal a new side each time.

You feel bad about asking about what the angel is doing. You shouldn't have assumed it's even here on purpose. *Is it a good peach?*

It's a good peach, the angel says.

Do you like your dad? This is a rude thing to ask. No one has ever asked you this question, because it is rude.

The angel gets juice on the ground. It watches, with some of its eyes, the tiny forming puddle it is making. The rest of the eyes are looking at you. The six wings look heavy and dirty. Hard to fold. Angels must not sleep on their backs.

I ran out of gas, you say.

You ran out of gas.

Google sent me here.

The angel takes another bite of the peach.

You get back in your car. You pray hard and drive to the nearest actually-open gas station (2.7 miles), and you get fifteen dollars' worth at three dollars a gallon. You turn over the engine and watch the needle come back up from under the line.

You sit in the idle car for a moment. You should get a scarf while it's still warm, you'll need it come fall. You text your boyfriend: *Can we meet? I need to talk to you.*

You bite your thumbnail. You look over your dashboard, then back down to your phone. You type into Google: *peach cobbler recipes.*

A life carved from obedience is not worship; it is pointless martyrdom. Suffering is not triumphant; it is only painful. You do not need to barter for your survival; glutting yourself on sorrow so you can *earn* "happiness."

Not even You, simulacrum.

A quickening. The night-black serpent asleep the Body is now on the move. Roiling scales slip through viscera and over your palms. You watch the venom drip along wristbone fangs and pool to the floor, forming a mirror. You drag your fingers through the puddle, oil slick and buzzing. Touch it to your lips. When a monster is a protector, we call that an angel.

When you finally look at him and say *I am done,* the words gallop out of your mouth and coalesce on his rug. A glistening, hard-eyed lizard.

You have shaped her in your image to be tough and long and hard. Thick legs and heavyweight and sporting horrible claws.

I am done has flames down the ridge of her back. *I am done* is effortless in the wave of her motion. *I am done* is newly born and immediate, and she is hungry, and she is needy.

I am done is already digging your beautiful forever-freedom. With her at your feet, however inappropriately: you find yourself smiling.

◆

PART THREE:

YOUR MOTHER WILL BE SAD
ABOUT THE ENDING.

COMMITTED ACTION WORKSHEET
(Adapted from Olerud & Wilson, 2002)

1. A component of my life that I value is ___COMMUNITY___ FAMILY + FRIENDS + DAVE ♥

My intention for this component is ___TO MAKE DEEPER CONNECTIONS___

The committed actions that I'm willing to take include the following (be sure to note when you'll begin these actions):

- GET BETTER @ TEXTING SIS GC STARTING TODAY @ LEAST 1 TXT a day.
- CALL PEOPLE TO LEAST 1/ WEEK ← LL MIKE TOMORROW. TALK TO DAD
- MAYBE TRY A NEW HOBBY? MAKE 3 FRIENDS by THE Time I'm 30... You have time...

2. A component of my life that I value is ___MY PLANTS + NATURE IN GENERAL___

My intention for this component is ___YOU GET DEPRESSED W/OUT PLANTS, IDIOT!___

~~I'm willing to take~~ ~~actions~~

- START MONDAY! GO UN BK WALKS A WEEK. NORMAL WALKS DONT DO WELL DONE FOOD BULLSHIT.
- GO OUTSIDE TO EVENTS W/OUT LIQUOR! HOZIER CONCERT?
- GET A DOG? → CHECK APARTMENT pet policy ON FRI.

3. A ~~~~ life is I value is ~~My ph. biography/painting~~ EMOTIONS!! LITERALLY UNY

My intention ~~~~ ___TO FEEL SOMETHING___ we are even in THERAPY omfg.

~~I'm willing to begin~~

- START DBT/ANY KIND of THERAPY (✓) (NICE!)
- YOGA TO CENTER + ground into ~~your~~ MY BODY my body!
- NO ROMANTIC RELATIONSHIPS to FILL the void. We're doing this SOLO, bitch!! GET YOUR SHIT ON LOCK.

absolute hitter, alveoli.
willhop, my as like works

The Dialectical Behavior Therapy Skills Workbook

when i finally left him, the didn't fade for weeks.

i used to pray a lot. the prayers all got eaten by wasps.

landfills are dressed in the blue and pink plastic of cheap rosaries. the bugs that crawl over each bead are tapping out a long *our father.* my pastor was sent from somewhere in this rotting pile. a beetle of recovery. scuttling and long-toothed—more afraid than angry.

the stress of survival had cost me. i developed an arrythmia.

in my new heartbeat, Echo's shrieked lament. a cockroach wish. a chitinous sort of worship.

the survivor's hunting mark.

◇

INCOMING TEXT FROM: MOUSE

You could just ▮ yourself. A single, terrible answer, skim milk in a desert.

The cemented Christ-glass of butterflies have sharp fingers. This isn't a metaphor; butterflies use their chitin to grip downward, so they can genuinely prickle or hurt when they land on skin.

For our sin of overconsumption, we will be raised in a different sky than our children. Scientists hypothesize that a large portion of the butterfly population has been decimated by the invention of the motor vehicle. *So no,* they say, *you're not imagining it.* There really used to be more butterflies in the wind.

The tired seeps into the harvest mouse, and the harvest mouse, shuddering over the steering wheel, spins her hands, which are her father's hands. It would all be over, and the memories would spill out onto the tarmac, illegible. Nobody else could get hurt by what you carry. Sacrifice a mouse to save the many.

But be honest.

When you yourself, you'll be dead forever. And are you sure
there's nothing left here for you? Are you really, *really* sure?

Metamorphosis remains a secret shared only by insects and Elijah.
The rest of us have to stand up and inhabit our own carcass.

◇

the reason that we quote books in the present tense is (at least in part)
because books are a frozen time line. when you quote a book, that
quote will always be on a specific page, during a specific passage—it
will always be in the present tense for the characters.

trauma can act like this, like a gravitational well. it bends light
around it.

sometimes what has happened is a neatly obvious recursive bow, a
loosed arrow with a clear arc. i cower at the loud noise. i flinch when
someone moves too quickly toward me. i get nasty, teeth showing,
instead of letting someone take advantage of me. the book opens back
up to the exact page it happened on: *trauma response.* no matter where
i look, because i wrote it down, the cat is still-dying.

but trauma is another thing too—it is the smoothest, quietest
wave. when there is no clear beginning point—when the trauma is just
being here, in this world: how do i track my own panicked responses?
how do i calculate my way home?

i know my life is a warning. i am honestly, genuinely trying.

i don't *want* to be constantly dipping through the laser grid of
my own wounds. i want to walk directly up to the diamond of my
own mind. i would ideally like to make this walk in form-fitting
and flattering spandex, but we can make something else work too. i
want to be unworried about beauty and always smiling. i want to
find humor again. i want to value myself without preface, without
mentioning the ways i serve *others* as the parts of *myself* that i love.

i hate this. i run my hands over the sharp easel of my own fiberglass hair and find myself, again, over and over, realizing—*fuck. it's gonna hurt no matter how i do it.*

◇

TEXT FROM: MOUSE

You are spending too much money on crafts so you don't have to think about things. Someone once called you "a JOANN fabrics kind of bitch," which you kind of took as a compliment. You have burn scars on your hands from hot glue—strange stigmata.

Thanksgiving is around the corner. Everyone is being gentle with you since *the breakup,* which is more than you deserve and better than you were hoping for.

You feel wild. Sometimes you miss him, sometimes you feel nothing. Sometimes you are the sexiest person on this planet and it's going to be very, very easy for you to snag another man. Sometimes you romanticize ▮▮▮.

You are holding Pepcid in the middle of a CVS. A horrible Christmas song is on the radio, and the thought comes through your body—*this is all actually happening.*

Holy shit. She's *actually* getting married. You're *actually* going to the wedding.

It's not going away just because you're going to be single for it. Nobody else's life is on hold. The world is still moving. You have to figure out how to move around two kinds of grieving. Get over it.

Did you expect some kind of dawn chorus? That you'd look up, and she'd have that expression again, the soft heat of her desire pooling over her lips.

It's probably the worst time of your life so far, and you still need to get groceries. You still need to pick up your laundry. You still need to remember to send your boss that stupid follow-up email.

This is real, and that's horrible. It's just so boring, so plain. The murky, thin air of a CVS and the blue carpet underfoot.

What's done is done. So, okay, you're heartbroken. There is only ever going to be the *after* of this. You are officially, forever, in the *rest of your life*. Her, and then not-her. Him, and then not-him. Just-you now, you and the Body you're borrowing.

You really should have made more friends in the last few years. Made more time for yourself. Actually had real thoughts and passions.

Something she and Adam have in common: it was never actually equally yoked. She doesn't think about you as much as you think about her. That much is *very* clear. You could disappear and she'd never notice your absence. It wouldn't be a mark in her book.

She chose someone else. No matter how much you talk to her or hang out with her or try to be *just* her friend—whenever you wake up, she will *still* be choosing him, the way she (loudly and obviously) did *not* choose you. The way you have never been chosen, no matter how many times you volunteer your hand over the horizon.

You aren't paying attention and a man reaches right over you to get to the top shelf. His motion feels on the nose, and you are too angry to function.

How does anyone have that much confidence. You see his entire armpit and his hips bump into your back. Doesn't he know you're having a fucking *terrible* day?

How does he just touch something without being a part of it? How does somebody learn to take up space without being aware of it? How can people reach for things without worrying what will stop them from getting it.

You're too pretentious. Just get your Pepcid and go home, kid.

the catholic god is a violent god. to show us he loves us, he crucifies his son. when he is disappointed, he washes the world with a bottomless flood. sends down angels that are distorted fire. commands armies, not orphanages.

i'm not sure i ever understood god's love as a benevolent thing. god's love was a form of expulsion: that he first cast out lucifer for disagreement and he killed his own son for our penance and—should we fail to heed his message, we too would live in eternity without him.

still, i was made to understand that almighty love did not have to make sense, nor did it have to extend a gentle hand—despite appearances, it was love nonetheless.

one becomes acclimated to the idea that love can be both unerring and omnipresent and infinitely kind and yet, at the same time: love can be cruel and one-sided. love can create an artifice of temperance. i knew i didn't have to *enjoy* the experience of being loved—i simply had to appreciate the breadth of it. i could even *fear* it—fear was another form of worship, after all.

and besides: i could love and admire a tree and not understand it. i had seen death love a sleeping face. i had seen that my cat could love me, transcending species, and i still killed him in an *act* of love. my youth is draining. i am trying to understand age as a love letter to staying on this planet. there's a chance love can be expressed in ways that can only really be viewed from another dimension.

there are many ways to picture the role of the church in a life. sometimes the bride is the church and we are the husband. sometimes the church is a benefactor. sometimes the church is a gate. sometimes it is a guillotine.

sometimes god is the actual biological father and all else must bow to him. we were to mimic the structure of god over person when we organize family under the father. the father was the protector, the progenitor, the Almighty.

the father's power and his authority were derived from what i could only understand as fear. leadership won from a strange anticipation of violence. fear is power, plain and simple.

i suppose there is the evolutionary argument that violence would somehow work to provide sustainability to the nuclear family. but in the earliest eras of human history, there's more archaeological evidence that humanity survived more as a result of *community*, not aggression. the modern-day understanding of the nuclear family was virtually absent—families were river deep, flush with overlapping hands and generations.

it isn't an ecologically sound social paradigm to be relentlessly war seeking: humans are one of the weakest predators in the animal world. it was only by combining each person's strengths that we were able to survive.

an aside—it's an illusion that somehow gender divides into father-as-protector and mother-as-caretaker. there is very little evidence that inborn skills (emotional or physical) are based on your genetic expression. even the narrative "women raise children while men hunt" has been shown to be mostly fiction.

still, we can learn to love what is familiar. we can learn that *fear* and *respect* are synonyms. we can learn that we do not need to be close to our fathers (divine or physical)—that their love is through a different lens than our own.

i do believe that fear and love are compatible. i do believe that one can fear love and that fear *creates* a love—in the overwhelming sense. awe and terror hold hands. both come from unknowing, unspeakable *beholding*.

when is an unknowable all-powerful creature a monster and when is it god and when is it the Father? when is he acting *as* your father and when is he following his own plans? why does the father know best? where is *the family's* say in all of this? when is a punishment a form of benevolence? when is violence just god's nature? how long should you remain silent when you are in pain? is it your fault for your weakness if you're easy to prey upon?

if a man can ███ me and wake up in the morning and talk easily and serve me breakfast, he is not a monster, he's a man. he wasn't born to be gentle.

god's love is like this, right? the open hand first; and we succumb without fight.

to be clear: abuse is not gendered.

but i do believe that my continued patience with it stemmed from a gendered lesson: a good girl does not need to be at peace. a good girl should always be cowering.

ready to get ███.

a woman's place is on her knees.

◇

FROM: MOUSE

From Marlowe: *Okay don't be mad. Promise you won't freak out.*

From Marlowe: *I know we should be celebrating you and I don't want to be a bitch, but I have to ask you something.*

Lacey walks out of the bathroom, half-nude. She is borrowing your hair curler. You are both going to a "spring fling" dance party, one of the many ways you are *trying.* Your brand-new therapist assures you there's no *winning* to trying, but you try very hard anyway, convinced you *will* win, somehow.

This dance party is, technically, if you look away, kind of how you're acknowledging your birthday coming up soon. You signed up for it last minute and begged Lacey to join, and now you are putting on makeup in the corner of your room.

Kaisa is making something in the kitchen, and the whole place smells like garlic. You have been better to her. She makes you laugh, which surprises you—you hadn't known her well enough to know she's funny. It feels bad you didn't know. It feels bad you were that selfish. There is a weird, tenuous sense of almost-friendship that is developing in a golden thread between the two of you, something skittish.

It turns out there are a lot of parts of your life you hadn't investigated. You are still too burned to get excited about most of them. You have to pick them up one at a time, examining them like shells on the beach.

"Guess who just texted me!" Singsong, you apply another layer of concealer under your eyes. You allow yourself one single, bitter thought about how you can't afford an actual birthday party this year. You didn't know being a bridesmaid would be so expensive. Marlowe keeps making you guys take her out to "celebration dinners."

"Is it Marlowe talking about the stupid fucking—that their parents are *just now* meeting each other? Like, the brunch thing?" At your shrug, she rolls her eyes. She adds lotion to her hands. "Can I say? I don't super like the *girly-girl* blushing-bride thing on her."

You check your phone. The text makes you kind of anxious. "Literally I don't know what it's about. Look at this." You hand her your phone.

She reads it, her eyebrows shooting up. "What the *fuck?*" She hands you it back, shaking her head. "What the fuck."

"Right? Okay, but yeah, every fucking third day she's like—*oh, will you check out my outfit?* As if she's low-key convinced this wedding hinges on, like, what she wears to a bar crawl with his friends. All of whom, by the way, like the parents, she legit *just met.*" You pause. "Wait. All of *who?* All of *whom?*"

"If it's a group of his friends, I think it's *whom?*"

You make hooting sounds rather than answer that, which makes her laugh. "Anyway," you wave it away with your concealer wand. "The point remains."

"I really, just, like. What is her problem. Like, ignoring whatever *that* fucking text is . . ." She takes a deep breath and gestures vaguely. "Literally just admit you don't even know him that well! You're *just now* introducing your parents to each other *four months* into the engagement? Like, I don't know how to tell her this, but a brunch is *not* gonna resolve that, sorry. Did she say anything else?"

She gestures at you, so you give her over the phone so she can look at the conversation again. She rolls her eyes. "Oh my God. I'm . . . *Don't be mad?* Like good, now I *am* mad." She scrolls upward before you can stop her. "Okay, whoa. Hang on. Why does she talk to you like you're going to fuck her."

A few of the pictures were nudes, asking you about her underwear choices.

"It makes me *uncomfortable*," you sing. "I have no idea how to respond to it!"

"Like. I know we used to send each other that shit, but." Lacey takes another breath, scrolls more, hands you back the phone. "I can't fucking believe her. That—that is *not* fucking appropriate. Like, I *know* you're the only one she's doing that to. Do not *think* I haven't noticed she's constantly inviting you to stupid things and making you pay for them. And, like, it better not be because you're single now. I will *actually* kill her."

"I *actively* don't like her fiancé, dude." Genuinely, unrelated to the rest of it. You had actually given him a chance. Like actually, for once. He was just a fucking piece of shit.

She nods emphatically. "He's the fucking *worst* and she drags him with her *everywhere* she goes. It's like. It's okay! If you're apart from him, believe it or not, you won't immediately bleed out!"

"*Literally*. For tonight I was like, *oh Lace' and I are going to a party, just to have something to do. Like, just to get out of the house, blah, blah, blah, Marlowe, why don't you come*. Like, it was clearly a girls' night kind of a thing." You hadn't wanted to tell her *it's for my birthday*. That felt desperate. You had, kind of, wanted her to just *know* that it was for your birthday, even though that wasn't technically "healthy communication."

Lacey checks her lipstick line. "No, that was literally immediately obvious. Also, I have to be honest—I texted her and said it was for your birthday. So she *definitely* knows it's for your birthday. So. There's that."

"Okay, wait. Wait. So explain to me," you scroll upward, "She literally asked me yesterday if he could come."

She sends you a dark look. "Oh my God. This is literally about *you*. For like *two minutes*. How about we *don't* drag *boyfriends* around the *single person*. Jesus."

You shrug, weirdly embarrassed. "I just . . . I don't know what her problem is. I ended up leaving her on read because I didn't want to handle it."

Lacey rolls her eyes. "Can she just, for like, *one* moment . . . be her own person?"

"Like, to be fair? Maybe the wedding is driving her crazy." Generous. You feel holy. Kind. Peaceful. Vindictive.

"And she's lost *so* much weight." Lacey says it casually, but the way her lips tighten suggests *I'm feeling judgment about this*.

You whip around. "Okay, *right?*"

"Literally." She nods so many times she has to hold the curler away from her skin.

Are you relieved she noticed too? You swallow whatever this half spite is. "Like, I know it's like this whole thing to—"

"Yeah, you obviously want to look your best, like. Obviously."

"Right. But, like, I mean. Have you *seen* her?" You go back to messing up your hair; move on to reapplying your eyeliner.

"She's like. I mean." She lowers her voice. "She looks sick."

"Do you think he's like . . . ?"

"No, no, no. I mean, I get it on her end."

"Yeah, I mean. There's a lot of pictures and stuff." You fuck up the eyeliner wing. It was better before you touched it. Now you gotta take the whole eye off.

"And she was always kind of, like. Super intense about that stuff."

"Like *super* intense, right?" You align Lacey in the mirror so you can still see her and take a deep breath. You will be good and normal, and you are not going to feel victorious while you say it. "Okay, actually? She asked me recently how, like, I lost weight."

You felt victorious. Fuck.

"What the hell." She stops to make eye contact in the mirror, clearly horrified, and then goes back to her hair. "Is she fucking *serious?*"

"I mean, I lost like—I mean, I did lose weight."

"No, that's obvious. Like, I've definitely noticed. It's, like, at least ten pounds on you."

Are you still victorious? Are you tasting the bitterness of having someone notice? Are you disgusted with yourself because it's not more or because it was so bad before that the change is obvious? "Yeah, like ten or fifteen. I don't weigh myself, really." You weigh yourself every morning. "You noticed?"

"Oh yeah. You dropped it, like. So quickly. I thought I was going to have to say something. Your thighs are, like, tiny."

You try to take it in stride. You can't say *thank you* or it will look like you were trying. "I think it's because I stopped drinking so much."

"Very sexy of you, as we both know."

"Right, but, so, anyway, yeah, she asks me, like. How I did it."

"I'm sorry, but why the fuck does she suddenly feel so comfortable with you *that's* something she's asking?" She clacks the claw on the curler a few times, turns to you. "Also, why is *she* noticing?"

"Okay, right?"

"Ugh." She goes back to the process at hand, her hair in lovely ringlets. "I'm, like, she's literally doing this to, like, *tell you* she's looking at your body. Because it's *Marlowe!* So she's doing what she *always* does. She just likes *playing* with you. It's fucking *routine* for her. She fucking led you on for years until—" At your look, she flinches. "Sorry. I just mean, what exactly is her *issue*. Like, at first, I was like, oh great! It's cool she's been making an effort again! But no, she's literally *still* a huge bitch. It's just . . . Gross." She lets out a low angry shudder-sigh, shivering through her body. "What did you say when she asked?"

It's weirdly nice to have a friend that gets defensive on your behalf. "I said, like. It wasn't that much weight, it's just that I had lost muscle first. And, like, again. Most of it is because I stopped drinking."

"Yeah. You had a problem."

You raise your eyebrows at her. "Don't I know it. It's, like, embarrassing."

"But she doesn't really drink, right?"

"Yeah. And I was like, *okay I had to go on this, like, medical diet.*"

"For your ulcers, right."

"And she's like. *What was the diet.*"

"Oh my God. No, she did not." Her teeth are gritted. At your look, she literally snarls. "*No,* tell me she did *not.*"

You nod once, sharp. "She *legit* asked me to send her info about it. And I was like. It was a conversation with my *literal doctor.* I had *medical issues.*"

"Holy shit."

"Like, it helped the bloating, though." For a while, you threw up all the time, felt constantly nauseous and heinous. Nothing was helping.

Your doctor sat you down and explained, however kindly—you were physically addicted to throwing up now, and would need to break the habit of nonpsychological bulimia. Your therapist allowed you one single harsh laugh at the punch line—you are, after all, in therapy partly for your extreme dietary restriction—and now you have to restrict your diet so you wouldn't have bulimia anymore. Nice going! You literally *can't* eat without disorder. Your body won't allow it.

Lacey gently hip checks you. "Your waist is fucking tiny now and I am obsessed with you. I *am* going to kill Marlowe, though. Like, there *is* going to be bloodshed."

Your phone buzzes.

From Marlowe: *would you be super mad if i don't come 2nite*

From Marlowe: *OH ALSO i think i found a spot for wedding dress shopping and i know it's super super super early in the process, but could you come with me?*

"Ah. There it is." You hand the phone over to Lacey.

She gasps and clicks her tongue. "Is she fucking serious? So like. We can just assume. She not only *knows* tonight is about your birthday, but that she's not even going to be *genuinely* sorry about skipping it? Or at least *try* to give you an excuse?"

You don't know how to answer that. You start picking lint off your outfit.

"And, okay, sorry, but *why* isn't this wedding dress thing in the group chat? We literally have a group chat for this reason. I hate this fucking secret, behind the-back bullshit." Lacey sounds genuinely upset.

It shouldn't surprise you, but you keep forgetting Lacey actually cares about getting invited; that she used to be Marlowe's friend too. You're a fucking bad friend, and yet—Lacey still stuck with you. She chose *your* side. You owe her so much better.

You pick at nonexistent dirt under your fingernails. "I just wish she stopped making me think about it, like, every two minutes. *Every* text is about the wedding, dude. She, like, never asks me how I'm doing."

"This is what I mean about the blushing-bride thing."

"And no offense but like—" you send a dark look to her. "I'm genuinely, like. Worried about the dress fitting thing. I . . . I like, don't think it's safe for her to like . . ." You don't know how to phrase it.

"Stand in front of a mirror and have people judge her appearance? Oh, it's bad." Lacey looks disgusted while she hands the phone back. "I still can't believe she fucking *asked* you how to lose weight."

"Oh right. Okay, wait, so she asks me that, and I'm like. You should talk to your doctor about it."

"Right, because you're not a nutritionist, and also. It's *genuinely* none of her business."

"Well, what bothers me is actually more like. She didn't know about the ulcers; so like, in context—I tell her, like, I had to go on this really extreme *medically required* diet for a while, and she just . . . skips over that and asks for the *diet?* And apparently doesn't care if I'm, like, dying or anything?"

"Oh my God, I didn't even think about that."

"Yeah, but you're fucking *normal* and would have actually *asked if I was okay.*"

"Hang on. So she doesn't even. Like *acknowledge* the doctor thing?"

"Nope!"

Lacey puts her free hand to her forehead. "I cannot. I am getting violent."

"I said I had lost the information but I'll look into finding it. Or whatever other bullshit."

"Don't give her even, like, a *little* bit of information about it. She deserves literally none of the emotional labor you go through on her behalf." Lacey turns off the curler and puts it down in the place you usually leave it. She knows you too well. "Is it okay if I'm fucking sick of her and it's only been, like. A few months. Like, I think I hate her since she got back. She's turned into—like—" she gestures vaguely.

"No offense, and I know this is a sore subject, but she was literally *so* much better when you guys were dating."

Except Marlowe's never actually been your partner. "I am just like. Horrified. Like, you *know* how hard it has been for me to not go crazy on this fucking diet. And like, *she* knows about my whole . . . past thing." You mean *eating disorder*, even though you didn't have one. "Like, we've had *so* many conversations about her stuff" (*eating disorder*) "and my stuff" (*eating disorder*) "And I *get* that she has a way more extreme problem" (*eating disorder*) "than I do—or like *did*, but."

She takes your hand. "Dude. It doesn't matter. What she's doing is fucking irresponsible. But, like, you know, you're her *favorite person*."

You do the Marlowe voice. "*My mama told me that some people are special.*" You kiss her knuckles and then her wrist and then her elbow while she squeals and giggles. You pick the curler back up, not wanting to run late, but you're super unprepared. You need to be more drunk for this. You have learned from your therapist that you might actually be *socially anxious*. In hindsight, this is really fucking obvious.

"I . . . need to be more drunk for this," you announce. You drag her over into the kitchen, where Kaisa is humming over her dinner. At your suggestion, all three of you take shots with your arms linked. Your cheeks starting to pink. You sail politely into being tipsy.

"I love you," Lacey says. She kisses your cheek in a big wet smack. You giggle.

"I love *you*."

"Get a room," Kaisa says, winking.

Lacey keeps one arm around your neck. "I have been her best friend since she was, like, *twelve*." Then she looks over at you. "Thirteen? Wait. Shit. When did we meet?"

You have no idea. "Math class?"

Kaisa laughs and sidles by you, carrying her plate of stir-fry to the table. She's going to be joining you guys on the adventure tonight, something you are weirdly proud of. Lacey was *delighted* by this, and has been trying to pretend not to care about it. You keep catching her sneaking looks toward Kaisa.

Lacey drags her eyes away and pops a Triscuit into her mouth. You bought them specifically for her, since you know she loves them. She nibbles the corner of a second one and then points it toward you, squinting. "You ever think about how, like, our relationship would be like, impossible to explain to a right-wing Republican?"

"Best friends that are gay but are *actually* platonic? Even though we kissed a lot in college?"

"We kiss now sometimes, too, to be fair."

You laugh and then blink. "Wait, hang on. Do I only make friends I end up kissing?"

Kaisa lifts her hand awkwardly. "You haven't kissed me."

Lacey buries her startled squawk into her Triscuit.

Kaisa chokes and points her fork at you. "Wait. Hang on. *Not* an invitation. Oh God. Respectfully, um. No thank you."

You giggle. Kaisa is Lacey's—you would rather die than ever make a move on her. And besides. It's not *like* that. It's nice enough just to be passingly comfortable with her, which is a huge improvement from before.

You check the music and let the other girls chatter and close one eye and text Marlowe back: *omg. of course I'd love to come. I am so so so so excited bb.*

You read the text aloud to Lacey, who nods. "Good. It's friendly. *And* it doesn't forgive her for missing tonight." Her mouth turns down. "I am still kind of hurt she didn't invite me wedding dress shopping. This bitch."

You reach up into her hair. "You're too pretty. You'd steal all the attention."

"Actually? Knowing Marlowe, that could *literally* be the reason." She gently bats your hand away. "Kaisa, have you *heard* all this shit?"

Kaisa sends you a wary glance, and then kind of waggles her head. She's been getting the details slowly. You didn't want to overwhelm her. "It all sounds . . . pretty fucked up."

Lacey beams. "I'm going to kill Marlowe in her sleep!"

Everything in your heart spills over. All eighteen or whatever years of knowing Lacey. You want to express this. You put your hands on her face and look deep into her eyes. "Your hair right now is gorgeous."

"*You're* gorgeous."

"Marry me."

"Oh my God. With everything that's happening?" She shudders. "Seeing *her* go through it? No. Bitch, I'm eloping." She kisses you on the cheek and asks you to queue up another song. Your nose buzzes pleasantly.

From Marlowe: *omg! thank goddddddddd lol i just feel like you're like the only one i can actually trust to be honest with me*

From Marlowe: *hey btw how does this dress look? Helllppp meeeeeee im going out w/his friends tonight and idk what to wearrrrrr*

From Marlowe: *ughh sorry i know ur probs busy but fr is this outfit okay?*

From Marlowe: *gsldkjfldsjk help me choose a different bra for this hang on*

The picture comes through while you and Lacey and Kaisa jostle your knees in the back of the Uber.

Lacey sees and gags. "Is she fucking *serious*?" She scrolls up, reaching over your arm. "Oh my God." She zooms in, cackling. "That's just a straight-up nude."

Kaisa looks over your shoulder. "I'm sorry if I'm not clear on the details, but I am . . . pretty sure she's getting married?"

"*Literally* what I'm saying," Lacey agrees. "Screenshot it and send it to him."

The bra is the color of tangerines. It has an ombre accent to it. Marlowe's flipping off the camera. *this is the one, right?*

You forget about it for a while, but in the bathroom later, you find yourself staring at the picture. The whole world is fuzzy. You scroll upward in the conversation, not sure what you're looking for exactly. Back down to the peach bra, and the dip of her hips and her collarbone jutting.

You type: *i'm uglier than i look*

You erase it and instead send: *omfggggg YESSS, absolute queeeeeen*

i can't just go to confession and give up being queer—i *am* queer. how can you remove the sin from the flesh without drawing blood.

i cannot tell the priest *i have had inappropriate relations with a woman and i am sorry* for two reasons. one: i am not sorry. two: i don't actually think the relations are inappropriate.

my simple solution was so joyful it sent a desert ablaze inside of me. if my *actual identity* was the sin, the answer was simply to *always* be sorry. repent now, for you are at the hour of the soul's death.

i understood any suffering i experienced was divine retribution for what i could not (and would not) change. i couldn't have needs. do you really *love* if you do not give *all* of yourself to others? you are *so* blessed, in this life—you simply aren't grateful enough.

let the pain spill out over everything, an amber and fleshy rug. tell no one what you are experiencing. remind yourself: suffering *is* love.

i do believe there's such a thing as feeling something so loudly that you no longer feel anything at all. you cannot even feel *the thing* itself. *the thing* swallows so deep that the soul becomes a pinprick, the center of a black hole.

you sense it, of course. it does reside in the body, somewhere. but it appears at a distance, far-off, incalculable. it becomes numb through familiarity.

i find it hard to envision a more precise doctrine of faith than this. *the thing* does exist, you know it does, and you know it must be, in some way or another, changing your universe; shaping how you move. monitoring your behavior intangibly. you just can't actually *see* it. nor is there any real evidence pointing to it.

the thing is obvious. it also has stopped existing. it is also always there. a white sheet over the earth; the shroud trembling with your breath.

the thing becomes a barrier. you touch *through* it. you love and hope and dream all with *the thing* dragging centipede legs deep into your cornea.

to upset *the thing* would mean pressing fingers against a heat that incinerates completely. it is better to remain unburned. what is the point of being happy when you have to force your way through the pain of it all? how do you ever arrive "at" happiness, if you must endure *the thing* first? won't you get "to" happiness as a different, injured self?

it is easy to assume—all situations are drawn along clear boundaries of right and wrong. it is *right* to be kind to your partner and your friends and your loved ones. it is *wrong* to ██ anyone at all. if you are ██ed, it is right to leave your partner. but it is *also* right to give our loved ones patience and trust.

it is wrong to accuse others. it is wrong to make a fuss. it is wrong to feel entitled to justice. it is wrong to assume intention.

it is right to be loyal. it is right to be empathetic. it is right to make an effort. it is right to stay through the bad times.

it is wrong to leave if it would hurt someone when you go.

when *the thing* echoes so brutally; right or wrong become insolent, uncanny. they dance around delineation. if everything is painful, how does one tell the difference between a good pain (like a stretch) and a bad pain (like a snapping)? if the whole world is water, are you ever wet?

where is the line? when you have spent so long being dominated by *the thing*—how do you ever draw a clear boundary? everything after *the thing* is muted, twisted, undefined. you could just be overreacting. you could just be unfair and unrelenting.

how would you know what is real? everywhere you look is *the thing*. and *the thing* transmutes the whole world into a monstrosity.

the saying: *misery loves company*. maybe also the nature of *the thing* is that it covets addition. you accidentally seek out trauma. despite your best efforts, you often mistake "being familiar with" for "being immune to further."

to escape this cycle—one must actually confront the ramifications of any *existing* trauma.

but . . . why would i do that?

i'm invincible here. nobody can hurt me; there is no *me* here to hurt. i am eating plums in space right now. i am letting the juice drip down my fingers.

birds have muscles in their feet that function in reverse of our hands: it takes effort for them to extend into our "relaxed" position; their relaxed pose is our "clenched fist." when they sleep at night; they do not need to worry about falling off a branch—they automatically close around their home. birds do not know what it is like to struggle to hold on.

when you have spent long enough in numbness, it begins to become comforting. it begins to become your only sense of reality. living inside of the flinch eventually makes cowering into a comfortable pose. relaxing feels like falling down.

it becomes genuinely difficult and painful, the practice of letting go.

◇

 O MOUSE

You fucking forgot that you'd stored the extra pans in the oven, because you're a dumb fucking bitch. It's preheated to 425 for scones, but has now *also* preheated several layers of cast iron pans and baking sheets.

The hand towel will have to do because the oven mitts are, as per usual, missing (more like *mitting*. Ha!) and you want to work quickly. You put the raw scones down and you wrap the towel around your hand and grab one of the preheated casserole dishes.

You hear not feel the burn. Yuck.

You drop the hot dish immediately, letting it clatter onto the ground with a *very* dramatic series of beats. You shove yourself into the sink. Your first aid classes said that it continues to actively burn for twenty minutes. Lots of people think ice is a good idea, but it's best to just run it under lukewarm water.

Kaisa comes into the kitchen. "Hey, I heard—"

Water is leaking down your forearms. Okay, so, it *hurts* now. "Sorry, sorry, sorry. Just tried to take out a hot pan from the fully hot oven. Like an idiot."

"Are you okay?" She comes over, her eyebrows knitting while she looks down at your wound.

Oh yeah. This one is *spicy*. "Hang on, can you put the scones in the oven and set a timer for thirty minutes?"

She moves to do that, still frowning. "What happened?"

"I'm okay." You remove the hand from the water for a second. The skin of your palm is in a full-on blister already. And. Oh God. Oh dear Lord. The blister is in a perfect penis shape. Balls and everything.

"I burned a dick into my hand," you say.

She closes the oven and glances at you and then hisses through her teeth, even though there's no way she can see the full damage from where she's standing. "That looks. Bad. Should we get a doctor?"

"I just gotta sit here until the twenty minutes are up—not for the scones, like, for *me*, the twenty minutes." You do not explain the twenty minutes, but she doesn't ask for more information." You set the timer for thirty, right?"

"I set the timer. Like. What happened?" She goes and drags two stools over, one for you and one for her.

"Oven mitts were missing. I think the towel slipped."

"Fuck dude, I'm so sorry. That shit hurts *bad* when it happens."

"It's not too bad." It hurts like a motherfucker. "Just in a bad place, I guess." The sink is a weird level to stand at this long, and you're guilty over wasting the water. You kind of hover-stand over your stool. You can't decide if you should bend fully over or just keep the weird holding-out-for-a-handshake angle.

"I think we were washing the oven mitts," she admits.

Oh yeah. *You* were actually the one who had thrown them into the load, but you like that she used *we*.

The pain is sizzling inside of your arteries.

"Hey, Kaisa? Like. Are we friends yet?"

She recoils as if you slapped her. "I . . . don't know how to answer that."

"Sorry. Oh my gosh. That was shitty of me, I just meant—"

"No, it's okay." She takes a deep breath. "You're in a lot of pain right now."

Sink and skin have the same letters! That's so fun.

Your hand fucking hurts.

Kaisa makes a noise in the back of her throat. "Well, actually. It's a weird time to bring it up . . . but, I mean, to your point, we've been living near or around each other for, like, years now." She picks at the bad, peeling vinyl of your shared countertop. "I was actually just talking to my therapist about how I feel, like, we're *just* starting to get to know each other as more than roommates." She gives you a smile. "I do like you as a roommate, though."

"I'm sorry," you say again. "I didn't mean to, like, imply anything weird—"

She waves her hand. "Didn't take it personally. I know what you meant."

You don't know what you meant, so this is a surprise. "I meant . . . like, I'd *like* to be friends." You throw a look at your hand. "Not, like. I'm not trying to pressure you, I guess."

"I think . . ." she sucks her teeth. "It's been nice to have someone to talk to about . . . stuff. One thing I really like about being queer is the community." She gives you that same gentle smile. "I think I kind of just assumed . . . we're queer, so we're friends."

"Right, like. We're queer, we're roommates, so we're friends. Like, no need to do anything else." You hadn't actually *tried* with her, not until recently. But then—you hadn't really *tried* with *anybody*.

You look at the burn. "But yeah, I get that." You try a different angle for the water to go over. "It's like: I see a queer person; I try to adopt them."

"Exactly."

"But, uh," you don't know how to phrase it. "Yeah. I just. I feel like you're, like. Someone I genuinely want to get to know better. You're really cool and I just . . ." you don't know what else to say. There isn't anything. "I've been, like." Caught up with Adam. Out of the house. Gone from your own life and purposes. Trapped in a body you were supposed to leave a long time ago before the owner got lost in space.

"You had your own stuff."

"I could have included you in more of that stuff."

She pats you gently on the back. "Let's discuss this after we get done washing the burn out. Or whatever it is you're doing."

"It looks like a dick."

"The hand?"

"The burn on my hand looks like a dick."

"It doesn't."

"I am telling you I have a dick on my palm, dude. A full blister penis."

"It does *not* look like a penis."

You show her. It burns as soon as it touches dry air.

"Okay," she admits. "You have a blister penis."

"Nobody wants to be friends with someone with a fuckin'— raised cock."

"It could be an elevated eggplant. It has eggplant vibes."

"You're trying to make me feel better about my fucking full-ball palm scrotum. I am telling you I will not feel good about this situation."

"This dick-uation, if you will."

You look at her. She looks at you. You both start laughing, and the sound of it makes something flip upside down in your heart. It almost feels like relaxing.

Hours later, when you've made the scones and said good night and are in your bed that is finally off the floor and are holding the hand oddly above you and are trying to make the pain stop, you realize— talking about it doesn't hurt as much as you thought that it would.

i have been thinking too much about the act of falling.

squirrels are immune to gravitational death. due to their body weight, they never reach a velocity that will end them. it would take a squirrel falling 4,800 miles before it died. rather than dying from the impact, it would instead starve to death.

the atmosphere is sixty-two miles. it is 238,900 miles to the moon. if an angel was the size of a squirrel, somewhere between the blue dewdrop of our earth and the peaceful gray of the moon: that's where heaven must be, nestled in the sweetness of space.

the safety from terminal velocity is not true for birds. roughly 90 percent of chicks will survive their first fall, but some will die on impact.

what color did angels turn, when their feathers met our air? is *that* why we say angels are made of fire? the streaking white light, a sphere of agony. leaves of feathers immolating. if they are made from certain particles, that fire could be green, blue, alight with nausea. any flesh would be evaporated.

our spaceships have been made with coats on the outside; designed to be lost in transit. we anticipate the destruction of earth's second mantle, her shield repelling the vacuum above us. maybe we picture hell as a hot place because, once ignited, angels burn in perpetuity.

or maybe they hit the ocean with a great and horrible splash. maybe their fall was what ended the dinosaurs. maybe lucifer was turned to obsidian, sharp and agile, cutting through to the earth's core. after that, the leftover gray firmament of angel wings spread over everything. the muted sound of their weeping. it all turned to ice; and the kingdom of eden was no more.

or maybe when they fell, they burned into pieces so small that it became like snow. when we look up, they are falling still. alive in the air, stuck in the loop of liquids.

or maybe god looked down at his falling son and said—*i will protect him for this last moment. after all, this is my plan. he need not suffer for it.*

i cannot help it: my heart breaks for the monstrous satan. lucifer was chosen by god to rebel. it is written that god knew, and that god still allowed the morning star to falter in the universe. it is written that lucifer was his first favorite; the strongest and wittiest and most wry. lucifer was the eldest. why did hell, then, belong only to him?

there are many stories on why the devil falls; in general his banishment is precipitated by some kind of mutiny. lucifer desires a different almighty plan, seeks to conquer. is rebuked.

god always knows better. if angels have no terminal velocity, he throws them toward the ground without grieving. he knows they will survive it— or, at least, *most* will.

do their wings and empathy burn up in the falling? do angels turn into different creatures, blistered and howling? is *that* what pain does to a person—makes a monster from a martyr?

if any angel is a man, it is lucifer. firstborn, most in god's image. i like a god that is small, and without wings. i like god to be simple, matter-of-fact, upright and dexterous, strange on four limbs. the angels can be buildings, or cranes, or architecture. i understand angels as ecosystems. but god should be small, and held in a palm.

one of the rarest metals on earth is iridium. it is virtually nonexistent in our crust, but it is common in meteors. almost all of the iridium we have in museums came from space rocks.

the greeks used to call the blood of the gods *ichor*, but i like the idea that angels are made from a similar material as iridium—shimmery, silver. alien. that their flaking bodies left blood as a solid in our lawns for children to pick up and tamper with. their ache as a mineral. as a precious filament.

if lucifer has our image, too—and he must have our image, to be so tempting—then his terminal velocity caps at fifty-three meters per second. i asked my brother, who is an engineer—*okay. so let's say satan made the crater that killed the dinosaurs. can we figure out where heaven is, based on the math around that?*

he says that *if* we believe that heaven happens just outside our atmosphere *and* satan is one hundred fifty kilograms—a huge man, but a man he could be—in order to make the same degree of damage as the chicxulub crater, satan would have to have particles that are *tachyonic.*

i had to google the term *tachyonic.* it is a hypothetical particle that can travel faster than light. my brother says, back-of-the-napkin-math, that it would have to be over 250 times the speed of light, *at least.*

so heaven must either be very far away, or satan must be bigger.

or, instead of falling, he was pushed. to slow his fall to a survivable speed—think of how massive his wings would have had to be.

what did lucifer think, while plummeting? was he not afraid?

after all, where do angels go if they die? what can an angel do, when the thing that has made him is also the thing that is rejecting him outright? how does he pray?

how could i *not* have pity for that moment: lucifer, blind and helpless, tumbling downward toward an alien planet.

Mouse looks at you and at the wedding invitation in your hand and at the world she has built for you. *i don't get it. i was good to you.*

She *was* good. She was good and she let a lot of bad things happen to this body. And the truth is that it's been fucking *hard.* You've watched what she is trying to do. She still throws up a lot.

can i have six more months? six more months and i'll leave, i'm out.

It hurts to see her panicked.

You put your hand to the mirror and start pushing.

 ROT

"ugh, would you—stop that?" marlowe's shoulders come up around her ears.

you take your finger out of My eye, blinking. "sorry. my contact is fucked up," you push your finger against your bottom lid, trying to get the little ring of fire back into place, careful not to smear your makeup, "it's like a million years old."

"daily lenses," she says, fluttering her eyes. she's working a tissue in her hands, adjusting her purse.

it's warmer than you expected, and the morning wind smells like the city.

you can't have daily lenses, you have astigmatism, which you're weirdly shy about. instead you push at your eye again and say, "right? okay. i'll talk to my eye guy."

her hands are already full, but she takes her phone out too. "i don't know where, like, everyone could be."

you both stand in front of the restaurant. earlier, you looked up the menu online and discovered it isn't really a place you can enjoy. a big red old-fashioned truck goes by, rattling.

"you know? all cars look the same to me," you tell her.

"and nobody's texted you, right?"

you check your phone even though you know the answer. you swipe through a few work emails and forget for a second what you're doing. oh, right. you check the same group chat she's already also looking at. you wrinkle your nose. "do you wanna call 'em?"

she sighs and shifts the coral-pink bag up her arm again. it's way too big for her.

she dials and holds the phone up, walking away from you. something in the figure-eight of her pacing while she waits for the other line to answer—you have to look back down at your phone, pretending to be busy.

you promised lacey you'd spy for her since she has—ironically—another wedding she has to be at right now. you text: *we're here but nobody else is it's super awkward.*

you play a level of the game *two dots,* which you are addicted to. you found it after you googled *games to play on your phone if you have anxiety.*

marlowe chirps, "hi! we're at the restaurant and i just wanna know if . . ."

to lacey: *sorry i'm gonna keep texting actually because i feel awkward right now lmfao*

you lose another life in *two dots* and then lacey's reply comes in: *ohhhh my god lol i'm cringing.*

to lacey: *helpppppp.*

to lacey: *it's only eight in the morning do you think it's okay if i start drinking now?*

you watch the typing icon come up and go away for a few times. oops. you start typing *that was a joke,* but then lacey's answer comes in.

from lacey: *the fact you haven't started yet is a testament to your strength and willpower.*

you text back: *it's a testament to sacrilege.*

marlowe returns and you black your screen. she shifts the purse up her shoulder, chewing her lip. "okay. so becca is gonna be able to make it, she's parking right now; but hannah can't, she's got food poisoning." she runs her hand through her hair.

"that's not so bad," you assure her, sounding more chipper than eight in the morning makes you feel, "it's just the first round of dresses anyway."

marlowe worries her lip still. she looks like she's about to speak when a girl comes trotting up, breathless. she's got tight blonde curls cropped in a bob and a runner's body (not that you notice) and a big broad grin on her face. "hi, hi, hi," she says. "i'm so sorry i'm late." she wraps marlowe in a hug, and they both squeal. she steps back and gulps the air, studying you.

you wave at her awkwardly, while marlowe says, "becca, this is another one of the bridesmaids, this—"

"oh, i know you from the group chat!" becca scoops you, unprompted, into a quick hug. despite everything, you love huggers. they just seem so earnest. you hug her back just as closely.

"it's so nice to meet you," when she steps back, she pushes her hair out of her face. "you're a good hugger, wow."

"hannah has food poisoning," marlowe says. you sketch a grateful bow at becca, who pouts big at the news.

"yikes. okay. well, if it's just us, should we go in?" she opens the door and holds it for you both, and you file in behind her. the reservation was for four people, so you're sat at a booth. for a second, nobody knows how to choose sides, but then you end up on the lonely side while becca and marlowe squeeze in together.

you aren't going to make an assumption about their size in comparison to yours and why they gave you all that room. you aren't. you glance at the menu. "should we just immediately go for mimosas?" you say.

becca laughs. "yes, absolutely." this makes you like her. then she points to marlowe. "not for you though, you don't want to be bloated." now you don't like her at all.

marlowe sighs. "yeah. honestly i don't know why i thought brunch before dress shopping was a good idea."

"okay to be fair, it's more like breakfast," you say. sweat forms in the small of your back despite the air conditioning. "most important meal of the day."

the cheapest thing on the menu is *eleven dollars*. what the fuck. for *fried eggs*?

"plus we have plenty of time before the wedding to lose the weight." becca gives marlowe a gentle hip nudge, winking. "i'm glad you're doing this so early in the planning."

"well, everywhere said it takes like nine months to get the dress in, and then three to get it altered . . ." marlowe trails off, her hands on the menu. "i'm sorry the plans were so last minute; this place had a cancellation and i just . . ."

becca waves the concern away while the waiter comes up. she orders the table a bucket of mimosas and a round of waters and then looks at us. "are we all ready to order too?"

you're not ready. fuck. "someone else go first."

becca gets a yogurt parfait. marlowe pauses for a bit and then gets two scrambled eggs and gluten-free toast.

you don't like anything on the menu. it's also fourteen dollars for a plain omelet. what the fuck. you choose the first thing you see. avocado toast. you inwardly flinch—avocados have so much fat.

"ugh, wait," becca holds up a finger. "actually, can i have that instead?" this makes you love her. she puts her palms into a little prayer position of thanks while the waiter slides away.

"i didn't know you're gluten-free," you say to marlowe.

she shrugs one slim shoulder. "not fully."

"gluten makes me so bloated," becca sighs. she winks at me. "but i can't resist bread."

"so . . . what kind of dress are you thinking of? like, style, i mean." you wish the waiter hadn't taken the menus. now there's nothing for your hands to do. you sort of awkwardly straighten your fork and knife.

"i'm not sure yet." marlowe tilts her head to one side. "today is more like . . . how i'm trying to figure that out."

"you know, i could really see you in one of those, like, mermaid styles," becca mimes the shape with her hands. "it'd look so good with your curves."

marlowe, to your ~~intimate~~ knowledge and observation, doesn't really have curves. you also just don't like the mermaid style, though, so maybe you're being unfair.

you let marlowe show you white dress after white dress on her phone. your heart is placing needles into your cheeks. when the waiter comes back with the water, you're mostly just glad to have something else to look at. when the mimosas come by, becca coos and claps her hands for the champagne opening. marlowe takes some but doesn't drink.

you all clink glasses—twice, once for becca's instagram—and you try to take a normal-and-average sip of your glass. now that becca mentioned bloating, you can't stop thinking about it. your shirt isn't tight but what if you just *think* it's not tight when it secretly *is*.

"i love your purse, by the way," becca says to marlowe over the rim of her glass, "i am a big purse girl myself. i mean like—big purse and also, like. big on purses, i guess."

marlowe smiles, her hand going to the behemoth. it's all rigid angles, more of a box than a bag. "it's vegan."

you bite back the automatic answer: *that's another way of saying it's plastic*. you miss lacey desperately.

becca reaches over her to touch the bag. "ugh. i wish i had mine right now. where'd you get it?"

"oh, t.j.maxx," marlowe nods at you like you would know that, "i was wine drunk and i was like, hold up. i need this."

you don't have anything interesting to add. "so how do you know marlowe, becca?"

the waiter returns with the food and you all sit back in your seats politely, trying to make room for the plates. the slice of bread is bigger than you expected, fuck. it's thick. you should have also ordered gluten-free.

becca evidently has no such reservations. she stabs her sunny-side-up egg while you hover over yours, her mouth in a relaxed grin. "oh, friend of the groom." she takes a bite, chews, and holds her hand up over her mouth while she speaks, gesturing with her fork between you and marlowe. "you guys know each other from college, right?"

you decide to start on the few bits of fruit next to your monstrosity of a meal. this and drinking? maybe if you only have half. you push a piece of melon over with your fork while you nod. "we met at—fuck, like, what, a thing for incoming students, right?"

marlowe laughs, shoots you a grin that you have to drop eye contact with. "oh yeah, like—she was making a little castle on one of the tables with the drink coasters they had."

"mouse house," you correct, before coughing and holding your hand to your chest. "wow, sorry, that came out way angrier than i meant it to." becca and marlowe both laugh lightly, but since you made it awkward, you're the one who has to fix it. you feign severity. "mouse houses are a deeply personal—" the joke isn't funny, so you don't finish it. "anyway, it's a big school, and freshman get lonely, so they had these like . . . little soirees." you put on a posh voice. "it was all quite charming."

marlowe laughs, which is good, because marlowe's laugh makes everyone relax. "oh my gosh, i will never forget—this guy comes up to us, we're building these, you know, *mouse houses*," she winks at you, "and he's tells us, like, you know, put the coasters back, people need to actually use them."

"which, like, he's not wrong," you admit.

"literally—and i will never forget this, becca—she goes—*this is technically using them.*" marlowe grins and looks at you, her eyes sparkling, big and wide and honest.

you never understood why people say *i will never forget* before a story. there is every chance you, for your part, will not only forget, but you will also think it never even happened to you. is this the part that's even real?

you spear a piece of pineapple.

"that's so cute," becca sounds genuinely wooed. "marlowe and i actually got introduced at, like, a party, kind of too."

she tells the story and you pretend to listen. you'd forgotten about the coasters you'd stacked into boxes and pyramids. you only really remembered the shock of marlowe's purple hair. she'd still had that undercut at the time, and had encouraged you to feel it after you'd complimented it. the way you'd first touched her was running your fingers over the fine velvet of her scalp. and then again, and then in her bed—

you realize this thought train is making you actively nauseous and then you have to pause for a moment, because the first thought you have is—*oh thank god, i don't want to eat.*

now, Mouse. you might be fucked up, but We're in therapy now, and you're not going to use *her* as an excuse.

marlowe holds her phone up to take a picture of the group, and you instinctively put peace signs in front of your face. she puts the phone down and winks at you.

you drink more of the mimosa. you're going to be unsafe to drive soon, but whatever. maybe it'll be worth the headache.

Transubstantiation escaped me. I *wanted* to be the kind of person who could believe the bread *literally* turned into the body of Christ, but that just was *evidently* untrue: it would have tasted different.

An irony: my OCD can somehow believe that if I eat a certain type of donut my family will suffer—but for some reason, the idea of a man speaking Jesus into the room via medium of stale bread is a *step* too far for me. It goes against my lived reality.

At least with my OCD, the rules have always made some sense— my brain would search for variables to change in order to shift my fate around. I have faith in chaos theory. If a butterfly can create a tornado, I can create bad luck by virtue of a breakfast treat. Whenever

I experience hardship on an otherwise-normal day, I end up dissecting all the small choices I made. *Oh, this is because I chose a Boston cream.* That donut is now dead to me.

But I never saw *proof* that God showed up in the eucharist. In fact, long after I was confirmed and was a full adult, I learned sort of guiltily—and with surprise—*oh, we're supposed to* literally *believe that?*

It can be easy to mock religion. I have heard my fair share of *so you're listening to an old man in the sky? Skydaddy will give you what you want if you ask nicely?* I cannot tell you how many "Are Catholics cannibals?" and "Does eating the eucharist count as eating meat?" kinds of jokes I have received.

Even deep in the traditional communities I was raised in, there are always people who admit—they don't *literally* believe in God-as-the-Father. They will readily tell you that much of the Bible functions as a metaphor. They understand that God cannot be drawn or imagined, but that one must conceptualize the everlasting *somehow*, so the old man image can stay for now.

The aggressive disdain of certain atheists was a hard point for me. It served no purpose I could ascertain. In the traditional circles I was raised in, atheistic spite was even used as an example of how atheists are morally depraved. How they mock our faith rather than trying to understand it. It made it harder to leave: we saw exactly how little acceptance we were facing. Nobody was going to be kind to us if we left. We were pointed toward that vitriol and were told, with delight— we *are* being persecuted.

I didn't see the point of it at first, except to signal to other atheists just how "cool and evolved" their group was. It didn't seek to "shock" someone into losing their faith—it just sort of suggested a lack of knowledge or empathy.

It's been a while, and I get it now. I don't blame the aggression, is the thing. Particularly against the casual American tradition of

Christian beliefs. It is an institutional bias; there will be people deeply and permanently injured by it. *I* am one of those people.

But for a long time, I associated any form of atheism as . . . just being cruel. I had been raised too traditionally. Often it felt like they saw my faith as purposeful self-delusion rather than deserving of sympathy.

It matters to me how much the narrative of *why didn't you leave the church if what was happening was so ugly* and *why didn't you leave him* both mistake an act of persistent agony for a single act of simplicity.

It wasn't like I ever really found a *home* in the church. I knew early it didn't want me.

But where else would I go? To what community?

◇

N   O: MORE

the dress store is the pristine offspring of a hotel and a spa. it's very trendy and instagram-able. everyone speaks in shy, cheery tones, murmuring to each other. one of the walls has been covered in huge white feathers, under which a pink neon signs says *i do.* everything is white and clean and sterile, but—even you, asshole that you are—you find yourself also cooing at the whole thing. your favorite feature is a black fountain in the waiting area, a naked cherub pouring water into a marble basin.

it's kind of awkward now that becca is in the bathroom. while you wait, a charming lady in a fashionably modern-but-professional dress has given you all another round of champagne. you now want to keep drinking for the rest of the morning. that is a horrible desire. stop it.

you and marlowe stand near the fountain, holding a glass each, not-looking at each other.

"his dick is out," she says. now you are both staring at the little molded penis.

"all men are the same," you sigh. "any excuse to show off."

she chuckles with the half snort that you're so familiar with. she sits down heavily on the black velvet bench. behind her, the wall is covered in fake ferns, a verdant lush green overlaid with a white neon sign that reads *love is all you need.*

"do you think listening to the water makes the people who work here, like, have to pee all the time?" you don't want to sit down yet. you want to pace, but there isn't really enough room for that. other excited groups have gathered, patiently waiting to be plucked and carted into whatever back room for their fitting.

"i can't believe mom couldn't come." she presses the heel of her hands into her eyes. "it's literally always like this with her."

you know you're supposed to comfort her, so you come over and do your duty, trying to casually sling your arm around her shoulder, gawky. she's so bony.

you think of lacey, and how touching her just feels like—*duh.* ~~there was a time when touching marlowe would have been the same thing.~~

you remove your arm and sip your champagne and nudge her to do the same. she obliges mechanically. you knit your brows. "i thought she was, like, really excited now that you're—" you don't want to say it, so you put on a posh accent, "betrothed."

"she was," she growls. "now it's just, like, nothing is good enough. everything is about her. the cake can't be lemon, she doesn't like citrus. the dress can't look like *her* dress. the sky can't be blue, her wedding had a blue sky." she puts her hand to her temple and lets out a single, aggressive moan, just quiet enough you know it's honest.

this confuses you. you glace at the phone in your hand, thinking of the group chat. "wait. i thought peggy was, like, genuinely—"

she waves her hand. "no, not peggy. oh my god. no, no, my *mother* has been great, she legit can't make it today because she's doing me a favor right now with a possible venue. no, like, *mom*. michelle."

"michelle." who the fuck is michelle?

one nod. "my mother-in-law."

she hadn't said "mother-in-law," right? or did you just hear wrong? are you misremembering?

maybe marlowe still knows you, on some weird level, because she answers the question you didn't ask. "i'm trying to get used to calling her *mom*. she's, like, insisted on it."

"um," you say. "i don't . . . love that."

"don't love what?" becca comes bounding back, adjusting her outfit. she is all smiles as she scoots down onto the bench next to you, nudging your leg in a gentle, friendly way.

you don't know how private marlowe is about this, and you're used to adam, so you find yourself immediately trying to hide the situation, to distract her. "becca, can i just say? your hair is so cute."

"my mother-in-law wants me to call her my mom." marlowe scowls. she starts turning the glass in her hand, swirling the liquid.

"oh, she's just being friendly," becca assures her. "honestly, it's really good she wants to be included like that."

"yeah, i guess," marlowe says.

"right," you say. "maybe."

"like, so many people i know have, like, mothers-in-law that don't actually accept them. it's kind of cute she, like, cares so much about this."

you cut your eyes directly to the cherub penis just so you don't say anything in response, hearing the sharp intake of marlowe's breath, feeling the way she stiffens.

is that the plural of *mother-in-law*? you assumed the *s* would go on *law*, not on *mother*.

"how about that little cherub penis, huh?" you blurt.

"yeah," marlowe says, her voice flat, "how about that."

you miss lacey. you text her a picture of the fountain cherub. "does this count as sexting?" you flash the screen to marlowe. she's not looking—chewing on her lip and scrolling through her phone instead. becca laughs, though.

"marlowe?" the woman from earlier shows back up. she's older than any of you, proper but friendly. sturdy looking in a pleasant way. fuck, why do you care so much about other people's bodies? you took actual classes on this. "i'm alexa—yes, like the device. i'll be taking care of you today." she beams at us. "and you two must be the bridesmaids, right? how are you liking the champagne?"

you want to french kiss her just for interrupting when she did. you owe her your very life. you offer your hand to marlowe to help her up, but she is too busy texting to see it.

alexa leads you through a few showrooms (you all coo), deposits you all in a velvet-lined private room. gold and mirrors and chintz. you think—*if i worked here, i'd fuck someone on the floor in one of these dresses, just to say i did.*

not a very christian thought, and god is watching. plus, you really shouldn't fuck anybody for a while, not after ████████.

you thought you were ready, but you weren't ready. when marlowe comes out in that first dress—a mermaid style—it doesn't matter that she doesn't like it. it doesn't matter that you all tell her to go change into something else. over alexa's laughing—*that's one off the list!*—you wish, fervently, you had more to drink. something else to get through this.

you open your *two dots* game and lose a life. becca talks about her boyfriend. you have come back around to becca, and decided you like her, because she's utterly harmless.

"do you have a boyfriend?" she smiles at you.

nevermind, you hate her. you wince before you can stop yourself. from the changing room, marlowe shouts, "she's gay!"

"oh my god," becca puts one hand over her mouth, "i'm so sorry. i meant, like, girlfriend? do you have a girlfriend? like, i didn't—you don't look—i'm—"

"i'm bi actually," you close the phone screen. "i gotta keep my portfolio options open."

becca laughs. you are kind of shocked by how genuine it sounds. she puts one hand on your leg. "oh my god. marlowe said you were funny, but you *really are*."

you are so shocked by this, you have literally no response. you blink. it has been a really long time since anyone said that about you.

"it's because she's gay," marlowe calls again. "that's how she lures girls in."

becca laughs again and winks at you. "oh, it's working."

you roll your eyes. "*bi*," you insist to the wall hiding marlowe, and then, in a conspiratorial mock-whisper to becca, you add: "marlowe just *wishes* i was gay."

"say the word and i will run away with you," marlowe shouts back, and then the door opens again, and she shuffles out, alexa in tow.

alexa had to clip marlowe into the dress using industrial wood clamps. this one is a tight satin slip. it's so obvious how thin she is under it.

you wish you were in the victorian times just so you could pretend to faint and be carted away from this place. maybe if you just started to pass out *a little?* like, just a normal amount of passing out. your ears are ringing.

you don't like the dress on her, are you biased? did you picture her in a ball gown? in something gauzy, fluttery, full of magic? did you ever picture her actually saying yes to all of it? standing next to you, blushing, looking up through her lashes?

becca thinks it's a strong contender. alexa is of course charming and funny. marlowe spins around herself, laughing.

you lose a life in *two dots* again. you text a picture of marlowe to your mom. she texts back *beautiful dress!*

after a few minutes, there's a general agreement that time is moving on and there's a lot to try on, time for the next dress. marlowe throws you a grin over her shoulder. in a witch voice, she announces: "back into the closet for me."

"oh," becca reaches out and touches your thigh, so casual and friendly, "i should tell you. my cousin is gay."

"oh! how fun," you smile at her. at this point in your life, you find this kind of interaction sort of funny, since you're pretty sure it's her way of being kind.

"oh my gosh, that reminds me. i have *got* to show you pics of my pride outfit. i went this year to support them and it was so cute and fun."

you appropriately react to each of the pictures, taking the gentle offer of companionship. it's a wedding dress fitting, after all, and it's actually nice to make friends. no, you and becca have very little in common—but that stuff has stopped mattering to you.

wait, where did you learn that from? is this you, placating adam's friends again?

or. it feels impossible, but it *could* be true—whatever strange glimmering anger you had is slowly growing silent. maybe it's just that you got hurt so badly you no longer want to be the person *doing* the hurting.

marlowe walks out in her dress, and suddenly everyone is crying. you wish, fervently, that you had food poisoning. you wish you had been drinking more.

you text lacey: *is there any way you can, like, fake an emergency?*

your mom hands you a tiny plastic dragon.

"uh," you say.

"for your project. you're collecting monsters, right?"

"are dragons monsters?"

"you could make them monsters."

"that's true of most things." you hip check her gently to show you're joking.

"flowers can't be monsters."

"what if you're allergic?" you turn the dragon over in your hand. "this is a nice dragon, though, damn. it's got heft."

"i got it from the dump. i thought you'd like it."

"i love it." you do love it.

"flowers can't be monsters," she repeats.

"okay but what about, like, oleander? nightshades."

"oh, that's a great idea, ███! you could write a book about, like, someone who works at a flower shop and kills people by selling them foxglove and things like that."

you don't write mystery, unfortunately. "although, actually, that kind of proves your point, though. flowers aren't the monster, the person doing the whole murder thing is."

"████████████████."

"i went to college for astute observations about that kind of thing." you make the dragon balance on your palm. "i'm gonna call him fernando."

"it might be a girl dragon," she offers. "you don't know."

"sorry, fernando."

"i like menace. you should call him menace."

you coo. "oh, that's perfect. menace the dennis."

"you should write a book about dragon detectives. you'd love that. maybe we could write it together."

you look up at her. "immediate international bestseller."

Give me back this moment, Mouse.
Give me back my mother. Give me back my loved ones.
Give me back my family. Give me back feeling.
Give me back my fucking body.

look closer. i'm not writing, though, am i. i'm confessing.

Plants can grow inside of the human body.

It's vanishingly rare, of course, but it's possible. Our bodies can act as soil. Plants can and often do consume meat. "Blood meal" and "bone meal" are not euphemisms. A body is an astounding fertilizer. It can be true that a seed will find purchase inside you.

In the state I grew up in, a man was found to have a sprout growing in his lungs. He had choked on a single pea, and it had slipped down the "wrong tube." It took root. It was safely removed. The man continued to eat peas after this incident.

Relatedly: in the eighth grade, my friend jokingly threw a freshly sharpened pencil at me, point first. I caught it. The school nurse couldn't get out all the graphite from my palm. I still carry around a tiny black mark.

There are times in this world when the poetics of the matter and the facts of the matter are indistinguishable. Both stand up and hold hands through the mirror.

 MOUTH

hold up your hand to the light, watch the sun come through your skin. subsurface scattering. take up drawing. take up kickboxing. cry over a work meeting.

go to therapy. talk for an hour straight. feel like you haven't accomplished anything.

text your friends from middle school. from work. from college. remember how many friends you *actually* have. go out and make more of them. remember why you liked having hobbies, before him.

go to therapy. talk for an hour straight again. feel glorious any time you're able to start a sentence with *well, my therapist says.* figure out how to french braid your hair.

go to a museum. go to a library. gag when you accidentally find an email draft of a letter you eventually hand-wrote to him. go on a hike in the full moon, get bitten by bugs. go to a dance class where you make friends with a seventy-six-year-old woman. go to a dance class where you are the most out-of-shape person there.

listen to *antianxiety music* for four days straight, but don't pick up wine the whole time. journal your thoughts, eventually stop scribbling your handwriting so much.

go to therapy. say *i'm trying to figure out the difference between being a monster and being made into a monster.* listen while your therapist is talking.

hold your hand up. it takes a bit, but you eat the burrito in private and then in public and then in front of your friends. take up cooking. take up baking. feed your new friends with an army supply of your cookies. listen to "bronze statue" by pavel lyubomudrov on repeat. think the universe is sending you messages about healing; at first by accident—and then believe it through *force.* you *will* see the good in the world, even if it leaves you absolutely ruined.

microwave your single meal dinners. stop counting your calories. let the batteries die in the bathroom scale without replacing them. cry happily. listen to audiobooks, many bad, some sappy. catch up on tv. stop constantly checking the angles of your body.

go to therapy, talk for an hour straight, laughing. you forgot you were funny, and smart, and kind, and willing. you forgot you were creative, and passionate, and ready.

feel the loneliness again, still, maybe always. maybe we *will* die alone. sometimes, this isn't scary anymore.

try new things. stop caring if people are watching you. play dnd on tuesdays. spend an irresponsible amount on removable wallpaper. start finally putting in applications to shelters to see about getting a dog. do better at work. find a better job. find good books.

go to therapy, cry about it, hold your shaking hands up, forming them around a new eucharist in the shape of a boston cream donut; something that you haven't touched since you were eight due to your ocd.

sometimes you let mold grow in the sink and spend hours on your floor, wondering what about you makes you so fundamentally wrong.

But on this day, finally: I eat the fucking donut.

Contract broken, both of us stand in the same body. Warm under the sun.

 MOUSE

like a dog, i dream about running. a thorn enters my foot; skin swallows the garden.

lacey is calling me. fuck. the alarm with three skulls has been mysteriously silenced. my past self is treasonous, caught in the nebulous lust of snooze buttons, snake quick. the scab on my elbow has come off. it's october.

how is it *october already.*

"are you sleeping in?"

the blackout curtains. kaisa specifically said i shouldn't get them, her smile sloping gently when she suggested reconsidering. "no. i'm up."

"you're sleeping in."

the dream was about good behavior. like a dog. the underground world had been filled with people in satin. their sounds and their laughter were still ringing in the air, but their bodies eerily frozen. a little boy told me they were being punished. they'd stay frozen until obedience training was over.

"i'm not sleeping in, i super promise." i absolutely had been sleeping in and she knows it. "i have way too much to do."

"you're lying. i love you. now get out of bed and text me when you're ready. i'm going to eat breakfast and shower. okay, love you, bye." lacey disconnects. okay, love you, bye.

the shower is too cold. someone downstairs is probably nursing their bad dreams too, holding them in the collarbone.

i should do some version of a workout. instead, i sit on the stupid yoga mat in stupid ass-out shorts that say *judges 15:15* that lacey bought me for my last birthday. i send in stupid work edits on my stupid phone while my laptop is open, stupidly, right in front of me.

i decide on a ten-minute *yoga flow* youtube. i am learning how to do a better crow pose.

lacey calls again. "you didn't text. are you dead?"

"i'm dead and a ghost."

"i'm seventeen minutes away. i will come up there and *get* you if i have to."

we say *love you see you soon* and then i have to *run.*

my hair is like weirdly dry lately and i need to remember to take my dbt workbook and journal and i didn't really pack last night and the article i was supposed to update isn't uploading. also, i think my panty line is probably visible through my jeans. i'm absolutely bad feminist for caring. where is margaret atwood.

speaking of male fantasies: lacey's new car is an orange-yellow mustang boss 302. i fucking love this thing. i am infinitely grateful she offered to drive.

i have to tuck my knees to my chest to fit and the seat is always lower than i expected. "i dreamed about like, dancers. but they were living, like, under the ground." i argue my overstuffed bag into the miniscule backseat and she hands me a coffee i'm not going to like but i order every time anyway because adam taught me to and i always forget to change it on the starbucks app. "do you think it's, like, a metaphor for having worms?"

"are they ever going to get your sleep study results back?" she doesn't flip her turn signal before yanking us into traffic, the car yowling at forty in a twenty-five.

i don't like the coffee. oh well. tiny miseries can be made into poems. "i think they forgot i exist."

"tanner has been dreaming too."

i shoot her a dirty look, grinning. "do i want to know the rest of this story?"

"*no!*" she gasps and swats my bicep, while i mock-hoot in pain, laughing. "not like *that.*" she gives me a wicked smile. "but if you want more information on *those* . . . ?"

i slap my hands over my ears. "mercy, oh my god, *no.*"

she cackles and then glances over at me. "hey, can i say something wild?"

i hope it's a fun sexy thing. i gesture outward. "as always."

she sends me another sideways glance. her smile is soft. "you've been looking really good lately. more *here,* i think."

i blush, which is embarrassing. "uh. yeah." shrug. "it's the therapy."

my phone gleefully disconnects between wi-fi and data; three emails roll in at once.

Hi, Thanks for bringing this to my attention!

"how *are* things with tan?" i scroll upward and then slap my forehead. "i forgot to bring spanx. fuck."

"shit," she grimaces with me.

"tanner though. answer the question."

she smiles in another way. a way i only see her do now and again. "things are . . . good."

"oh, you *like* him like him, huh?"

it's her turn to blush. "he's okay," she coughs. at my look, she swats me again. we both turn our eyes to the street and shriek while a squirrel darts out in front of the wheels. lacey's hands work the wheel easily while she keeps going.

i look back to check. "it's alive!"

"my bad." she makes the square-face, double-chin flinch that means *whoops.* i recognize it from my own body language and laugh.

the engine reminds me of shaking grave dirt. i like how it feels to be in this car, adjacent to power. masculine simulacrum by proxy of loud car—bad feminism, maybe. but it *is* kind of fun. "oh, hey, how's the new exercise bike?"

she rolls her eyes. "can you believe it was a thousand dollars? why did we spend that much? it's just a bike." she flicks her glance over to me. "thank you for asking."

i have started to be good about this. i keep a list on my phone about things that are happening in the lives of my friends since my memory is shit. i want them to know that i actually, you know, pay attention. "next time tell him you got the bike for a thousand dollars and then just get like a walmart brand and keep the cash."

she snorts down her nose. she has a habit of driving with only one hand at a time, free arm either playing with her piercings or checking her phone. i watch her swipe an email notification.

which reminds me. i check mine. janice suggests that i update the new excel sheet that she makes us keep that has no value whatsoever. and *then* i can sign off for vacation.

i frown over my updates, trying to figure out what to enter without repeating myself a million times. "what's another word for accessible?"

lacey is changing the song on her spotify. "obtainable?"

"no, like. when you're reading at your skill level."

"smart."

"no." i bite my thumbnail. i have finally kicked the habit of tearing them off but it's still, like, a little teeth shelf. "like, easy to read."

"oh. i don't know. um . . . simple?"

i look up, tilting my head to the music she's playing. "is this mahler's fifth?"

"yeah. i don't know. foggy weather, fall, halloween vibes? felt right." she gasps and looks over at me. "shit. wasn't this like, you and adam's—"

"okay, don't—no worries, i'm okay." *the things that happened to this body happened to someone else anyway.*

"i love you," she says, and puts on "spooky scary skeletons" instead.

"i love *you*. also, okay, to be cheesy for a second? the leaves are so fucking pretty. holy shit. did they turn like, overnight?" golden and hazy. the sun just right, Instagram filtered. "*fuck*, it's a beautiful day. i'm mad it's like, so goddamn perfect."

"so how are you . . . like . . . doing?"

"i mean." when we were kids she and i went sledding and i was scared shitless and when she shouted *bail!* i stayed in and held on. "i'm *purely* there to cause chaos."

"and!" she holds up one finger, "don't forget! you are *also* there to steal."

"casual theft! we love larceny!"

she gives my thigh a gentle pat. soothing. "i'm not going to leave your side. it's going to be me and you hunched over and sipping out of a fishbowl together and it's going to fucking rock." points at me again. "drinking *and* stealing."

"i brought, like. probably too many dresses to try on."

we are fourteen again. i feel so lucky these days, to be surrounded by people who love me.

we did also throw up ███ times this week. but hey. it's down from ████.

lacey adjusts her hair. "i like, emptied my closet into a bag. it takes up literally the entire trunk. and don't talk to me about how much underwear i brought, like i'm gonna shit myself every single day. shit myself *twice*."

"did you bring the green velvet?"

"i *did* bring the green velvet."

"ugh." i feign agony. "you're going to *kill* in that. can you not save some of the smolder? hold it back for those of us who are shuffling about with our little mole noses on the ground?"

"i know, right?" she flips the ring up into her nose and then back out. "oh, shit wait, did you bring a curling iron?"

i can't remember. "probably. i threw everything into the bag and ran."

"same here, honestly." the squeeze migrates from my thigh to my hand without looking. her fingers are cold. "i'm letting you know that i'm only going to this because *you're* going. marlowe owes you *big* time."

"god owes me karma points." i snort like oh so casual. "i'm gonna get to the pearly gates and god will be like—*oh, yeah, no, she's a huge mess. but we gotta let her in, she went to that bachelorette.*"

"um, excuse me." lacey holds her pointer finger up prissily again, grinning, perfectly mocking. "not a *traditional* bachelorette though!"

i honk a laugh. "what did the—on facebook, it was like, what, *surprise party for friendship and feminine bonding*? like first of all, i said that to be *funny.*"

"and, like, no offense to that girl who was planning it, but then you said—"

"i *know,* right? *ghouls and gals goblin gathering* really had so much potential." i put a hand to my forehead in a swoon. "my talents are fucking squandered. *wasted.*"

"it's a crime."

"also i know we've said this already but the fact it's so close to halloween—"

lacey is already nodding. "and the fact it's *not fucking halloween themed!*"

"literally should be considered a federal offense."

"hang on." she switches to something chopin, eyes entirely off the road. "okay. so, like, how drunk are we getting?"

"you know, i don't really dream if i drink?"

"that's . . . ? so weird. was that part of the study?"

it wasn't. "do you think they're going to, like, tell me if i'm really weird about sleep, or do you think they're going to, like, let me live in blissful ignorance."

"you *know* you're really weird about sleep."

"dude, i'm so excited to plan your bachelorette one day. i have literally a binder of ideas." well, not physically. but plans A through R are pretty good.

she makes a noise in the back of her throat and then slams us onto the highway, barely checking the mirrors. "i mean, if tanner ever actually, like, does propose, i cannot *wait* to see what you do."

i loosen my grip on the door and go back to the work i was supposed to be doing. "i think i put more exclamation marks into emails than, like, is strictly necessary."

"i'm a solid two-to-three." the sun slants across the dash and we both flip the visor down. she puts on sunglasses she's had since we were, like, sixteen. they say *citibank* and would be heinous on anyone else. her hair picks up the green of the plastic.

"do you think tanner is, like, *close* to proposing?"

she sighs dreamily. "i don't know. we talk about it sometimes, like . . . what we want, where this is going. but i think we're just . . . like we're *good* right now. no sense in rushing."

"london would have been *so* good, though."

"london *would* have been so good," she agrees.

for a bad moment, i think about texting adam *hi, been thinking about you.* instead, i sit on my hands and watch the gentle neck of yellow leaves and the navy tongue of the wettened road, humming along to the radio.

In the middle of the drive home, about twenty minutes after the first exit but thirty before the second, Route 2 slopes downward. There's another highway I don't know the name of that's just visible in the distance, cresting a hill I also don't know the name of. In the feral dark, the lights of the other highway end up floating just above the tree line.

This delicate slope of white wings, the powerful and silent lift of one thousand glowing geese, arching their mechanical bodies into the expanse of the horizon.

One thousand people also going to or coming from home; their winking suspended lives dangling in the intangible *away*. One pearl necklace, and the soft ache of mechanical rosary beads, passing over the head of the New England skyline.

The prayer of one thousand people; all of us not-quite-here, distracted. Driving together. Getting home together. Closing our eyes to the muted, gentle laughter of our childhood. Kissing our little lives goodnight before the bird of our heart comes home, her crinkled feathers all coated in mist.

◇

 ME

lacey pulls into the parking lot. turns and faces me. her shirt has her old summer camp logo on it. she unbuckles her seatbelt. grabs her keys. puts the keys back down. punches the radio off. clicks her tongue and takes a deep breath and tucks her right hip so she's facing me. her arms reverse atlas over the wheel.

oh shit. looks serious. i put the phone down.

"i love you," she says. her knuckles are white around the edges of her keychain. she jabs the keys toward me. "and i want you to know we are going to get through this together."

"i'm going to be okay!" i laugh. it doesn't sound like a laugh. it sounds like a bark. woof.

"you don't need to be." she pushes the sunglasses back onto her head, a precious green tiara. her eyes scan mine. "if you need to leave, if you need to breathe, literally if you need *anything*—just say the word. i will pack up my shit. i will call us an uber if we are drunk. but i love you, and i will go."

i reach up and braid a section of her deep hair, up behind her ear.

"i love you too," i say. i tie the braid off, look back into her eyes. "for real, lace'. i'm going to be okay."

"look at me."

okay. her eyelashes are so long.

"i'll kill her if she hurts you. i'll kill anyone who hurts you." lacey holds my cheek, her thumb whisking my skin. "i love you. i mean it."

"i will also kill anyone who hurts you," i repeat, "i love you too." we both sit there in the cooling car, and we both mean it.

The daughter is standing in the garden, and the weeds that are in her hair are tangled and nasty. Her hand is around an apple. She is cowering and dusty.

For a long time, she will mistake the grime of survival for being dirty.

if i can learn to hover, i will never fully be in the place my mother cannot touch me.

you can figure out a way to wash your hands without scraping the whole skin off, but you'll actually have to pay attention in therapy instead of just performing the motions. there is an ache that is seeping between the floorboards. they pretend that getting better is easy, that you make the choice to go to therapy and then, six months later, like a magic trick—you're just *healed*, happy and ready.

i tell my therapist i still have no idea what the space between *overwhelmed* and *completely numb* would even *look* like. she suggests that maybe it's good enough, for now, that i can even recognize the fact i'm getting overwhelmed.

i want to be brave enough that the whole world rings with the
note of the bell i am carrying inside my left hip. i want someone to cry
over me. i want a drink. i want to ███████ ██ ███████████████.
i instead make soup.

recovery isn't pretty. but the discord does become a melody if you
play it on loop.

the hotel suite is beige-yellow, affordable-classy. bags are already
taking up every flat surface. there are a lot of cheek kisses and
champagne. i hug becca, give her a spin so she can show off her
sparkly outfit. she introduces lacey and me around the circle of girls
whose names i immediately forget. we crowd around the three mirrors
and flutter eyelashes in our own e.l.f eye kits.

"okay but i love the purple dress on you." lacey is weaving my
curling iron around her head. "i think you should go with the purple."

it's too tight. i don't like the idea that if i sit, my body will be a real
body. i should have worn different underwear, but i am learning to just
wear something else and not make a big deal about it. "i'm just in, like,
sort of a dark, witchy mood."

"we'll do a shot and then decide. i think you should go with, like,
sexy minx meets biggest regret vibes."

"i'm really feeling more like. garden gnome lost in the earthly
delights."

"artistic, i like it. could we add possums to the mix? you love
possums."

"um, *yes*, of course. i'm kind of thinking, like. a feral cat suddenly
understands her own mortality. but make it an *aesthetic*."

"oh, that's a good one! i know you loved the *cats* movie. really
brings it back."

i saw *cats* with adam. "genuinely, the musical of the decade. don't let others tell you, uh, otherwise."

she laughs. "you fucking *hated* that movie, dude."

"i've come back around on it. enemies to lovers, slow burn."

"you know? thematically correct for you. we're going to match lipstick, right?"

"i was gonna go with that one we got at—yeah, exactly. the sephora one." i'm suddenly weirdly shy. "uh, also, this is maybe—i don't know, gross. but, um. i also have like, a set of earrings i brought? i was thinking we could match those, too, maybe. like, um, maybe do," i swallow the tail of the sentence, embarrassed, a blush spiking my cheeks, ". . . like an earring swap?"

"okay, first, this color is killer on you. secondly, you are fucking amazing and i love you and we are absolutely doing an earring swap." lacey checks her phone. "hey, marlowe is about to show up. are you okay?"

i smile at her. "i'm in therapy."

we all scatter to hide. i don't do a good job of it, make a joke and pretend to hide under a lampshade. becca presses in with me. we 3-2-1, marlowe does look appropriately surprised, she laughs and does shots with all of us. lots of touching and laughing and playing music too loudly. happy engagement!

i lend marlowe the purple dress. her hip bones show through it. lacey does marlowe's hair with my iron. i start a list in my phone of things i want to buy the happy couple as a wedding gift. i send my mom a picture of the earrings.

marlowe puts her palm flat on my cheek. "i'm so glad you came. i love you and i have been missing you lately."

i noose two fingers around her skinny wrist. "i miss you too! sorry for having been so hard to pin down for, like, months now. how's the cat?"

she grins. "toothpaste is good. getting old, though."

"when dave was getting older, we had to put him on that old-cat food. with like—"

"oh, my dad calls that the *creatine treatment*," she laughs. "senior cat food or whatever?"

"how *is* papa marlowe?"

"did i tell you he started collecting puzzles recently?"

"did she tell you she might get a dog soon?" lacey interjects, pointing to me. "how fun is that?"

"oh," marlowe blinks.

something about the look on her face bothers me. i switch topics. "but yeah, like, i'm sorry i haven't been able to, like, hang out or, like, make it to, like, anything, recently." not since that first dress fitting.

"i know the job has been, like. keeping you *so* busy."

"yeah it's, like, totally, like . . . it's a lot." it isn't. i'm actively avoiding her. i am avoiding this. i am avoiding going to bars with her and getting drunk with her and seeing her fill up on marital bliss. bad, bad feminist.

listen—i'm *trying* to get better. i'm not perfect.

"she sold out." lacey shows up and shoves me a completely full cup. i have to slurp it to get it safely below the rim. "now she's too cool and rich for us."

for us. what a use of the plural inclusive. how is it possible i always forget they *also* used to be friends. "you know how it is. dog eat dog, and i am a bitch." i waggle my head, trying to make the bad joke funnier by preemptively mocking it.

"d'you remember when you bit that guy in—" marlowe looks devious.

"oh, *i* know this one." lacey angles herself, putting her body between me and marlowe. her tone is the exact level of parsed politeness that i recognize to mean she's actually just saying *not today, bitch.* "didn't he like, try to hurt you, marlowe? and she bit him while she was defending you?"

i get a little thrill at her protectiveness of me and have to smile into my cup, pretending not to notice it.

"um, we talked about it after, and he was actually, like, joking, but yeah," marlowe cuts her eyes to me. "i *did* tell him to fight me." she laughs, but lacey and i don't.

"one time i bit a man just for, like, *being* there." i sip my drink. "it was just, like, a tuesday. we were in a cafeteria line. didn't know the dude either. i was just like—*munch.*"

"are you fucking insane?" lacey's eyebrows say *babe why*, but she's smiling.

"i have literally no idea. he was just available to be bitten."

"you're going—i mean you're *going* to jail." marlowe's amused. "i fully expect this behavior from you."

bitch. *you don't know me.* i snap my teeth at lacey, directing my response toward her. "you gotta keep 'em guessing. keeps the dating pool active and lively. like shark feeding."

"one time, before tanner, i told a guy i thought i could drink blood, just for, like, the drama. i wanted to know what, like, *happened.*"

i reel at her, gaping, grabbing her bicep. "this is insane but i legit," before adam, "like i *did the same thing.*"

"ugh. thank god i never have to date again." marlowe sighs, throws her head back. "can you . . . like can you believe that? i'm getting *married.*"

"i'm literally so happy for you!" i add a vocal exclamation point. "i feel really lucky to be here with you and celebrating, dude, for real."

"okay but did the dude, *like,* that you were a—like did he think it was hot that you thought you were a vampire?" lacey uses her free hand to hook her pointer finger into a mock fang. "because mine, like, he *liked* it."

"no, tell me he did not," i choke on my sip, "he did *not.*"

"*i* had to drop the act because *he didn't*. he was—i shit you not—*turned on by it.*" she gives a tangy vampiric hiss.

i have to put the cup down while laughing, winded. lacey starts laughing too. we lisp dracula lines at each other—*i vant to suck your cock!*

"i never, like, did any of that weird stuff, but i like a little light choking," marlowe says, over lacey's *i onvly eat pussy!* and my *i'm a monster bella; eh heh heh heh.*

"you gotta be careful with that shit," i say.

"ugh. did you hear about those people that literally died from doing all that fifty-shades shit? like. oh my god." lacey steps forward and pushes my hair back from behind my ear. the weirdness of not being in a circle overrides my good sense and i have to step so we return to an equilateral triangle.

marlowe looks fucking perfect in that dress. i hope she doesn't give it back. i always feel kind of bad for the environment when i burn things. carcinogens or whatever. "where and when is the honeymoon?"

marlowe shrugs. the music shifts and we all take a sip and then marlowe angles her phone upward so we can be in her instagram story. i look down, away.

"okay. here's the drinking game." i hold up my free hand. "kinkiest shit you've ever done. if someone else has done it, you both drink and put a finger down. if only you did it, you drink but keep the finger up."

"not numbers?" marlowe looks surprised.

i don't know how to answer that.

"no, i wanna play *this* one." lacey shoots marlowe a dark look and then shakes her hair down her back. "for the record, this is a judgment-free kink zone. i am saying this because i am *going* to annihilate you both."

"you're going to die," marlowe looks *very* assured, "this is a fool's game."

"anal beads," lacey says, right out of the gate. i don't drink, but marlowe does.

"okay, let me think," she says. "choking, i guess, since i said that one already."

lacey and i immediately sip. "practically *vanilla*," i say, and i make it sound like a joke. my phone buzzes. a text from kaisa:

Hi! Just saw that Marlowe posted a story with you guys. I'm glad you got there safe. Let me know if you want to talk later or if you need a break! I'll be up pretty late.

from kaisa: *Tell Lacey I said she looks nice :)*

underneath her texts, i have three others; one from a new friend, two from old ones i've just now reconnected with. someone recently said to me *you're easy to get along with* and i've been riding that high for *weeks*.

i flash the screen and kaisa's texts to lacey, who coughs into her drink. a blush flames across her face, which she hides under one palm. she fans herself, grinning, before taking a deep breath and pulling herself together.

"where were we? oh. wait, so. okay, so get this—" lacey sits back, almost onto someone else's makeup bag, she and the other girl laugh and hold each other's elbows. "once i accidentally forgot that choking is, like, a kink thing? and i ended up telling my *dad*."

my eyes bulge. "say more *immediately*." this is way better than coming out in a wendy's. i have never been more invested in a story in my whole life.

"no. no way," she laughs, "i'm not *nearly* drunk enough to tell y'all yet." at the reminder, we all drink, and then lacey gestures to me. "all yours, my liege."

"sex in a garden." that feels safe. risky but not *weird*. just frisky.

neither of them move, so i drink and keep the finger up.

"i—*where*?" marlowe is blinking. "like, in public?"

i mumble into the rim of my cup. "uh. at my local garden share."

they both immediately explode. in between lacey's *you absolute whore i'm obsessed with you* and marlowe's *your fucking—public garden plot?* i hold up my hands. *"once,"* i say. "like *one time,* very quickly."

"you absolute *slut.* that is for the *community,"* lacey chides, but there's only humor in her shock. "next time have sex in public someplace *normal* . . . like, you know, a mall parking lot. drink, by the way."

neither marlowe nor i can attest to that, so lacey shrugs and drinks twice.

"honestly, one of these days you need to tell me how i grow something without killing it," marlowe says. her lips twist. "i never got any better at it."

"i mean, like. you just gotta find what sticks. like. minus the sex? this summer i got really into the plot—okay, *stop* it. it was just like. that was *before* this. oh my god. but it's a lot of just, like, practice."

"i fucked a guy in a canoe," marlowe says. again, she is alone in this, but lacey and i drink in support anyway.

"isn't that the punch line to a beer joke? fucking close to water?" lacey adjusts the strap on her heel. "when's the uber coming?"

"an hour." marlowe nods at me, smiling. "your turn."

"okay, so we're doing three bars, the dj party, and then the last bar—and then back here for closing drinks, right?" lacey is scrolling through something on her phone. "can i say? i fucking love whoever made this excel sheet. it's perfect."

i think becca did. "well, ladies, the mission is to drink. so i gotta go with the obvious—handcuffs." i drink for less time than they do, which surprises me. i want to be able to remember the night, i think.

"okay, my turn. paddling," lacey doesn't really take a breath before she goes back to drinking. i wish i'd chosen a different flavor of mixer. the sugar in it makes my jaw hurt. also for some reason i am worried a fly smell it and then it will land in it and super die.

marlowe clears her throat. "um. i don't know if it's *kinky*, but like. you know, i once spent like. two hours fingering a girl." marlowe very much does not look at me. Her cup says *bridezilla in the making*.

"that's just *sex*," lacey says. "that isn't *kinky*."

"she wasn't, like. Allowed to touch me back. She just had to sit there and take it."

my cheeks burn. I don't think i actually like artificial mango? maybe if there were some, like, ice chips or something to cut it. oh my god, i'm old. it's fucking funny.

i hold the cup out, wincing. "remember when we would, like, bathe in this stuff? holy fuck it's sweet."

lacey grabs a pinch of my dress on marlowe's body purple. it wouldn't be pinchable on me. "you gotta get *weird* with this stuff. it's your *bachelorette*, girlfriend."

"it's my fucking *bachelorette*," marlowe agrees, and just starts chugging. we squeal, the girls around us squeal, lacey chugs too, and then everyone in the room is drinking. marlowe pours herself a new round, the rum splashing heavy. someone turns the music up.

"can i ask you something?" lacey loops her arms around marlowe's neck, "now that your quest is over, what's the body count at?"

"i've only just begun killing people." i don't like my interjection. it sounds immature, unfunny. i am secretly glad when neither of them acknowledges it. i start refilling lacey's cup.

"um," marlowe loops her tongue around her teeth. "i don't remember."

"you *slut*," lacey gasps, taking the full cup from me, "i'm so proud of you."

"yeah," marlowe says. she looks down at her hands and then back up at me.

i shrug like *that's lacey*. there's a weird pause while lacey goes to the bathroom. marlowe dips her head and slides off to socialize. i stand in a corner, playing *two dots*.

i jump when i hear her. "will you come get ice with me?" marlowe
holds the brown cannister up.

oh, she's talking to *me*. "oh, sure, of course."

"let's do shots while they're out!" lacey's call is immediately met
with cheers. i should have tried to actually learn the names of the
other girls here. i'll do it when i get back.

the door snicks shut. the music is tepid now, and the muted
yellow-gold-red of the hall smells faintly of something chemical;
chlorine or bleach.

marlowe puts one shaking hand to her forehead. "sorry. holy shit.
thank you for coming."

"to . . . ice?"

she shoots me a look. "to *this*."

i don't know what to say to that. the ice machine is just around
the corner, black and heavy with plastic. red and blue *ice* in a
calligraphy scarf over some polar bears.

she sticks the cannister under the dispenser and then just *drops* to
the floor. her body minimizes into a cower, panting, pushing her head
between her knees, her hands up in a flinch.

oh. a panic attack. we've had these.

i take the full ice bucket and close it, crouching next to her. i'm
not sure if touching her will make it better or worse; i'm worried i'll
overstimulate her further.

"why do like. all ice buckets. always have the same round tops?" i
say, just to talk. "i've been to, like, forty-six hotels and they always have
the same top."

marlowe doesn't say anything. i hear her breath hissing over her
teeth.

"also i think that the insert always looks like a trash bag."

she begins to scratch the back of her neck, hard.

"hey." i take her small wrist in my hand. "none of that."

"i can't breathe. i'm—i think i'm dying."

i put the ice down and place the cool of my palm against the curved ferris wheel of her spine. "do you want me to keep talking? we can sit in silence."

she shakes her head.

"*no* as in *stop talking* or *no* as in, *let's use silence?*"

"t-talk. please." she gropes for my free hand and squeezes it, groaning. the panicked, harsh moan of unspeakable anxiety.

my skin turns white around her fingers and something inside my hand goes *crunch*. oh well. i have the other hand; i massage tiny circles into where her muscles are spasming.

i have no idea what to say. what would i even tell her? i don't think i'm going to be around much longer; the body doesn't belong to me, and the landlord is getting louder. "can i be honest with you? nobody ever thinks i'm kinky."

she tilts her head so one eye peeks up at me from the side of her knee.

i sniff. "and i want to know exactly, like, what *i* did. is it because i mostly wear black?" since the massage isn't helping, i let her keep my squeezed hand and with the other i take a single ice cube out of the bucket. my teeth hurt—a tactile repulsion to *cold thing*. i trap it in my fist and blow into it. "you know, i don't even, like, use ice on wounds. like when i get bruises and stuff? i just, like, fucking hate how it feels. once i broke my ankle and they were like—you *gotta* ice. and i remember just being like cut the leg off."

the ice has started to melt enough it is sweating. i unwrap her a little, pull her hand so her wrist is facing upward, and let the cold water drip from my fist onto her skin. she flinches at first, but then closes her eyes. i see her jaw working. the rivulet slips from me to her. bit by bit. my skin hurts. "sorry, this is gonna take a long time. my brother has hands so hot that he can melt wax. once i watched a documentary where they said women couldn't work with chocolate because our hands are too warm and like—every person in my family. *immediately.* was just like—your hands are so cold and horrible; you should work with chocolate."

she sighs and sniffs. she offers the other wrist. drip, drip.

"your hands *are* kind of cold." her voice is shaky. she glances one round eye up at me up through her thick lashes. "i remember."

i cannot *wait* to tell my therapist about how i do not react to that.

instead, i focus on not spilling water everywhere. "i shouldn't have said they called my hands horrible. they didn't." i, on the other hand (ha!), *did.*

she tucks her head back down. "my dad once told me i have the hands of a fisherman." she relaxes the smallest amount more. i hear her start to breathe deeply, and i internally count with her—*in for five, out for seven.*

she has extremely delicate hands. i don't know where her father got that. "hey, i got you something for your wedding."

"i can't, um, do that righ—"

before she can finish, i slap the ice cube into her open palm. she shrieks and it goes flying, skittering across the sienna tile to rest under the machine. we both stare at it for a second.

"he was with us for so little time, but we loved him so deeply," i say.

she laughs, finally, choked and shaky.

"i can't believe you turned down my gift. i made that little ice sculpture just for you."

she wipes at her eyes. "sorry," she sniffs. "i suck. want me to go get it?"

"only if you plan to eat it. what? don't look at me like that. waste not, want not. now the ants can have a swimming pool. oceanfront property with a view."

she laughs again, this time with the timbre i'm used to. she draws a shaky breath, and then two. "sorry." she clears her throat, squeezes my hand, drops it. "sorry. i'm okay now. sorry. like. sorry."

i look at her, and she looks at me. the ice machine is whirring.

"i missed you," she whispers.

oh fuck.

i clear my throat. "i'm very missable. that's just good taste."

she leans her head on my shoulder. "the whole time. all of france. i would walk around paris, missing you. i miss you now too."

i scramble for something to say. "no ice cube artisans in france, huh?"

she isn't laughing. she looks up at me through those lashes again. "i meant it," she murmurs, drawing her face close to me. "thank you for coming."

"it's legit no problem."

the moment is long and slow while she bites her lip. "depot. i meant—a while ago, at the party, i meant what i said. you—like you really *are* my favorite person. everything with you just . . . feels so different."

she cranes her neck.

i look down at her and at her lips and at the person i learned love from and at my history and i think of monsters and i think of being unhinged and i think of how badly i wanted to stop existing and how long i spent wanting to ruin our friendship and how much i tried to shove into the maw of my loneliness and how much i wanted to put anything in the wound even if it was acid just so that the edges would be definitive and how i have spent so many nights wanting things that ███ me and how i have wanted to ███ myself *so* fucking badly that it was a swarm inside of my lungs and how i wanted to be gone so badly i would crash the car for it i wanted it like a scream i wanted it like falling i wanted it like a starship in a bright sky of yearning.

but how no matter how badly i wanted it, i still fucking *didn't*.

i stand up.

there are going to be a lot of long days in my life. this is not the start of one of them.

i check the hem of my dress and then offer her my hand. "have you found a therapist?"

she pauses for a second, then slowly shakes her head, taking my palm, pulling herself up. "his insurance doesn't cover it and nobody takes medicaid."

i drop her hand to adjust my skirt again. "i found mine literally through luck. i basically hunted her for sport."

she takes a deep breath. out of the corner of my eye, i see her shoot me a look. i stare at the bad wallpaper. she pats around her (my) dress. "fuck. i forgot the room key."

"they'll let us in."

"what if the music is too loud?"

"we'll pull the fire alarm." i can finally actually look at her again.

during all of this, she's always been just a person.

she nods like that's the sensible answer. "okay. how's my makeup?" she tilts her head toward the light, but it actually makes it harder to see, not easier.

"it's okay."

"okay." she heaves another deep breath and holds it for a moment before letting it out in a rush. "sorry for being so dramatic."

the music isn't too loud. they cheer when she knocks and then they drag her in, laughing. someone asks to redo her makeup. someone hands her a drink.

i put the ice down on the already sticky desk with the half-full cups and abandoned plastic shot glasses.

i text kaisa back—*i'm okay! yes let's definitely talk tomorrow . . . SO many thoughts lol. and thank you for asking (: Lacey says hi. we miss you. and girl! MESSY.*

Theoretically, recovery allows a person with mental illness to experience further loss or trauma without becoming leveled by it, instead teaching healthy mechanisms and coping skills to overcome hardship. A person who is "recovered" knows that recovery isn't a singular goalpost, nor can any person "be" recovered—but there are actions and beliefs I no longer partake in when in mourning (or at all). It's not that it never hurts: it's that I know the name of it now, and can shape my hands around it.

I am still inhabiting the same body and mind as I did when I was hurting; I have simply taken the bitterness out of the baggage.

But it is still, by its own resolution, baggage.

Did you know butterflies turn into goo in the cocoon? I love that. When I hit rock bottom, I squish too. De-body myself into a formless, horrible scream. It's happened within the last three months of writing this manuscript.

I am not writing to you from a fondly estranged future. I am writing to you from just recently getting up. Scrambling back to my knees. Wet and cold and shaking.

the lights make an esplanade across the blue of the room. aurora beams strike clear plastic cups and ruddy cheeks. my tinnitus is going to hate this.

marlowe's wearing a white sash with *bride!* on it and tossing her hair. i am standing at the edge of the dance floor, watching people make their small groups. how cute that we are so keen to cuddle. i love the small communities of parties. i am honey-sweet about a lot of things, recently. it feels romantic, to be alive.

it's loud here. the dj isn't very good, but he's trying. i watch becca bend to shout something in marlowe's ear, and marlowe nods along. i think i've seen this exact plateau in an art gallery, once.

in interpreting the concept of fate, there's often a "three-in-one" feminine divinity: *maiden, mother, crone.* three women, one eye. three women around a skein. three women who are the same past-present-future in different bodies.

here also are your options if you are a woman. it had to be a woman, didn't it. our lives pass in calculated chapters. it is not *bachelor, father, codger.* we know why.

marlowe looks down into her drink. something from 2011 is playing. the dj is good at picking songs but not good at transitioning.

the world is pretty big. my phone has eight missed messages from people i love. i have to remember to call my therapist and reschedule our appointment. i should journal when we get back to the hotel, i need to prevent myself from being overwhelmed.

the world is pretty small. we are standing on the second floor of a bar that only fits about forty people and is housing about one hundred fifty. the floor is uneven. i like the way it slants carefully toward the front windows, like it will tip us all out along a wooden tongue. becca keeps jokingly suggesting we walk another half mile so we can hit the strip clubs next.

is a woman still a maiden when she's already married but not a mother? is a crone no longer a mother?

i watch the lights hit each person in the party. how becca shifts her weight; the unconscious display that her feet hurt. how lacey plays with her hair. the way that the others touch each other so gently— gentle elbow grabs and hugs and dancing. how we balance each other with our fingertips.

i'm definitely not a maiden, and i cannot have children from this body. so i guess, for now—that makes me a crone.

a crone—from the french *caroigne*, meaning *carcass* or *cantankerous woman*. something about that feels pretty funny. something about that feels pretty freeing.

it's okay, actually. what's the worst thing that happens? i'm too old to find love?

i have already spent my whole life lonely. so far—despite so much—it hasn't managed to actually kill me.

i look up and watch the lights stripe the ceiling. i find myself smiling.

just like that—it's okay.

or, if it *isn't*—it might be. one day. eventually.

you have been trying, genuinely. but whenever you sit down to write about it (again, over and over for *years*), the thing that you write is:
i am dead by the side of the road already.

a long time ago, there was a rainbow outside of our house. i got up and went to find my mom, excited to share the moment. she couldn't find her glasses in time. the sun shifted. she looked up at the gray sky and said, "oh. i missed it."

i still feel bad about it.

the enduring nature of love is just this: we know we could never hurt someone like that. not in a permanent way. and not on purpose.

everyone else is still inside, dancing.

i was once told by a friend that the best time to leave a party is while everyone is still having fun. i have chosen two in the morning to be staying late enough.

"i've been thinking a lot about. like. the similarities between vampires and angels, recently." i scoot closer to lacey. the steps we're crouched on are super cold. i've been shivering for hours. i always do when i'm drunk. the light mist is going to make my curls poof up into circus poodle ringlets.

"oh, hang on. i love that. something that's undead and something that's never been alive."

"exactly." the uber is sixteen minutes away, but he's been sixteen away for a while. i keep checking the updates.

the city dark makes an orange halo around her beautiful cheekbones. "okay. wait. i love this. say more."

i splay my hands like a magician. "okay, be honest. if i came back wrong, would you kill me?"

her eyes are half-closed, leaning back on her elbows, a small drunk smile curling the edges of her lips. the green velvet dress on her really is killer. "hmm. how wrong are we talkin' here?"

"vampire wrong." i mime canine teeth.

"no, i mean, like, *sexy* vampire or like. *evil bad* vampire."

"bad and evil. not sexy." a rotten corpse rising to the surface. i know too much about vampire mythology, the idea of an un-death almost seems boring. angels, though—how could they even know the fear of mortality?

"hmm." she shakes her head, tossing her hair back. the drizzle coming off her makes a tiny firework show in the night. "are you *happy* as a vampire?"

good question. "i think i'm not *me*, so it's hard to say. the *version* of me that's a vampire is happy, sure."

"so it's not *you*. okay. hang on. but it *is* happy?"

i run out of thumbnail to bite off and start sorting through my hair for split ends, running the fried tips over my fingerprints. "just, like, a vampire in *my* body."

lacey stares at You, and for a second, You worry You gave Mouse away.

then she lunges for my throat, growling. i squawk, trying to out-maneuver her gnashing teeth as she chomps the air in sharp clicks.

i giggle while she pauses to wipe her mouth. she blinks. "holy shit. being a vampire literally just put me out of breath."

"i have *got* to get back to zumba classes," i agree, panting. a person runs a red light down the road. nobody's awake to yell about it.

she sighs and lies all the way down. i follow her, our hips brushing as we pour our bodies over the steps. she loops her legs with mine, i slide my arm under her neck. it's kind of warm like this. she flicks her eyes over to me. "but yeah, i mean, if you wanted me to, i'd kill ya. i don't know. did you *want* to be a vampire?" she gives a half grin and shrug. "i mean, *technically*? i *am* pro-choice."

"is . . . being a vampire . . . assisted suicide?" i try to solve it in the air while i ask it. "like . . . if you don't come back the same . . . you're essentially . . . ending the consciousness, right?"

"oh, don't you dare," she levels a finger at me. "i am *too* drunk for you to pull me into a Ship of Theseus question. i'll kill you in the real life."

"it's technically, like, the *soul* of theseus, but," i hold my hands up in surrender, gently hip checking her while i glance at my phone. now it says *twenty* minutes for the uber. fuck. "if you were a vampire, i'd become a vampire too so that we could be vampires forever together."

"don't be stupid." she loops her fingers into mine. "if i turn into a vampire, you need to be a werewolf. we gotta have day-to-night, round-the-clock *coverage*."

"oh my gosh. you're, like, so right—i mean, yeah, duh, of course."

"*someone* has to be around to menacingly open the door to like. helpless girls in white dresses." i didn't notice it before, but her hair still has the frizzy braid i gave to her in the parking lot. she must have tied it off without me noticing.

i love her into my bones. i close my eyes for a second, just feeling it resonate around my chest. when i open them, i start counting streetlamps. "do you think vampires, like, have to deal with tax evasion?"

"don't they just, like, eat the IRS?"

"like, the problem i have when vampires amass huge amounts of wealth is that . . . like. that's just how the government is *run*, you know? i genuinely do not think anyone would notice if one of those old guys in the senate was *actually* drinking blood." i adjust the strap on my heel. "they'd probably just say it was, like, a vaccine alternative."

"the thing that always bothered me in *Twilight* was that vampires didn't have to breathe. They could have just gone into the ocean and, like, been at peace. they could have made *atlantis*, i mean."

i blink. "oh my god. they could have just made a vampire atlantis." i reach up and wipe off some of her melting eye makeup. "are vampires, like, affected by water pressure?"

she shrugs, blinking upward, letting me fix her cheeks. "ask stephenie meyer."

"they're described as being living stone, so i feel like . . . no?"

she gently taps my wrist, excited. "oh my god. remember when we went to the midnight premiere of the last book? i literally forgot we did that until someone was talking about it the other day."

we had been the only ones in our small suburban school to read the books—neither of us had any idea about how popular the series had been nationally. we were just teenagers who liked reading fantasy. our parents had been *delighted* by the fact that when we finally asked to stay out late, it was for a literal *book party*.

then we'd shown up, and everyone had been dressed up in capes.
the two of us had been dressed in tight abercrombie, completely
baffled by the size of the reception, by the number of adults present.
this was just a stupid vampire series we'd both enjoyed—how the hell
was it *this* busy at our local Barnes & Noble. did the *adults* know the
books were dumb?

"missed our chance to be one of the evil guys," i sigh, looking down
the street. "i'm still mad about the fuckin—"

she slaps her hand down on the steps, sitting fully up. "about the
fucking *scavenger hunt!* the prize was fucking—'*the friends we made
along the way*' and i just—holy shit! i almost killed them for that one."

in hindsight, the scavenger hunt had probably been put together
by kids not much older than we had been, working a horrible retail
job, just trying to make some fun with very few resources. but still.
"shouldn't have said there was a prize at the end if—"

"—if there was no fucking prize," she agrees, growling. her hands
go up in the dark air, waving angrily. "you literally didn't even have to
say there was a prize, is the thing! we would have done it anyway!"

i kiss her cheek. "you're *my* prize."

"it is not enough to undo the massive amounts of trauma i have
clearly experienced as a result of this bait-and-switch technique from
a large book retailer."

"i'm gonna burn the whole place to the ground for your birthday
present."

she sighs. "no, it's not worth it. i still go there sometimes. they
have good coffee."

"ah. the one thing stopping gays from world domination."

"oh, by the way—i forgot to tell you, i'm down for that thing we're
doing next thursday too. tanner got off work."

"oh, perfect." i should make a note on my phone about that.
recently my social calendar has been suspiciously full. i used to be *so*

afraid to be alone. these days feel unreal—so much love in them from
the rest of the world that i'm excited for the parts when i come home
and *am* alone. it's fucking wild.

"*straight*," lacey snaps like *eureka.*

"huh?"

"she acts *straight*." her hands press together like she's folding her
idea into prayer. "marlowe. i can't explain it. she just like. i mean. i've
seen bi people with partners of the opposite gender or whatever. and
they don't, like, always *act* straight. they're still, like. there's *something*.
not to say, like, you know, there's a way to *act* gay but—"

"no, honestly? i get this." i wave away the rest of it.

"like, yes there's no way to act gay but!" she huffs. "marlowe *is*
acting straight!" she squints at me. "this is one of those things you
cannot explain to a republican."

i nod vigorously. "i think it would kill them. but you are correct,
go on."

"she just like. she's been flat-ironed. when you were bad—
sorry—like, it was like. oh, oh no, ███'s not really *in* there, she's just
playacting. but marlowe looks like . . . like she thinks *this* is happy. but
i don't think it's like . . . she's not in *recovery*. she's just putting things
together haphazardly. like, she's making the *picture* of bliss."

i look away, nodding. "it turns out that you need to actually *go to*
therapy and, like, *listen*. and do the *actual* hard work."

"exactly. and she *isn't*."

i sigh. i search for lacey's hand in the darkness. it's cold, and i
breathe on it, rubbing it to warm it up. "i mean. i know it sucks. i
literally know it *sucks*. but the alternative is . . ." is bleeding. is being
broken. is never healing.

another car goes by. the city used to scare me a lot. these days
i kind of like how loud it is. everyone's beautiful and unreal lives in
one location.

we spend a moment like that, just quiet, holding hands. her head tilts. "you know something? you remind me that i kind of actually believe in god."

"don't, i'll cry."

"i mean it." lacey reaches the other hand over to make a little hand sandwich. "there's something like. really brave about you."

i look over at her, her soft outline in the rain and the velvet dress and one earring from my set and one earring from her set and the braid in her hair.

"lacey," i say. and then i can't say anything, i'm too choked up.

she looks away. "i just. you came back. i tried to . . . i tried to tell you. and i feel bad about it, because i didn't do a good job. in the ikea once, i—i even thought about, like, straight-up kidnapping you. i *tried*."

i squeeze her hand. "it's not your fault." my voice is thin, crackling.

"i hate that i just. i just fucking. i had to watch it happen and just fucking *pray* that if i supported you good enough you'd pull through. i felt like—" she exhales slowly. "i felt like i was fucking dying, dude. i can't just . . . watch something like that hurt you. not *you*."

i don't know how to respond. the world gets that glow of tears around the edges. my throat hurts for all of it.

she examines her shoes. "it's just, like. you've been my best friend for so fucking long, dude. and this is going to make you *viscerally* uncomfortable, but—" when she peers up at me, tears are in her eyes too. "it's just . . . fucking nice. to see you actually remember that the person you need to love is *you*."

i have to blow out a breath to stop from crying at that. i manage a half laugh, trying to break the tension. "i'm sorry i was, like, insane. for a long time."

"you weren't insane." her voice is a croak. "you just . . . can't think right. and you loved the wrong people. it could happen to any of us."

another car goes by. i like her turn of phrase. "it could happen to any of us."

"yeah," she sighs. "and so often it does."

i stand up. "hey, lacey? will you pose for me?"

her brows knit, despite her soft and confused smile. "i thought you didn't do photography anymore?"

"i don't know," i say. "i'm thinking about restarting."

one picture. long exposure. her head tilted back; her hair soft around her. somebody who loves you, before/after. the night explodes in a flash.

"you'll stay here, right? you'll be okay this time?" she puts her hand in yours as both of you blink stars out of your eyes.

You look down at her, and you know—it's time to come back to life.

◆

HOW TO DIE BY THE SIDE OF THE ROAD AND NOT HAUNT AN INTERSECTION.

since you are handcuffed to the experience, and to the *almost*: you decide to write a book about it. it'll be called *a beginner's guide to talking to angels*. it will be about how angels also evolved along the same path as an oil slick—a rainbow presentation of time, a flattened life layered on the surface of water. it will be about how for angels; a miracle is a dollar store. how all angels love punk rock. how angels always bowl with the bumpers up.

it will be about finding god again. how god's hands were wet and she passed through you like a skein of satin.

hypothesis: whenever you are going somewhere, the angel must already be there, to find.

hypothesis: angels have wings that drag on the ground and hurt to wield. angels must not sleep on their backs.

hypothesis: an angel is a monster.

at the top of your page, you write:

1. whatever you lost in the church you can get it back by the side of a gas station.
2. don't ask about their father. the only thing we all have alike is our wounds.
3. collect only what serves you and annihilate what does not.
4. always approach an angel with your hands out and your palms up.
5. anything can be a church if you ask it nicely.
6. you didn't lose god; you lost the way home, which is different.
7. faith is a bag of peaches.

That which I seek solace for is the thing most likely to cause me real and direct pain. During my original process of discovering and

evaluating my condition, I believed I had to love my body in defiance of
the problems it presented. At the time of writing, I now understand that
love isn't a piecemeal operation: that which kills you is also lovable.

we are driving from one home to another. we have just said goodbye
to our mother. we could call someone if we wanted to, spend the time
just talking.

but tonight is just for us, just ours.

it gets sleepy, out here. after driving it so many times, the
road smears a strange and silent orange. the edges bleed together,
overlapping hands, forgotten poetry stanza.

the radio and the little lamb and the lord.

a lot of bad things have happened. no metaphor to the truck
horn this time. it would be so easy, and we could close our eyes, and
the earth would simply swallow us. we would become one of those
wooden crosses, decorated pink and surrounded by candles and psalms.
people would miss us.

Let me take the wheel, Mouse says. Just for a moment.

for a moment, you let her, so she can practice what it feels like to
fall asleep.

and then you pull over and get out of the car. you put the harvest
mouse on the ground. it's too cold here, and it won't survive for long.

"I love you," you say. "I am grateful you were there when I
couldn't be."

Mouse turns and looks at you-who-is-me.

The things that happened in this are all true, unless they happened
to her or to me, and, in that case—they happened so loudly I had to

leave them somewhere else. Don't go looking. When you cut your hand on something like that, it never heals correctly. It is swift, bloody work, but from time to time—you must do swift and bloody things.

I kill her.
I take home me.

FAREWELL, I LOVE YOU

it takes a lot of grieving. but one day you will look up, and you will finally understand what it is you have been collecting.

ACKNOWLEDGMENTS

The entire world of my gratitude is overwhelming. I am extremely fortunate to have received *so* much love and support in making this.

Every person in my family who has read this manuscript and listened and took it seriously. Thank you to my parents who both have listened to hours of my ranting about each choice I made and for their celebration of each step of the process. Jonathan, thank you for talking to me every day and letting me call you at 2 a.m. during a panic attack; it kept me grounded and sane and is one of my favorite parts of my routine. Thank you for book recs and thank you for getting it. Gabrielle, thank you for seeing the beauty in this thing faster than I did; for loving it enough to remind me why I wanted to write it in the first place. Thank you for the ways you consistently stand up for me, even when I don't stand up for myself. Erin, your calm and thoughtful support and consideration is a bastion of strength and kindness. Thank you for being a part of this family and for choosing to be my sister. Thank you all for knowing it was worth keeping even when I wanted to delete it. Thank you for being there since day one, and, also, thanks for consistently agreeing to babysit Goblin.

To many, many, many beautiful friends who have been through each opaque draft and each moment I wanted to quit writing and lie down in a ditch. Amy, you're a delight, thank you for loving the angels. Nat, thank you for the fig tree. Alex, I am manifesting us both a life of quiet writing and soup. David and Molly and Jelly and Gremlin: you all saw the start of this. Thank you for helping me step into it so I could see the end of it too. Thank you to Amity House and each person who helped me sort the early stages of this collection into something sensible.

Alison: anything I could possibly say, I hope you already know, but I'll say it anyway. I love you; every day I am glad I met you. It is lucky to be in your life. I am also, like, completely moved in at this point, so kicking me out would be dangerous for local wildlife. Thank you for giving me Lacey. The book (and my life) would have been different without hope.

I also want to acknowledge the University of Massachusetts Amherst and their Creative Writing MFA. Thank you for letting me run away to the woods to write for three years of my life. I came into that program asking, "How do I make the most of this?" You were all right when you told me: *Use the time how you need to. Just make sure you continue to write.*

Thank you to my agent, Amanda Orozco, who has been patient and kind and unfailingly calm in ways that I genuinely hope to figure out and apply to myself one day. Thank you for being the first moment this was real, and for standing by it for so long and through so much; knowing it's a shot in the dark.

Thank you to my editor, Danys Mares, who has been thoughtful and considerate and has asked me questions that were so observant that I had to walk around myself a few times before I felt confident I had an answer. Thank you for helping the newborn calf of it actually get to see the sun. Thank you for believing in the poetry of it.

Thank you to each person in my life who has held my hand and held back my hair and kept me company. It couldn't have existed without the constant, consistent efforts of other people. I would not have been able to continue alone.

This book used to be a confession about one of the worst parts of my life. It became a book about surviving. It became a book about light. I am still not perfect, but the ways that I am better: I owe so many of them to each of you, and the ways you make room for me and my story.

Thank you.

About the Author

Rowan is living in Massachusetts with her rescued greyhound. She is a graduate of the University of Massachusetts Amherst's MFA Program for Poets and Writers and was the recipient of the 2021 Harvey Swados Prize in Fiction.

She's okay now, and her plants are thriving.